# THE GOLDEN SHOEMAKER

## or, "Cobbler" Horn

## J. W. KEYWORTH

1st WORLD
LIBRARY
Literary Society

# The Golden Shoemaker

## J. W. Keyworth

© 1st World Library, 2008
PO Box 2211
Fairfield, IA 52556
www.1stworldlibrary.com
First Edition

LCCN: 2007935393

Softcover ISBN: 978-1-4218-9346-4
Hardcover ISBN: 978-1-4218-9446-1
eBook ISBN: 978-1-4218-9246-7

Purchase *"The Golden Shoemaker"*
as a traditional bound book at:
www.1stWorldLibrary.com/purchase.asp?ISBN=978-1-4218-9346-4

1st World Library is a literary, educational organization
dedicated to:

- Creating a free internet library of downloadable ebooks

- Hosting writing competitions and offering book publishing
scholarships.

Interested in more 1st World Library books? contact:
literacy@1stworldlibrary.com
Check us out at: www.1stworldlibrary.com

# 1ˢᵗ World Library Literary Society

## Giving Back to the World

"If you want to work on the core problem, it's early school literacy."

**- James Barksdale, former CEO of Netscape**

"No skill is more crucial to the future of a child, or to a democratic and prosperous society, than literacy."

**- Los Angeles Times**

"Literacy... means far more than learning how to read and write... The aim is to transmit... knowledge and promote social participation."

**- UNESCO**

"Literacy is not a luxury, it is a right and a responsibility. If our world is to meet the challenges of the twenty-first century we must harness the energy and creativity of all our citizens."

**- President Bill Clinton**

"Parents should be encouraged to read to their children, and teachers should be equipped with all available techniques for teaching literacy, so the varying needs and capacities of individual kids can be taken into account."

**- Hugh Mackay**

# CONTENTS

# CHAPTER I

## BEREAVED!

In a small house, in a back street, in the large manufacturing town of Cottonborough, the young wife of "Cobbler" Horn lay dying. It was the dusk of a wild evening in early winter; and the cruel cough, which could be heard every now and then, in the lulls of the wind, from the room upstairs, gave deepening emphasis to the sad fact that the youthful wife and mother—for such also she was—had fallen a victim to that fell disease which sweeps away so much of the fair young life of our land.

"Cobbler" Horn himself was engaged just now in the duties of his calling, in the little workshop behind the kitchen. The house was very small. The kitchen and workshop were the only rooms downstairs, and above them were three small chambers. The one in which the dying woman lay was over the workshop, and the sound of her coughing came down with sharp distinctness through the boarded floor, which was the only ceiling of the lower room.

"Cobbler" Horn knew that the death of his wife was probably a question of a few hours at most. But he had promised that the boots on which he was at work should be finished that night; and he had conscientiously withdrawn from his wife's bedside that he might keep his word.

"Cobbler" Horn was a man of thirty or so. He was tall, and had somewhat rugged features and clear steadfast eyes. He had crisp black hair, and a shaven face. His complexion was dark, and his bare arms were almost as brown as his leathern apron. His firmly set lips and corrugated brow, as he bent now over his work, declared him to possess unusual power of will. Indeed a strength of purpose such as belongs to few was required to hold him to his present task. Meanwhile his chief misgiving was lest the noise he was compelled to make should distress his dying wife; and it was touching to see how he strove to modify, to the utmost degree which was consistent with efficient workmanship, the tapping of the hammer on the soles of the boots in hand.

Sorrowing without bitterness, "Cobbler" Horn had no rebellious thoughts. He did not think himself ill-used, or ask petulantly what he had done that such trouble should come to him. His case was very sad. Five years ago he had married a beautiful young Christian girl. Twelve months later she had borne their little dark-eyed daughter Marian. Two years thereafter a baby boy had come and gone in a day; and, from that time, the mother had drooped and faded, day by day, until, at length, the end was close at hand. But "Cobbler" Horn was a Christian, and did not repine.

His task was finished at last, and, with a sigh of relief, he rose to his feet. In that moment, he became aware of a tiny figure, standing in the open doorway of the kitchen. It was that of a little four-year-old girl, clad in a ruby-coloured dress, which matched to perfection her dark skin and black hair. Her crimson cheeks were dashed with tears, and she looked like a damask rose just sprinkled by a shower of rain. The light in her dark eyes, which glistened with intense excitement beneath her jet-black hair, indicated that her tears

J. W. Keyworth

were those of indignation rather than grief. How long she had been standing there he could not tell; but, as soon as she saw that her father had finished his work, little Marian—for she it was—darted forward, and throwing her arms around his neck, with a sob, let her small dusky head fall upon the polished breast-piece of his leathern apron.

"What's amiss with daddy's poppet?" asked the father tenderly, as he clasped the quivering little form more closely to his breast.

The only answer was a convulsive movement of the little body within his arms.

"Come, darling, tell daddy." Strange strugglings continued within the strong, encircling arms. This little girl of four had as strong a will as her father; and she was conquering her turbulent emotions, that she might be able to answer his questions. In a moment she broke away from his clasp, and, dashing the tears from her eyes with her little brown hands, stood before him with glowing face and quivering lip.

"Me 'ant to see mammy!" she cried—the child was unusually slow of speech for her age. "Dey 'on't 'et Ma-an do upstairs."

"Cobbler" Horn took the child upon his knee, and gently stroked the small dusky head.

"Mammy is very ill, Marian," he said gently.

"Me 'ant to see mammy," was the emphatic response.

"By and bye, darling," replied the father huskily.

"What 'oo going to c'y for, daddy?" demanded the child, looking up hastily into her father's face. "Poor daddy!" she continued, stroking his cheek with her small brown hand, "Isn't 'oo very well?"

"I'm not going to cry, darling," said the father, bowing his head over his child, and taking into his strong hand the little fingers which still rested against his face. "You don't understand, my poor child!"

There followed a brief pause.

"P'ease, daddy," pleaded Marian presently, "Ma-an *must* see mammy. Dere's such pitty fings in se shops, and me 'ants to do with mammy to see dem—in morning."

The shops were already displaying their Christmas decorations.

Marian's father gave a great gasp.

"Marian shall see mammy now," he said solemnly, as he rose from his stool still holding the child to his breast.

"I'se so glad!" and she gave a little jump in his arms. "Good daddy!"

"But father's little poppet must be quiet, and not talk, or cry."

"No," said Marian with childhood's readiness to make a required promise.

The child had not seen her mother since the previous day, and the altered face upon the pillow was so strange to her, that she half turned away, as though to hide her face upon her father's shoulder.

The gleaming eyes of the dying mother were turned wistfully

towards her child.

"See, poppet; look at mammy!" urged the father, turning the little face towards the bed.

"Mother's darling!"

There was less change in the mother's voice than in her face; and the next moment the little dark head lay on the pillow, and the tiny, nut-brown hand was stroking the hollow cheek of the dying woman.

"'oo is my mammy, isn't 'oo?"

"Yes, darling; kiss mammy good-bye," was the heart-breaking answer.

"Me tiss 'oo," said the child, suiting the action to the word; "but not dood-bye. Me see 'oo aden. Mammy, se shops is so bootiful! Will 'oo take Ma-an to see dem? 'nother day, yes 'nother day."

"Daddy will take Marian to see the shops," said the dying mother, in labouring tones. "Mammy going to Jesus. Jesus will take care of mother's little lamb."

The mother's lips were pressed in a last lingering kiss upon the face of her child, and then Marian was carried downstairs.

When the child was gone, "Cobbler" Horn sat down by the bedside, and took and held the wasted hand of his wife. It was evident that the end was coming fast; and urgent indeed must be the summons which would draw him now from the side of his dying wife. Hour after hour he sat waiting for the great change. As the night crept on, he watched the deepening shadow on the beloved face, and marked the gathering signs which heralded the brief triumph of the king of terrors. There was but little talk. It could not be otherwise; for, every moment, utterance became more difficult to the dying wife. A simple, and affectionate question and answer passed now and then between the two. At infrequent intervals expressions of spiritual confidence were uttered by the dying wife; and these were varied with a few calmly-spoken directions about the child. From the husband came, now and then, words of tender encouragement, mingled with morsels of consolation from the good old Book, with, ever and anon, a whispered prayer.

The night had almost passed when the end came. The light of the grey December dawn was struggling feebly through the lattice, when the young wife and mother, whose days had been so few, died, with a smile upon her face; and "Cobbler" Horn passed out of the room and down the stairs, a wifeless husband and the father of a motherless bairn.

# CHAPTER II

## AUNT JEMIMA

It was Aunt Jemima who stepped into the vacant place of Marian's mother. She was the only sister of "Cobbler" Horn, and, with the exception of a rich uncle in America, from whom they never heard, and a wandering cousin, a sad scapegrace, she was her brother's only living relative.

"Cobbler" Horn's sister was not the person to whom he would have chosen to entrust the care of his motherless child, or the management of his house. But he had no choice. He had no other relative whom he could summon to his help, and Aunt Jemima was upon him before he had had time to think. She was hurt that she had not been called to the death-bed of her sister-in-law. But the omission rather increased, than diminished, the promptitude with which she wrote to announce that she would come to her bereaved brother without delay, and within a week she was duly installed as mistress of his house.

"I thought I had better come at once," she said, on the night of her arrival. "There's no telling what might have happened else."

"Very good of you, Jemima," was her brother's grave response.

And so it was. The woman meant well. She loved her brother sincerely enough; and she had resolved to sacrifice, for his sake and his child's, the peace and freedom of her life. But Aunt Jemima's love was wont to show itself in unlovely ways. The fact of meaning well, though often a good enough excuse for faulty doing, is not a satisfactory substitute for the doing of that which is well. Your toleration of the rough handling inflicted by the awkwardness of inconsiderate love does not counteract its disastrous effects on the susceptible spirit and the tender heart, especially if they be those of a child. It is, therefore, not strange that, though "Cobbler" Horn loved his sister, he wished she had stayed away. She was his elder by ten years; and she lived by herself, on the interest of a small sum of money left to her by their father, at his death, in a far off village, which was the family home.

"You'll be glad to know, Thomas," she said, "that I've made arrangements to stay, now I'm here."

They were sitting by the fire, towards supper-time; and the attention of "Cobbler" Horn was divided between what his sister was saying and certain sounds of subdued sobbing which proceeded from upstairs. Very early in the evening Aunt Jemima had unceremoniously packed Marian off to bed, and the tiny child was taking a long time to cry herself to sleep in the cold, dark room.

"Never mind the child," said Aunt Jemima sharply, as she observed her brother's restless glances towards the staircase door; "on no account must she be allowed to have her own way. It was high time she went to bed; and she'll soon be fast asleep."

"Yes, Jemima," said the troubled father; "but I wish you had been more gentle with the child."

"Fiddlesticks!" was the contemptuous exclamation of Aunt Jemima, as she regarded her brother severely through her spectacles; and she added, "Since you have wished me to take the oversight of your house and child, you must leave me to manage them as I think fit."

"Cobbler" Horn did not venture to remind his sister that he had not expressed any such wish. Being so much his senior, and having at least as strong a will as his own, Jemima Horn had always maintained a certain predominance over her brother, and her ascendancy still prevailed to some extent. Making no further reference to the child, he sat listening by turns to a prolonged exposition of his sister's views on the management of children, and to the continued wailings which floated down from the room above, until, at length, as a more piteous cry than all frantically voiced his own name, "faver," his self-restraint gave way, and he rose hastily and went upstairs.

Aunt Jemima watched him in grim silence to the foot of the stairs.

"Mind," she then called after him, "she is not to come down."

"Cobbler" Horn did not so far set his sister at defiance as to act in flat contradiction to her decree. Perhaps he himself did not think it well that the child should be brought downstairs again, after once having been put to bed. But, if Marian might not come down, Marian's father might stay up. As soon as his step sounded on the stairs the child's wailing ceased.

"Zat zoo, daddy?" and the father felt, in the darkness, that two tiny arms were stretched out towards him in piteous welcome. Lighting the candle, which stood on the table by the window, he sat down on the edge of the bed, and, in a moment, Marian's little brown arms were tightly clasped about his neck. For a brief space he held the child to his breast; and then he gently laid her back upon the pillow, and having tucked the bed-clothes well about her, he kissed the little tear-stained face, and sat talking in the soothing tones which a loving parent can so well employ.

Leaving him there, let us make a somewhat closer inspection of Miss Jemima, as she sits in solitary state before the fire downstairs. You observe that she is tall, angular, and rigid. Her figure displays the uprightness of a telegraph pole, and her face presents a striking arrangement of straight lines and sharp points. Her eyes gleam like points of fire beneath her positively shaggy brows. Her complexion is dark, and her hair, though still abundant, is already turning grey. Her dress is plainness itself, and she wears no jewelry, all kinds of which she regards with scorn. Her old-fashioned silver watch is a family heirloom, and a broad black ribbon is her only watch-guard.

Yet there is nothing of malice or evil intent in Aunt Jemima's soul. She is no less strictly upright in character than in form. She cannot tolerate wickedness, folly, or weakness of any kind. So far well. The lack of her character is the tenderness which is woman's crowning grace. When she is kind it is in such a way that one would almost prefer for her to be unkind.

Such is Aunt Jemima, as we see her sitting in front of her brother's fire, and as we know her to be. Need we wonder that, "Cobbler" Horn's heart misgave him as to the probable fate of his little Marian in such rough, though righteous, hands?

When "Cobbler" Horn at length came downstairs, his sister was still sitting before the fire. On his appearance, she rose

J. W. Keyworth

from her seat.

"Thomas, I am ashamed of you," she said, as she began, in a masterful way, to make preparations for supper. "Such weakness will utterly spoil the child. But you were always foolish."

"I am afraid, sister," was the quiet reply, "that we shall hardly agree with one another—you and I—on that point."

# CHAPTER III

## HOW MISS JEMIMA MANAGED
## HER BROTHER'S HOUSE

On entering upon the management of her brother's house, Aunt Jemima laid down two laws, which were, that the house was to be kept spotlessly clean, and that everything was always to be in its right place; and her severe, and even fierce, insistence on the minute fulfilment of these unexceptionable ordinances soon threatened utterly to banish comfort from her brother's house.

The restrictions this masterful lady placed upon her patient brother constituted a state of absolute tyranny. Lest her immaculate door-step should be soiled, she would rarely allow him to enter the house by the front-door. She placed a thick mat inside his workshop, at the doorway leading into the front-room; and she exercised a lynx-eyed supervision to ensure that he always wiped his feet before coming in. She would never permit him to go upstairs without putting off his boots. She removed his hat from the wall of the front-room, and hung it on a nail in a beam, which was just over his head as he sat at work in his shop; and whenever she walked, with her policeman-like tread, in the room above, the hat would fall down, and strike him on the head. He bore this annoyance for a day or two, and then quietly removed hat and nail to one of the walls.

Strong-natured though he was, "Cobbler" Horn felt it no weakness to yield to his sister in trifles; and he bore with exhaustless patience such vexations as she inflicted on him alone. But he was firm as a rock where the comfort of any one else was concerned. It was beautiful to see his meek submission to every restriction which she laid upon him; it was sublime to behold his stern resistance to such harsh requirements as she proposed to lay upon others.

More than one battle was fought between the brother and sister on this latter point. But it was on Marian's account that the contention was most frequent and severe. Sad to say, the coming of Aunt Jemima seemed likely to drive all happiness from the lot of the hapless child. Rigid and cruel rules were laid upon the tiny mite. Requirements were made, and enforced, which bewildered and terrified the little thing beyond degree. She was made to go to bed and get up at preternaturally early hours; and her employment during the day was mapped out in obedience to similarly senseless rules. Her playthings, which had all been swept into a drawer and placed under lock and key, were handed out by Aunt Jemima, one at a time, at the infrequent intervals, during which, for brief periods, and under strict supervision, the child was permitted to play. Much of the day was occupied with the doing of a variety of tasks few of which were really within the compass of her childish powers. Aunt Jemima herself undertook to impart to Marian elementary instruction in reading, writing, and kindred acts. Occasionally also the child was taken out by her grim relative for a stately walk, during which, however, she was not permitted, on any account, to linger in front of a shop window, or stray from Aunt Jemima's side. And then, in the evening, after their early tea, while Aunt Jemima sat at her work at the table, the poor little infant was perched on a chair before the fire, and there required to sit till her bed-time, with her legs dangling till they ached again, while the tiny head became so heavy that it nodded this way and that in unconquerable drowsiness, and, on more occasions than one, the child rolled over and fell to the floor, like a ball.

One lesson which Aunt Jemima took infinite pains to lodge in Marian's dusky little head was that she must never speak unless she was first spoken to; and if, in the exuberance of child-nature, she transgressed this rule, especially at meal-times, Aunt Jemima's mouth would open like a pair of nut-crackers, and she would give utterance to a succession of such snappish chidings, that Marian would almost be afraid she was going to be swallowed up. A hundred times a day the child incurred the righteous ire of this cast-iron aunt. From morning to night the little thing was worried almost out of her life by the grim governess of her father's house; and Aunt Jemima even haunted her dreams.

Marian had one propensity which Aunt Jemima early set herself to repress. The child was gifted with an innate love of rambling. More than once, when very young indeed, she had wandered far away from home, and her father and mother had thought her lost. But she had always, as by an unerring instinct, found her way back. This propensity it was, indeed, necessary to restrain; but Aunt Jemima adopted measures for the purpose which were the sternest of the stern. She issued a decree that Marian was never to leave the house, except when accompanied by either her father or Miss Jemima herself. In order that the object of this restriction might be effectually secured, it became necessary that Miss Jemima should take the child with her on almost every occasion when she herself went out. These events were intensely dreaded by Marian; and she would shrink into a corner of the room when she observed Aunt Jemima making preparations for leaving the house. But she made no actual show of

J. W. Keyworth

reluctance; and it would be difficult to tell whether she was the more afraid of going out with Aunt Jemima, or of letting Aunt Jemima see that she was afraid.

It was a terrible time for the poor child. On every side she was checked, frowned upon, and kept down. If she was betrayed into the utterance of a merry word she was snapped at as though she had said something bad; and ebullitions of childish spirits were checked again and again, until their occurrence became rare. And yet this woman thought herself a Christian, and believed that, in subjecting to a system of such complicated tyranny the bright little child who had been committed to her charge, she was beginning to train the hapless mite in the way she should go.

It was a very simple circumstance which first indicated to "Cobbler" Horn the kind of training his child was beginning to receive. Happening to go, one morning, into the living-room, he found that his sister had gone out, and, for once, left Marian a prisoner in the house. The child was seated on a chair, with her chubby legs hanging wearily down, and a woebegone expression on her face. Taking courage from the absence of her dreadful aunt, Marian asked her father to give her some of her toys, and to let her play. Finding, to his surprise, on questioning the child, that she had been forbidden to touch her playthings without express permission, and that they were put away in the drawer, he readily gave her such of them as she desired, and crowned her happiness by remaining to play with her till Aunt Jemima returned.

This incident created a feeling of uneasiness in the father's mind; but it was a circumstance of another kind which fully revealed to him the actual state of things. Passing through the room one evening when Marian was on the point of going to bed, he paused to listen to the evening prayer of his child. She knelt, in her little night-clothes, at Aunt Jemima's knee.

The father sighed, as he waited for the sound of the simple words which had been learnt at the dictation of the tender mother-voice which was now for ever still. What, then, were his astonishment and pain when Marian, instead of repeating her mother's prayer, entered upon the recital of a string of theological declarations which Aunt Jemima dictated to her one by one!

"Cobbler" Horn strode forward, and laid a strong repressive hand upon the child; and Aunt Jemima will never forget the flash of his eye and the stern tones of his voice, as he demanded that Marian should be permitted to pray her mother's prayer.

After this he noticed frequent signs of the tyranny of which Marian was the victim, and interposed at many points. But it was only in part that he was able to counteract the cruel discipline to which Aunt Jemima was subjecting his child.

J. W. Keyworth

# CHAPTER IV

## "ME LUN AWAY"

Winter passed drearily away—a wet one, as it happened, with never once the white gleam of snow, and scarcely a touch of the healthy sting of frost. "Cobbler" Horn had not ceased to sorrow for his dead wife; and, when the spring was well advanced, there befell him another, and scarcely less severe bereavement, though of a different kind.

There had been no improvement in the relations between Aunt Jemima and the child. Aunt Jemima still maintained the harsh system of discipline which she had adopted at first; and the result was that the child had been led to regard her father's sister with as near an approach to hatred as was possible to her loving little heart. Marian's heart was big, almost to bursting, with concealed sorrow. Like her father, young as she was, she found it easier to bear grief than to tell it out. She did not want her father to know how miserable she was. Her childish soul was filled with bitterness, and her young life was being spoiled. Such of her pleasures as had not been taken from her were divested of all their charm. Almost her sole remaining joy was to snatch, now and then, a bit of clandestine love with her father, when, on some rare occasion, Aunt Jemima happened to be out of the way.

Recognising the uselessness of resisting a hand so hard and strong as that of Aunt Jemima, Marian had lately meditated another way of escape from the wretchedness of her lot. She contemplated an expedient which occurs more readily than any other to the youthful victim of oppression, but which had probably never before presented itself to the mind of a child so young. The expedient is one, indeed, which seldom effects its purpose, and is usually productive of a plentiful crop of troubles. But Marian had no fear. She was full of one thought. She could not any longer endure Aunt Jemima; and she must make it impossible for Aunt Jemima to scold, or smack, or restrain her any more. She must escape, without delay, from the sound of Aunt Jemima's harsh voice, and place herself beyond the reach of Aunt Jemima's rough hand. True, there was her father. How could she leave him? This would have been impossible to her if she had realised what she was about to do. But it seemed so easy and pleasant to slip out into the bright spring morning, and trot away into the mysterious and delightful country, which lay outside the town. Nor did she dream of the hardships and danger which might be awaiting her out in the strange, unloving world, into which she had so lightly resolved to launch her little life. So it came to pass that, on a certain bright May morning, Marian took her opportunity, and went out into the world.

Marian's opportunity was furnished by the fact that Aunt Jemima had gone out, leaving Marian at home, and, for once, had forgotten to lock the door. As soon as Aunt Jemima's back was turned, the child huddled her little pink print sun-bonnet upon her small black head, and, with one furtive glance over her shoulder towards her father's workshop, whence she could distinctly hear the quick "tap-tap" of his hammer, she opened the front-door, and slipped into the street. Her first action was to shoot a keen glance, from her sharp little eyes, to right and left. There was no one to be seen but one of the funny little twin men who kept a huckster's shop across the way. This little man was a great friend of Marian's, and he called to her now in joyous tones, as he stood in the doorway of his shop, to come over and see what he had in his pocket. Marian gave a decided shake of her head.

"No; Ma-an going away. Tum another time."

Then, murmuring to herself, "Me lun away," she set off down the street, with a defiant swagger of her small person, and her bonnet-strings streaming out upon the wind; and the little huckster watched her with an admiring gaze, little thinking into what wilds of sorrow those tiny twinkling feet had set off to run.

# CHAPTER V

## "THE LITTLE TWIN BRETHREN"

The name of the little hucksters across the way was Dudgeon. As to age, they were on the verge of thirty—Tommy having entered the world a few minutes previous to John. They were so much alike that it was difficult to distinguish them when apart. John was just a shade lighter in complexion than Tommy, and Tommy overtopped his brother by something like an inch. The twins were so small as to seem insignificant; but their meek amiability was an efficient set off against their physical deficiencies. If there was any measure of self-assertiveness between them, it belonged chiefly to Tommy. Though both the little men were kind to Marian, Tommy was her especial friend; and it was he who had watched her as she ran away. The twins were both bachelors; though John had kept company for several years with a young woman of exemplary patience. Tommy, who was a sincere Christian, was a member of the church to which "Cobbler" Horn belonged. John occasionally attended the services at the same place, but could not be persuaded to join the church.

The close resemblance between the brothers was the cause of many ludicrous mistakes. In their boyhood, they had frequently been blamed for each other's faults and misdeeds;

J. W. Keyworth

and it was characteristic of Tommy that he had quietly suffered more than one caning which his brother ought to have received. But, when it had been proposed to administer to him a dose of medicine which had been prescribed for John, he had quietly protested and explained the mistake.

When the twins grew up, similar blunders continued to occur; and the little men had frequent opportunities of unlawfully profiting by the errors in which their close resemblance to each other often involved their friends. But, to the credit of these worthy little men be it said, they conscientiously declined to avail themselves of the opportunities of illegitimate benefit thus thrown in their way.

It was a curious sight to see these two queer little men standing, sitting, or walking, side by side. The minister of their chapel would often speak of the first occasion on which he had seen John Dudgeon. It was one Sunday evening, shortly after he had assumed the pastorate of the church. The service had just commenced, and the eye of the minister happened to rest, for a moment, on the humble figure of Tommy Dudgeon, who was, as usual, in his place. The minister had already made the acquaintance of Tommy, but of the existence of John he was not yet aware. What, then, was his astonishment, the next moment, to see another Tommy Dudgeon, as it seemed, come in and take his place beside the one already in the pew! For a breathing space the new pastor imagined himself the victim of an optical illusion; and then he rubbed his eyes, and concluded that Tommy Dudgeon had a twin brother, and that this was he.

It was not surprising that these two peculiar little men should have excited the amusement of those to whom they were known. Their amazing and almost indistinguishable resemblance to each other, and the consequent unconscious mutual mimicry of tone and gesture which prevailed between them, while they were a source of frequent perplexity, were also irresistibly provocative of mirth. What wonder that those who saw the little hucksters for the first time should have felt strongly inclined to regard them in a comic light; or that the mere mention of their names should have unfailingly brought a smile to the faces of those to whom their peculiarities were known!

The boys of the Grammar School, which was situated in a neighbouring street, had, from time immemorial, furnished Tommy and John Dudgeon with an epithet accommodated from classic lore, and dubbed them, "the *little* Twin Brethren."

# CHAPTER VI

## THE FATHER'S QUEST

When Aunt Jemima came home, she was surprised, in no small degree, at the absence of Marian. With gathering indignation she called up the stairs, then searched the house, and finally presented herself before her brother, who was quite alone in his workshop, and sat calmly working on his stool.

"Then she is not here?"

"Who? Marian?" responded "Cobbler" Horn in no accent of concern, looking up for a moment from his work. "No, I thought she was with you."

"No; I left her in the room for a moment, and now she is nowhere to be found."

There seemed to "Cobbler" Horn no reason for alarm, and, as his sister returned to the kitchen, he quietly went on with his work. But Aunt Jemima's mind was ill at ease. Once more she searched the house, and called and called again. There was no response, and the silence which followed was profound and ominous. Swiftly she passed, with growing alarm, through her brother's workshop, and out into the yard.

A glance around, and then a closer search; but still no sign of the missing child. The perturbed woman re-entered her brother's presence, and stood before him, erect and rigid, and with outstretched hands.

"The child's gone!" was her gloomy exclamation.

"Gone!" echoed "Cobbler" Horn blankly, looking up. "Where?"

"I don't know; but she's gone quite away, and may never come back."

Then "Cobbler" Horn perceived that his sister was alarmed; and, notwithstanding the occasion, he was comforted by the unwonted tenderness she had expressed. As for Marian, he knew her for a born rambler; and it was not the first time she had strayed from home.

"Perhaps," he said placidly, "she has gone to the little shop over the way."

Then he resumed his work, as though he had simply told his sister where she would be likely to find her spectacles.

Aunt Jemima took the hint, as a drowning person catches at a straw. She made her way to the front-door, and having opened it, was on the point of crossing the street, when Tommy Dudgeon emerged from the shop, and came over towards where she stood.

"Good morning, ma-am," he said, halting at a respectful distance. "You are looking for little miss?"

"Well," snapped Aunt Jemima, "and if I am, what then? Do you know where she is?"

J. W. Keyworth

"No, ma-am; but I saw her go away."

Miss Jemima seized the arm of the little man with an iron grip.

"Man! you saw her go away, and you let her go?"

With difficulty Tommy freed his arm.

"Well, ma-am, perhaps I ought—"

"Of course you ought," rapped out the lady, sharply. "You must be a gabey."

"No doubt, ma-am. But little miss will come back. She knows her way about. She will be home to dinner."

Having spoken, Tommy was turning to recross the street.

"Stop, man!"

Tommy stopped and faced around once more.

"Which way did she go?"

"That way, ma-am," replied Tommy, pointing along the street, to Aunt Jemima's left-hand, and his own right.

The troubled lady instantly marched, in the direction indicated, to the end of the street; but, finding that five ways branched off therefrom, she returned baffled to her brother's house, and sought his presence once more.

"Thomas," she cried, almost fiercely, "the child has certainly run away!"

Still "Cobbler" Horn was not alarmed.

"Well," he said calmly, "never mind, Jemima. She has a habit of going off by herself. She knows her way about, and will not stray far. She will be back by dinner-time, no doubt."

Though by no means satisfied, Miss Jemima was fain to accept this view of the case for the time. With a troubled mind, she resumed her suspended domestic duties. Unlikely as it might seem, she could not banish the dread that Marian had actually run away; and, as the morning passed, the fear grew stronger and stronger in the troubled lady's breast that she would see her little niece no more. Accordingly when dinner-time arrived, Aunt Jemima was not surprised that Marian did not appear. The dinner consisted of Irish stew— Marian's favourite dish. On the stroke of twelve it was smoking on the table. For the twentieth time the perturbed lady went to the door, and gazed wistfully up and down the street. Then, with a sigh, she re-entered the house, and called her brother to dinner.

"Cobbler" Horn, feeling sure that Marian would soon return, had dismissed the fact of her disappearance from his mind; and when, on coming in to dinner, he found that she was still absent, he was taken by surprise.

In reply to his inquiry, Aunt Jemima jerked out the opinion that the child would not come back at all.

"Why shouldn't she?" he asked. "I've known her stay away longer than this, and there's no occasion for alarm."

So saying, he addressed himself to his dinner with his usual gusto; but Miss Jemima had no appetite, and the show of eating that she made was but a poor pretence.

"Don't be so much alarmed, Jemima," said her brother, making progress with his dinner. "I've no doubt the child is amongst her friends. By and bye I'll go out and hunt her up."

He still had no fear that his little daughter would not soon return. He accordingly finished his dinner with his usual deliberation; and it was not until he had completed one or two urgent pieces of work, that he, at last, put on his hat and coat, and taking his stout blackthorn stick, set out in search of his missing child.

All the weary afternoon, he went from house to house, amongst friends and friendly neighbours; but no one had seen Marian, or knew anything as to her whereabouts. Every now and then he returned home, to see if the child had come back. But each time he found only Aunt Jemima, sitting before the fire like an image of grim despair. She would look up with fierce eagerness, on his entrance, and drop her gaze again with a gasp when she saw that he was alone.

Long before the afternoon was over the father's unconcern had given place to serious alarm. He was not greatly surprised that he had failed to find Marian in the house of any of their friends; but he wondered that she had not yet come home of her own accord. While he would not, even now, believe that Marian had run away, he was compelled to admit that she was lost. But what was that? He had turned once more towards home, and had entered his own street, and there was Marian, playing with some other children, on the pavement, just in front. Her back was towards him, as she bent down over her play. But there was no mistaking that thick, night-black hair, and the little plump brown legs which peeped out beneath the small frock. With the promptitude of absolute certainty, he put out his strong hands and lifted the child from the ground. Then he uttered a cry. It was not Marian after all! He put her down—he almost let her drop, and the startled child began to cry. "Cobbler" Horn hastily pushed a penny into her hand, and strode on. He staggered like one who has received a blow. It seemed almost as if he had actually had his little one in his arms, and she had slipped away again.

When he reached home, his sister was still sitting in grim silence, before the now fireless grate. On her brother's entrance, she looked up as aforetime. "Cobbler" Horn sank despondently into a chair.

"Nowhere to be found!" he said, with a deep sigh.

"We must have the tea ready," he added, as though at the dictate of a sudden thought.

"Ah, you are tired, and hungry."

Aunt Jemima hesitated on the last word. Could her brother be hungry? She thought she would never wish to taste food again.

"No," he said quickly; "but Marian will want her tea. Put the dinner away. It is cold, Jemima."

"I put her plate in the oven," said Aunt Jemima, in a hollow voice, as she rose from her seat.

"Ah!" gasped the father. The little plate had become hot and cold again, and its contents were quite dried up. Aunt Jemima put the plate upon the oven-top; and then turned, and looked conscience-stricken into her brother's face. Severe towards herself, as towards others, she unflinchingly acknowledged her great fault.

"Brother, your child is gone; and I have driven her away."

She lifted her hands on either side of her head, and gently swayed herself to and fro once—a grim gesture of despair.

"I do not ask you to forgive me. It is not to be expected of you—unless she comes back again. If she does not, I shall never forgive myself."

"Jemima," said "Cobbler" Horn, rising from his seat, and placing his hand lightly on her shoulder, "You are too severe with yourself. That the child is lost is evident enough; but surely she may be found! I will go to the police authorities: they will help us."

He turned to the door, but paused with his hand on the latch.

"Jemima," he said, gently, "you must not talk about my not forgiving you. I would try to forgive my greatest enemy, much more my own sister, who has but done what she believed to be best."

The authorities at the police-station did what they could. Messages were sent to every police centre in the town; and very soon every policeman on his beat was on the look-out for the missing child. At the same time, an officer was told off to accompany the anxious father on a personal search for his little girl. First of all, they visited the casual ward at the workhouse, and astonished its motley and dilapidated occupants by waking them to ask if they had fallen in with a strayed child on any of the roads by which they had severally approached the town. When they had recovered from their first alarm beneath the gleam of the policeman's bulls-eye, these waifs of humanity, one and all, declared their inability to supply the desired information. The officer next conducted his companion into the courts and bye-ways of the town. Many a den of infamy was filled with a quiver of alarm, and many a haunt of poverty was made to uncover its wretchedness before the horrified gaze of "Cobbler" Horn. But the missing child was not in any of these. Next they went a little way out on one or two of the country roads. But here all was dark: and they soon retraced their steps.

Having ascertained that nothing had been heard at the police-station of his child, "Cobbler" Horn at length turned home-ward, in the early morning, with a weary heart. Miss Jemima was still sitting where he had left her, and he sadly shook his head in response to the appeal of her dark hollow eyes. During the hour or so which remained before dawn, "Cobbler" Horn restlessly paced the house, pausing, now and then, to open the front-door and step out into the street, that he might listen for the returning patter of the two little feet that had wandered away.

Before it was fairly light, he left his sister, still distraught and rigid in her chair, and went into the streets once more. What could he do which he had not already done? From the first his heart had turned to God in prayer, and this seemed now his sole remaining resource. Yes, he could still pray; and, as he did so now, his belief grew stronger and stronger that, if not now, yet sometime, he would surely find his child again.

Not many streets from his own he met a woman whom he knew. She lived, with her husband, in a solitary cottage on the London Road—the road into which "Cobbler" Horn's street directly led, and she was astir thus early, she explained, to catch the first train to a place some miles away. But what had brought Mr. Horn out so soon? "Cobbler" Horn told his sorrowful story, and the woman gave a sudden start.

"Why," she said, "that reminds me. I saw the child yesterday morning. She passed our house, trotting at a great rate. It was washing day, and, besides, I had my husband's dinner in the oven, or I think I should have gone after her."

"Cobbler" Horn regarded the woman with strange, wide-open eyes.

"If you had only stopped her!" he cried. "But of course you didn't know."

With that, he left the woman standing in the street, and hurried away. Very soon he was walking swiftly along the London Road. The one thought in his mind was that he was on the track of his child at last. He passed the wayside cottage where the woman lived who had seen Marian go by, and went on until, moved by a sudden impulse, he paused to rest his arms upon the top of a five-barred gate, and look upon the field into which it led. Then he uttered a cry, and, tearing open the gate, strode into the field. Lying amidst the grass was a little shoe. It was one of Marian's without a doubt. Had he not made it himself? He picked it up and hid it away in the pocket of his coat. Marian had evidently wandered that way, and was lost in the large wood which lay on the other side of the field. To reach the wood was the work of a few moments. Plunging amongst the trees, he soon came upon a pool, near the margin of which were some prostrate tree trunks. Near one of these the ground was littered with shreds of what might have been articles of clothing; and amongst them was a long strip of print, which had a familiar look. He picked it up and examined it closely. Then the truth flashed upon him. It was one of the strings of Marian's sun-bonnet! Holding it loosely between his finger and thumb, he gazed upon the foul green waters of the pond. Did they cover the body of his child? He had no further thought of searching the wood. With a shudder he turned away, and hurried home.

Aunt Jemima had bestirred herself, and was moving listlessly about the house.

"Jemima, do you know this?" She took the strip of print into her hand.

"Yes," she said, "it is—"

He finished her sentence. "—the string of her bonnet."

"Yes."

He told her where he had found it, and showed her the shoe.

The pond was dragged, but nothing was discovered. They searched the wood, and scoured the country for miles around; but they came upon no further trace of the missing child.

# CHAPTER VII

## WHAT HAD BECOME OF THE CHILD?

When Marian left her father's house, she had but one idea in her mind. Her sole desire was to escape from Aunt Jemima; and it seemed to her that the most effectual method of doing so was to get into the country as fast as she could. It was not likely, she thought, that there would be any Aunt Jemimas in so pleasant a region as she had always understood the country to be. She knew vaguely which direction to take, and supposed that if she kept on long enough, she would ultimately reach her destination. What she would do when she got there she had not paused to think. At present she was simply thrilling with the sweet consciousness of liberty, and enjoying her scamper in the fresh spring morning air. It was not likely, perhaps, that Marian would run right away from home, and stay away. Like any other little chick, she would make for home at roosting time, if hunger did not constrain her to turn her steps thitherward at a much earlier hour.

Marian's surmise that the way she had taken led into the country proved to be correct. The street widened out into a road, the houses became fewer and brighter till they ceased altogether; and the child realized, with a little tremor, that, at last, she was out in the country all alone. Her feeling was one of timid joy. All around her were the green fields and waving trees; and the only house in sight was a little white-washed cottage far on in front. It cost Marian an effort to pass a man with a coal cart who presently loomed in view; but when she found that he slouched by without taking any notice of her, she took heart again and tripped blithely on.

Presently she found herself opposite to the little white-washed cottage; and she remembered that she had been there once or twice with her father. She would have been better pleased, just now, if the cottage had been on some other road. How could she pass it without being seen? This was plainly impossible; for there was the woman of the house— being the same whom Marian's father met the following morning—hanging out the clothes in the garden, close to the hedge. Marian trotted on, pretending not to know that there was any one near. Then she felt hot all over, as she became aware the woman had seen her, and was calling across the road. But she just gave her dusky little head a determined shake, and pursued her way. The woman, being weighted with an accumulation of domestic cares, without a second thought, and much to her subsequent regret, let the little runaway go by.

When Marian had left the cottage out of sight behind, she began to feel lonely, and to be very much afraid. There was not a human being in sight, except herself; and the only dwelling she could see was a farm-house, perched on the top of a hill, away across the fields. She slackened her pace, and looked furtively around. Then she went on more quickly again; but, in a few moments, a slight bend in the road brought before her a sight at which she stopped short and uttered a cry of alarm. An exceedingly ill-favoured man, and a no more prepossessing woman, were sitting upon the bank, by the road-side, discussing a dinner of broken victuals. They were thorough-going tramps, of middle age. Marian would have fled; but their evil eyes held her to the spot.

J. W. Keyworth

"What a pretty little lady!" said the man, holding out a very dirty hand. "Come here, missy!"

But Marian shrank back with a smothered cry.

"I've finished my dinner, I have," said the man, getting up.

"So have I," echoed the woman, following his example; "and we'll go for a walk with little miss."

"What a precious lonely road!" she remarked, when she had glanced this way and that, to make sure that no prying eyes were near. "Catch hold o' the little 'un, Jake; and we'll take a stroll in the fields."

There was a perfect understanding between this precious pair; and Marian was promptly lifted over a five-barred gate, and led by the woman across a grass field, towards a wood on the other side, while the man followed stolidly in the rear. A few paces from the gate Marian's shoe came off; but she was as much too frightened to say anything about it, as she was to ask any questions of her captors, or to resist their will. Having reached the wood, they plunged into its recesses, and at length halted before a large pool, at the edge of which there lay upon the ground the trunks of some trees which had been cut down. Taking her seat on one of these, the woman drew Marian to her side, and, while the man stood by with an evil smile, proceeded to strip off some of the child's clothes. Marian began to cry, but was silenced with a rough shake and a threat of being thrown into the pond. Having divested the child of most of her garments, the woman took from a dirty bundle which she carried a draggled grey wool shawl, which she wrapped tightly, crosswise, around Marian's body, and tied in a hard knot behind her back.

Perceiving that Marian had lost one of her shoes, the hag

sent her husband back to look for it, while she proceeded with the metamorphosis of the hapless infant who had fallen into her hands. She smeared the little face with muddy water from the margin of the pool; she jerked out the semi-circular comb which held back Marian's cloud of dusky hair, and let the thick locks fall in disorder about her head and face; she dragged the little sun bonnet in the green slime at the margin of the pool, and, on pretence of tying it on the child's head, wrenched off one of the strings, which she heedlessly left lying on the ground.

At this point the man returned without the missing shoe.

"It doesn't matter," said his spouse. "Lend me your knife."

She then proceeded to cut and slash Marian's remaining shoe in a most remorseless manner, after which she replaced it on the child's foot, and wrapped around the other foot a piece of dirty rag.

"Come now," said the woman, having rolled up Marian's clothes with the rubbish in her bundle; "we wanted a little girl, and you'll just do." So saying, she took tight hold of the child's hand.

"I want my daddy!" cried Marian, finding her voice at last.

"That's your daddy now," said the woman, pointing to the man: "and I'm your mammy. Come along!" and, with the word, she set off at a vigorous pace, dragging the child, and, followed heavily by her husband, through the wood, and across the field, and then out upon the road, away and away, with their backs turned towards Marian's home.

# CHAPTER VIII

## THE SHOEMAKER BECOMES "GOLDEN"

One morning, about twelve years after the disappearance of Marian, there came to her father a great, and almost over-whelming surprise.

It is not necessary to dwell on the manner in which the twelve years had passed. Nothing had ever been heard of Marian. The most thorough search was made, but without result; and at length, the stricken father was constrained to accept the conviction that his child was indeed gone from him into the great world, and, bowing his head in the presence of his God, he covered his bruised heart with the fair sheet of a dignified self-control, and settled down to his work again, like a man and a Christian.

Yet he did not cease inwardly to grieve. If his child had gone to her dead mother, there would have been strong conso-lation, and, perhaps, in time, contentment might have come. But she was gone, not to her mother, but out into the cold, pitiless world; and his imagination dwelt grimly on the nameless miseries into which she might fall.

Miss Jemima still kept her brother's house; but she had been greatly softened by her self-accusing grief. And now, as the brother and sister sat at breakfast one autumn morning, came the surprise of which we speak. It came in the form of a letter, which, before opening it, "Cobbler" Horn regarded, for some moments, with a dubious air. The arrival of a letter at his house was a rare event; and but for the fact that the missive bore his name and address, he would have thought there was a mistake, and, even now, the addition of the sign, "Esq." to his name left the matter in some doubt. The stoutness of the blue envelope, and the bold character of the handwriting, gave the packet a business-like look. For a moment, "Cobbler" Horn thought of his lost child. A slight circumstance was sufficient, even yet, to re-awaken his hopes; and he still clung to the conviction that, some day, his child would return. The letter, however, contained no reference to the great sorrow of his life; and, indeed, its contents were such that he forgot, for the time being, Marian, and everything else. He looked up with a gasp of astonishment; and then, turning his attention again to the letter, deliberately read it through, and, when he had finished, calmly handed it to his sister. She read a few words, and broke off with a cry.

"Thomas!"

"Yes, Jemima, I am a rich man, it seems. Read on, and say what you think;" and "Cobbler" Horn rose from his seat, and went quietly into his workshop.

Miss Jemima devoured her brother's letter with greedy eyes. It was from a firm of London lawyers, and contained a brief announcement that the rich uncle of "Cobbler" Horn had died, in America, without a will; that "Cobbler" Horn was the lawful owner of all his wealth; and that they, the lawyers, awaited "Cobbler" Horn's commands. Would he call upon them at their office in London, or should they attend him at his private, or any other, address? In the meantime, he would oblige by drawing upon them for any amount of money he might require.

With what breath she had left Miss Jemima hurried into her brother's workshop.

"Thomas," she demanded, flourishing the letter in his face, "what are you going to do?"

"Think," he answered concisely, without looking up from the hob-nailed boot between his knees, "and pray, and get on with my work."

"But this letter requires an answer! And," with a glance of disgust around the rough shop with its signs of toil, "you are a rich man now, Thomas."

"That," was the quiet reply, "does not alter the fact that I have half-a-dozen pairs of boots to mend, and two of them are promised for dinner-time. Leave me, now, Jemima, and we'll talk the matter over this evening. I don't suppose the gentlemen will be in a hurry."

Miss Jemima withdrew as she was bidden, thinking that there was one gentleman, at least, who was not in a hurry.

All day long "Cobbler" Horn quietly worked on in the usual way. He did this partly because he loved his work and was loath to give it up, partly because he had so much work on hand, and partly that he might think and pray, which he could always do best on his cobbler's stool. He found it difficult to realize what had taken place; but when, at last, he fairly grasped the fact that he was now a rich man, mingled feelings of joy and dread filled his breast. There was little taint of selfishness in "Cobbler" Horn's joy. It was no gratification to him to be relieved of the necessity to work.

Nor was he fascinated with the prospect of luxury. His joy arose chiefly from the thought of the amount of good he would now be able to do. It was impossible that he should form anything like an adequate conception of the vast power for good which had been placed in his hands. The boundless ability to benefit his fellowmen with which he had been so suddenly endowed could not be realized in the first moments of his great surprise, yet he perceived faint glimmerings of possibilities of benevolence beyond his largest-hearted dreams.

Thoughts of his long-lost child stole over him ever and anon. If she had been left to him, he would have rejoiced in his good fortune the more, on her account. But she was gone.

The joy of "Cobbler" Horn was chastened by a solemn dread. A great responsibility had been laid upon him from which he would have infinitely rather been free. He prayed, with trembling, that he might prove worthy of so great a trust.

At dinner-time Miss Jemima questioned her brother as to his intentions. His answers were brief and indefinite. The matter could not be settled in a moment. In the evening they would talk things over, and decide what to do.

The evening came, and brother and sister sat before the fire.

"Jemima," said "Cobbler" Horn, "I must accept this great responsibility."

"You surely did not think of doing anything else?" exclaimed the startled lady.

"Well—yes—I did. The burden seemed so great that, for a time, I shrank. But the Lord has shown me my duty. I could have desired that we might have remained as we were. But there is much consolation in the thought of all the good we shall be able to do; and—well, the will of the Lord be done!"

Miss Jemima was astounded. Her brother had become rich beyond the dreams of avarice, and he talked of resignation to the will of God!

"Then you will answer the letter at once?" she said.

"Yes, to-morrow."

"And you will go to London?"

"Yes, next week, I think."

"Next week! Why not this week? It's only Monday."

"There is no need to hurry, Jemima. There might be some mistake. And it's as well to give the gentlemen time to prepare."

"Lawyers don't make mistakes," said Miss Jemima: "And as for preparing, you may be sure they have done that already."

But nothing could induce "Cobbler" Horn to hasten his movements; and his sister was fain to content herself with his promise to write to the lawyers the next day, which he duly fulfilled.

# CHAPTER IX

## A STRANGE CLIENT FOR MESSRS.
## TONGS AND BALL

The day on which "Cobbler" Horn had proposed to the lawyers to pay them his promised visit, was the following Monday, at three o'clock in the afternoon, and by return of post there came a letter from the lawyers assenting to the arrangement. During the week which intervened, "Cobbler" Horn did not permit either himself or his sister to mention to a third person the change his circumstances had undergone. Nor did he encourage conversation between his sister and himself on the subject of his suddenly acquired wealth. And neither his manner of life nor the ordering of his house gave any indication of the altered position in which he was placed. He did not permit the astounding news he had received to interfere with the simple regularity of his life. Miss Jemima might have been inclined to introduce into her domestic arrangements some outward and visible sign of the altered fortunes of the house; but her brother's will prevailed, and all things continued as before. The "golden shoemaker" even continued to work at his trade in the usual way. And all the time he was thinking—thinking and praying; and many generous purposes, which afterwards bore abundant fruit, began to germinate in his mind.

J. W. Keyworth

At length the momentous day arrived, and "Cobbler" Horn travelled by an early train to London, and, having dined frugally at a decent eating-house, presented himself in due time at the offices of Messrs. Tongs and Ball. The men of law were both seated in the room into which their new client was shown. One of them was a very little, round, rosy, middle-aged man, with an expression of countenance so cherubic that no one would have suspected him of being a lawyer; and the other was a tall, large-boned, parchment-faced personage, of whom almost any degree of heart-lessness might have been believed. The two lawyers rose and bowed as "Cobbler" Horn was shown in.

"Mr. Horn?"

"Thomas Horn, at your service, gentlemen."

"This is Mr. Tongs," said the tall lawyer with a waive of his hand towards his rotund partner; "and I am Mr. Ball," he added, drawing himself into an attitude which caused him to look much more like a bat than a ball, and speaking in a surprisingly agreeable tone. Upon this there was bowing all around, and then a pause.

"Pray take a seat, Mr. Horn," besought Mr. Ball.

"Cobbler" Horn modestly obeyed.

"And now, my dear sir," said Mr. Ball, when he himself and his partner had also resumed their seats, "let us congratulate you on your good fortune."

"Thank you, gentlemen," said "Cobbler" Horn gravely. "But the responsibility is very great. I am only reconciled to it by the thought that I shall now be able to do many things that I have long desired to do."

"Ah," said Mr. Ball, "it is one of the gratifications of wealth that a man is able to follow his bent—whether it be travelling, collecting pictures, keeping horses, or what not."

"Of course," echoed Mr. Tongs.

"No, no, gentlemen," dissented "Cobbler" Horn, "I was thinking of the good I shall now be able to do. But let us get to business; for I should be sorry to waste your time."

Both lawyers protested. Waste their time! They could not be better employed!

"You are very kind, gentlemen."

"Not at all," was the candid reply.

"You have come into a very large fortune, Mr. Horn," continued Mr. Ball, as he began to untie a bundle of documents. "You are worth very many thousands; in fact you are almost a millionaire. I think I am right, Mr. Tongs?"

"Yes," assented Mr. Tongs, "oh yes, certainly."

"All the documents are here," resumed Mr. Ball, as he surveyed a sea of blue and white paper which covered the table; "and, with your permission, Mr. Horn, we will give you an account of their contents."

The lawyer then proceeded to give his client a statement of the particulars of the fortune of which he had so unexpectedly become possessed.

"We hope, Mr. Horn," he said, in conclusion, "that you may do us the honour to continue the confidence reposed in us by your late uncle."

"I beg your pardon, sir?" said "Cobbler" Horn.

"I ventured to hope that my partner and I might be so fortunate as to retain the management of your affairs. I believe you will find that since—"

"Oh yes, of course," "Cobbler" Horn hastened to interpose. He had not dreamt of making any change. The lawyers bowed their thanks.

"May we now ask," said Mr. Ball, "whether you have any special commands?"

"I think there are one or two requests I should like to make. I have a sister, and I believe my uncle left another nephew."

"A sad scrapegrace, my dear sir," interposed Mr. Ball, whose keen legal instinct gave him some scent of what was coming next.

"Cobbler" Horn held up his hand.

"Can you tell me, gentlemen, whether there are any other relatives of my uncle's who are still alive?"

"We have every reason to believe that there are not."

"Very well, then, I wish my uncle's property to be divided into three equal portions. One third I desire to have made over to my sister, and another to be reserved for my cousin. The remaining portion I will retain myself."

"But, my dear sir," cried Mr. Ball, "the whole of the property is legally yours!"

"True," was the quiet reply; "but the law cannot make that

right which is essentially wrong, and my sister and cousin are as much entitled to my uncle's money as I am myself."

Mr. Ball was dumfounded.

"My dear sir," he gasped, "this is very strange!"

But "Cobbler" Horn was firm.

"You will find this scapegrace cousin of mine?" he asked.

The lawyers said they would do their best; and, when some further arrangements had been made, with regard to the property, "Cobbler" Horn took his departure, leaving his two legal advisers to assure one another, as they stood together on the hearthrug, that he was the strangest client they had known.

J. W. Keyworth

# CHAPTER X

## MISS JEMIMA IS VERY MUCH ASTONISHED

Miss Jemima Horn was sufficiently curious as to the result of her brother's visit to the lawyers, to render her restlessly eager for his return. He came back the same night. He had work to finish in the cobbling line; and besides he had no fancy for any bed but his own.

After supper, the brother and sister sat down before the fire, for the talk to which Miss Jemima had been looking forward all day long.

"Well, brother," she queried, "I suppose you've heard all about it?"

"Yes, in a general way."

"And what is the amount?"

"I'm almost afraid to say. The gentlemen said little short of a million!"

Miss Jemima threw up her hands with a little jerk of wonder, and gazed at her brother with incredulous surprise.

"Where is it all?" was her next enquiry.

"Some in England, and some in America."

"It's not all in money, of course?" she asked, in doubtful tones.

"No," said her brother, opening his eyes: "it's in all sorts of ways. A great deal of it is in house property. There's one whole village—or nearly so."

"A whole village!"

"Yes, the village of Daisy Lane. It was the family home at one time, you know."

This was true. The village of Daisy Lane, in a Midland county, had been the cradle of the race of Horn. "Cobbler" Horn and his sister, however, had never visited the ancestral village.

"Well?" queried Miss Jemima.

"Well, uncle had a fancy for owning the village; so he bought it up bit by bit."

"Only to think!" exclaimed Miss Jemima. "And what else is there?"

"Well, there's money in all sorts of forms that I understand very little about."

"It's simply wonderful!" declared Miss Jemima.

"And then there's the old hall at Daisy Lane. Uncle meant to end his days there; but God has ordered otherwise, you see."

J. W. Keyworth

"And you will go to live there?"

"No," answered her brother, slowly; "I think not, Jemima."

"But—"

"Sister, I don't think we should be happy in a grand house—at any rate not all at once. But there's something else I want to talk about."

Of late years the ascendancy had completely passed from Miss Jemima to her brother; and now, though she would fain have talked further about the old family mansion, she submissively turned her attention to what her brother was about to say.

"It is probable, Jemima," he begun, "that there has never been a rich man who had so few relatives to whom to leave his wealth as had our uncle."

"Yes: father and Uncle Ira were the only members of Uncle Jacob's family who ever married; and the brothers and sisters are all dead now. We are almost alone in the world."

"Except one cousin, you know," said "Cobbler" Horn.

"You mean Uncle Ira's scapegrace, Jack. But no one knows where he is. He may be dead for all we know."

Somehow Miss Jemima did not seem to desire that there should be any other relatives of her uncle to the front, just now, but her brother and herself.

"If Jack is dead," said "Cobbler" Horn, "there will be no more to say. But if he is alive, he must have his share of uncle's money; and I have left it with the legal  gentlemen  to find him if they can."

"Thomas," protested Miss Jemima, "do you think it would be right to hand over uncle's hard-earned money to that poor wastrel?"

"His right to the money, Jemima, is as good as ours."

"Perhaps so; but I feel convinced that uncle would not have wished for any part of his money to go to Jack. It would be like flinging it into the sea."

"Yes; but that cuts both ways, Jemima. Uncle would never have willed his money to me, any more than to Jack. But God has given it to me, and I mean to use it in the way of which I believe He will approve."

"And that is not all," he hastily resumed. "I have another relative;" and he directed a look of loving significance towards his sister's face. "Do you think that, if I admit the claim of our poor scapegrace cousin to a share of our uncle's money, I shall overlook the right of the dear sister who has been my stay and comfort all these sorrowing years?"

"But—but—" began Miss Jemima, in bewildered tones.

"Yes, you are to have your share too, Jemima."

"But, brother I don't desire it. If you have the money, it's all the same as though I had it myself."

With all her severity, there was not an atom of selfishness in Miss Jemima Horn.

"It's all arranged," was her brother's reply. "I instructed the lawyers to divide the property into three equal portions."

Miss Jemima, supposing that an arrangement with the lawyers was like the laws of the Medes and Persians, which "altered not," felt compelled to submit; but it was with the understanding that her brother took entire management of her portion of the money, as well as his own.

There was little further talk between "Cobbler" Horn and his sister that evening. Their early bed-time had arrived; and "Cobbler" Horn, having read a chapter in the Bible, offered a fervent prayer, in which he asked earnestly that his sister and himself might receive grace to use rightly the great wealth which had been entrusted to their charge.

"If we should prove unfaithful, Lord," he said, "take it from us as suddenly as Thou hast given it."

"Oh, brother," cried Miss Jemima, as they were going up to bed, "some letters came for you this morning."

"Cobbler" Horn took the four or five letters, which his sister was holding out to him, with a bewildered air.

"Are they really for me?" he asked.

"Small doubt of that," said Miss Jemima.

The opening of letters was, as yet, to "Cobbler" Horn, a ceremony to be performed with care. He drew a chair to the table, and deliberately took his seat. He took up the first letter, and, having read it slowly through, placed it in Miss Jemima's eager hand. It was a request, from a "gentleman in distress," for a loan of twenty pounds—a "trifle" to the possessor of so much wealth, but, to the writer "a matter of life or death."

"This will never do!" pronounced Miss Jemima; and the lady's lips emitted a gentle whistling sound.

"How soon it seems to have got wind!" exclaimed "Cobbler" Horn.

"It's been in the papers, no doubt."

"So it has," he said; "I saw it myself in a newspaper that I bought this evening, to read in the train. It called me the 'Golden Shoemaker.'"

"Ah!" cried Miss Jemima. "I've no doubt it will go the round." The good lady was not greatly averse to such a pleasant publication of the family name.

"Well," she resumed, "what do the other letters say?"

They were all similar to the first. One was from a man who had invented a new boot sewing-machine, and would take out a patent; another purported to came from a widow with six young children, and begged for a little—ever so little—timely help: and the other two were appeals on behalf of religious institutions.

"Penalty of wealth!" remarked Miss Jemima, as she took the letters from her brother's hand.

"I suppose I must answer them to-morrow," groaned "Cobbler" Horn.

"Answer them!" exclaimed Miss Jemima. "If you take my advice, you'll throw them into the fire. There will be plenty more of the same sort soon. Though," she added thought-fully, "you'll have to read your letters, I suppose; for there'll be some you'll be obliged to answer."

"Well," said "Cobbler" Horn quietly, as they turned to the stairs, "we shall see."

# CHAPTER XI

## "COBBLER" HORN ANSWERS HIS LETTERS, AND RECEIVES THE CONGRATULATIONS OF HIS FRIENDS

When, after a somewhat troubled night, "Cobbler" Horn came down next morning, his attention was arrested by the letters lying, as he had left them, on the table, the night before.

"Yes," he said, in answer to his thoughts; "I think I'll deal with them straight away." So saying, he drew a chair to the table, and, having found a few sheets of time-stained note paper, together with a penny bottle of ink, and an old crippled pen, he sat down to his unwelcome task. The undertaking proved even more troublesome than he had thought it would be. The pen persisted in sputtering at almost every word; and when, at crucial points, he took special pains to make the writing legible, the too frequent result was an indecipherable blotch of ink. When the valiant scribe had wrestled with his uncongenial task for half an hour or more, his sister came upon the scene. Quietly she stepped across the floor.

"Ah!" she exclaimed, peeping over her brother's shoulder, "so you are answering them already!"

"Cobbler" Horn started, and a huge blot fell from his pen into the midst of his half-finished letter.

"I'm afraid I shall not be able to send this, now," he said, with a patient sigh.

"No," said Miss Jemima, laconically, "I'm afraid not. You are writing to the 'widow,' I see; and you are promising her some help. That's very well. But, in nine cases out of ten, what strangers say of themselves requires confirmation— especially if they are beggars; so don't you think that, before sending money to this 'widow,' it would be as well to ask for the name of some reliable person who will vouch for the truth of her statements? You must not forget, what you often say, you know, that you are the steward of your Lord's goods."

This was an argument which was sure to prevail with "Cobbler" Horn.

"No doubt you are right, Jemima," he said; "and, however reluctantly, I must take your advice."

"That's right," said Miss Jemima.

"You haven't answered the other letters?" she then asked, with a glance over the table.

"No."

"Well, hadn't you better put them away now, and get to your work? After breakfast you must get a new pen and a fresh bottle of ink. Then we'll see what we can do together."

In an emergency which demanded the exercise of the practical good sense, of which she had so large a share, Miss

Jemima regained, to some extent, her old ascendency over her brother. He quietly gathered up his letters, and, placing them on the chimney-piece, retired to his workshop.

At breakfast-time Miss Jemima's prognostication began to receive fulfilment in the arrival of the postman with another batch of letters. This time the number had increased to something like a dozen. Having received them from the hands of the postman, "Cobbler" Horn carried them towards his sister with a somewhat comical air of dismay.

"So many!" exclaimed she. "Your cares are accumulating fast. You will have to engage a secretary. Well, we'll look at them by and bye."

Scarcely was breakfast over than there came a modest knock at the door, which, on being opened by Miss Jemima, revealed the presence of the elder of the little twin hucksters, who still carried on business across the way.

Miss Jemima drew herself up like a sentry; and little Tommy Dudgeon, finding himself confronted by this formidable lady, would have beaten a hasty retreat. But it was too late.

"I beg your pardon, ma'am," he began humbly; "I came to see your brother."

"I don't know," was the lady's lofty reply. "My brother has much business on hand."

"No doubt, ma'am; but—but—"

At this point "Cobbler" Horn himself came to the door, and Miss Jemima retreated into the house.

"Good morning, Tommy," said "Cobbler" Horn heartily,

"step in."

"Thank you, Mr. Horn," was the modest reply, "I'm afraid I can't. Business presses, you know. But I've just come to congratulate you if I may make so bold. Brother would have come too; but he's minding the twins. It's washing day, you see. He'll pay his respects another time."

John Dudgeon had been married for some years, and amongst the troubles which had varied for him the joys of that blissful state, there had recently come the crowning calamity of twins—an affliction which would seem to have run in the Dudgeon family.

"We are glad you have inherited this vast wealth, Mr. Horn," said Tommy Dudgeon. "We think the arrangement excellent. The ways of Providence are indeed wonderful."

"Cobbler" Horn made suitable acknowledgment of the congratulations of his humble little friend.

"There is only one thing we regret," resumed the little man; "and that is that your change of fortune will remove you to another sphere."

"Cobbler" Horn smiled.

"Well, well," he said, "we shall see."

Whereupon Tommy Dudgeon, feeling comforted, he scarcely knew why, said "Good morning" and ambled back to his shop.

About the middle of the morning "Cobbler" Horn and his sister sat down to deal with the letters. First they glanced at those which had arrived that morning, and then laid them aside for the time, until, in fact, they had dealt with those previously received. First came that of the assumed widow, to which Miss Jemima induced her brother to write a cautious reply, asking for a reference. To the man who asked for the loan of twenty pounds, Miss Jemima would have sent no reply at all; but "Cobbler" Horn insisted that a brief but courteous note should be sent to him, expressing regret that the desired loan could not be furnished. It did not need the persuasion of his sister to induce "Cobbler" Horn to decline all dealings with the importunate inventor; but it was with great difficulty that she could dissuade him from making substantial promises to the religious institutions from which he had received appeals.

"I think I shall consult the minister about such cases," he said.

The investigation of the second batch of letters was postponed until the afternoon.

During the morning, and at intervals throughout the day, others of "Cobbler" Horn's neighbours came to offer their congratulations, and were astonished to find him seated on his cobbler's stool, and quietly plying his accustomed task. To their remonstrances he would reply, "You see this work is promised; and if I am rich, I must keep my word. And then the habits of a lifetime are not to be given up in a day. And, to be honest with you, friends, I am in no haste to make the change. I love my work, and would as lief be sitting on this stool as anywhere else in the world."

There came some of his poorer customers, who greatly bewailed what they regarded as his inevitable removal from their midst. They could not congratulate him as heartily as they desired. They would rather he had remained the poor, kind-hearted, Christian cobbler whom they had always known. Many a pair of boots had he mended free of charge for customers who could ill afford to pay; not a few were the small debts of poor but honest debtors which he had forgiven; and not seldom had clandestine gifts of money or food found their way from his hands to one or another of these regretful congratulators. Perceiving the grief upon the faces of his friends, "Cobbler" Horn contrived, by means of various hints, to let them know that he would still be their friend, and to remind them that his enrichment would conduce to their more effectual help at his hands.

On one point all his visitors were agreed. Great wealth, they said, could not have come to any one by whom it was more thoroughly deserved, or who would put it to a better use. "The Lord," affirmed one quaint individual, "knew what He was about this time, anyhow."

In the afternoon, "Cobbler" Horn and his sister set about the task of answering the second batch of letters. They were all, with one exception, of a similar character to those of the first. The exception proved to be a badly-written, ill-spelled, but evidently sincere, homily on the dangers of wealth, and ended with a fierce warning of the dire consequences of disregarding its admonition. It was signed simply—"A friend."

"You'll burn that, I should think!" was Miss Jemima's scornful comment on this ill-judged missive.

"No," said "Cobbler" Horn, putting the letter into his breast pocket; "I shall keep it. It was well meant, and will do me good."

By tea-time their task was finished; and "Cobbler" Horn heaved a sigh of relief as he rose from his seat. But just then the postman knocked at the door, and handed in another and still larger supply of letters, at the sight of which the "Golden Shoemaker" staggered back aghast. The fame of his fortune had indeed got wind.

"Ah," exclaimed his sister, who was setting the tea-things, "you'll have to engage a secretary, as I said."

# CHAPTER XII

## "COBBLER" HORN PAYS
## A VISIT TO HIS LANDLORD

The day following his trip to London "Cobbler" Horn paid a visit to his landlord. His purpose was to buy the house in which he lived. Though he realized that he must now take up his actual abode in a house more suited to his altered circumstances, he wished to retain the possession and use of the one in which he had lived so long. The humble cottage was endeared to him by many ties. Here the best part of his life had been passed. Here his brief but blissful married life had been spent, and here his precious wife had died. Of this house his darling little Marian had been the light and joy; and her blithe and loving spirit seemed to haunt it still. These memories, reinforced by a generous purpose on behalf of the poor neighbours whom he had been wont to help, decided him to endeavour to make the house absolutely his own.

"Cobbler" Horn did not tell his sister of his intention with regard to the house. He simply said, after breakfast, that he was going out for an hour; and, though Miss Jemima looked at him very hard, she allowed him to depart unquestioned.

"Cobbler" Horn's landlord who was reputed to be enormously rich, lived in one of the most completely hidden parts of the town, which was approached by a labyrinth of very narrow and dirty streets. As "Cobbler" Horn pursued his tortuous way to this secluded abode, he pondered, with some misgiving, the chances that his errand would succeed. He knew his landlord to be a man of stubborn temper and of many whims; and he was by no means confident as to the reception with which his intended proposal would meet. It was characteristic that, as he thought of the difficulties of his enterprise, he prayed earnestly that, if God willed, he might obtain the gratification of his present desire. Then, with growing confidence and quickened step, he proceeded on his way, until, at length, he stood before his landlord's house.

The house was a low, dingy building of brick, which stood right across the end of a squalid street, and completely blocked the way. Over the door was a grimy sign-board, on which could faintly be distinguished the vague yet comprehensive legend:

"D. FROUD,
DEALER."

The paint upon the crazy door was blistered and had peeled off in huge mis-shapen patches; the door-step was almost worn in two; the windows were dim with the dust of many years.

The door was opened by a withered crone, who, to his question whether Mr. Froud was in, answered in an injured tone, "Yes, he was in; he always was;" and, as she spoke, she half-pushed the visitor into a room on the left side of the entrance, and vanished from the scene. The room was very dark, and it was some time before "Cobbler" Horn could observe the nature of his surroundings. But, by degrees, as his eyes became accustomed to the gloom, he perceived that the centre of the apartment was occupied with an old mahogany table, covered with a litter of books and papers. There stood against the wall opposite to the window an ancient and dropsical chest of drawers. Facing the door was a fire-place, brown with rust, innocent of fire-irons, and piled up with heterogeneous rubbish. The walls and chimney-piece were utterly devoid of ornaments. The paper on the walls was torn and soiled, and even hung in strips. On the chimney-piece were several empty ink and gum bottles, an old ruler, and a further assortment of similar odds and ends. The only provision for the comfort of visitors consisted of two battered wooden chairs.

At first "Cobbler" Horn thought he was alone; but, the next moment, he heard himself sharply addressed, though not by name.

"Well, it's not rent day yet. What's your errand?"

It was a snarling voice, and came from the corner between the window and fire-place, peering in which direction, "Cobbler" Horn perceived dimly the figure of the man he had come to see. Mr. Daniel Froud had turned around from a high desk at which he had been writing in the gloom. How he contrived to see in so dark a corner was a mystery which belonged to the wider question as to the penetrating power of vision in general which he was known to possess. The small boys of the neighbourhood declared that he could see in the dark like a cat. He now moved a step nearer to "Cobbler" Horn, and stood revealed, an elderly, and rather undersized, grizzled, gnarled, and knotted man, dressed in shabby and antiquated clothes.

"Good morning, Mr. Froud," said "Cobbler" Horn, extending his hand, "I've come to see you on a little business."

"Of course you have," was the angry retort; and taking no

notice of his visitor's proffered hand, the man stamped his foot impatiently on the uncarpeted floor. "No one ever comes to see me about anything else but business. And I don't want them to," he added with a grim chuckle. "Well, let us get it done. My time is valuable, if yours is not."

"My time also is not without value," was the prompt reply. "I want to ask you, Mr. Froud, if you will sell me the house in which I live."

If Daniel Froud was surprised, he completely concealed the fact.

"If I would sell it," was his coarse rejoinder, "you, 'Cobbler' Horn, would not be able to buy it."

"I am well able to buy the house, Mr. Froud," was the quiet response.

Daniel Froud keenly scrutinized his visitor's face.

"I believe you think you are telling the truth," he said. "Mending pauper's boots and shoes must be a profitable business, then?"

"I have had some money left to me," said "Cobbler" Horn.

The interest of Daniel Froud was awakened at once.

"Ah!" he exclaimed, "that is it, is it? But sit down, Mr. Horn," and the grizzled reprobate pushed towards his visitor, who had hitherto remained standing, one of his rickety and dust-covered chairs.

"Cobbler" Horn looked doubtfully at the proffered seat, and said that he preferred to stand.

"If you are willing to sell me the house, Mr. Froud," he said, "name your price. It is not my intention to waste your time."

Daniel Froud still pondered. It was no longer a question whether he should sell "Cobbler" Horn the house: he was beginning already to consider how much he should ask for it.

"So you really wish to buy the house, Mr. Horn?" he asked.

"Such is my desire."

"And you think you can pay the price?"

"I have little doubt on that point."

"Well"—with a sudden jerk forward of his forbidding face— "what do you say to L600?"

Unsophisticated as he was, "Cobbler" Horn felt that the proposal was exorbitant.

"You are surely joking?" he said.

"You think the price too small?"

"I consider it much too large."

"Well, perhaps I was joking, as you said. What do you think of L500?"

"I'm afraid even that is too much. I'll give you L450."

Daniel Froud hesitated for some minutes, but at last said, "Well, I'll take your offer, Mr. Horn; but it's a dreadful sacrifice."

A few minutes sufficed to complete the agreement; and then, in taking his departure, "Cobbler" Horn administered a word of admonition to his grasping landlord.

"Don't you know, friend," he said, "that it is a grievous sin to try to sell anything for more than it is worth? And how contemptible it is to be so greedy of money! It does not seem to me that money is to be so eagerly desired, and especially if it does one no more good than yours seems to be doing you. Good morning, friend; and God give you repentance."

Mr. Froud had listened open-mouthed to this plain-spoken homily. When he came to himself, he darted forward, and aimed a blow with his fist, which just failed to strike the back of his visitor, who was in the act of leaving the room.

Confronting him in the doorway was the old crone who kept his house.

"Was that Horn, the shoemaker?" she asked.

"Yes, woman."

"Horn as has just come into the fortune?"

"Well—somewhat."

"'Somewhat!' It's said to be about a million of money! Look here!" and she showed him a begrimed and crumpled scrap of newspaper, containing a full account of "Cobbler" Horn's fortune.

With a cry, Daniel Froud seized the woman, and shook her till it almost seemed as though the bones rattled in her skin.

"You hell-cat! Why didn't you tell me that before?"

The wretched creature fell back panting against the door on the opposite side of the passage.

"Daniel Froud," she said, when she had sufficiently recovered her breath, "the next time you do that I shall give you notice."

With which dreadful threat, she gathered herself together, and hobbled back to her own quarter of the dingy house, leaving Mr. Froud to bemoan the absurdly easy terms he had made with "the Golden Shoemaker."

"If I had only known!" he moaned; "if I had only known!"

That evening "Cobbler" Horn told his sister what he had done, and why he had done it; and she held up her hands in dismay.

"First," she said, "I don't see why you should have bought the house at all; and, secondly, you have paid far more for it than it is worth."

# CHAPTER XIII

## FREE COBBLERY

"I suppose you'll be looking out for a tenant for this house, when you've found somewhere for us to go?" queried Miss Jemima, at breakfast the next morning.

"Well, no," replied her brother, "I think not." "Why," cried Miss Jemima, "I hope we are not to go on living in this poky little place!"

"No, that is not exactly my intention, either," said "Cobbler" Horn. "We must, I suppose, remove to another house. But I wish this one to remain very much as it is; I shall want to use it sometimes."

"Want to use it sometimes!" echoed Miss Jemima, in a mystified tone.

"Yes; you see I don't feel that I can give up my lifelong employment all at once. So I've been thinking that I'll come to the old workshop, now and then, and do a bit of cobbling just for a change."

Here he paused, and moved uneasily in his chair.

"It wouldn't do to charge anything for my work now, of course," he continued; "so I've made up my mind to do little bits of jobs, now and again, without any pay, for some of the poor people round about, just for the sake of old times, you know."

Miss Jemima's hands went up with their accustomed movement of dismay.

"Why, that will never do," she cried. "You'll have all the thriftless loons in the town bringing you their boots and shoes to mend."

"I must guard against that," was the quiet reply.

"Well," continued Miss Jemima, in an aggrieved tone, "I altogether disapprove of your continuing to work as if you were a poor man. But you ought, at least, to make a small charge. Otherwise you will be imposed upon all round."

Finding, however, that she could not move her brother from his purpose, Miss Jemima relinquished the attempt.

"Well, Thomas," she concluded, "you can never have been intended for this world and its ways. There is probably a vacancy in some quite different one which you ought to have filled."

The next few days were largely spent in house hunting; and, after careful investigation, and much discussion, they decided to take, for the present, a pleasantly situated detached villa, which stood on the road leading out past the field where, so many years ago, "Cobbler" Horn had found his little lost Marian's shoe. The nearness of the house to this spot had induced him, in spite of his sister's protest, to prefer it to several otherwise more eligible residences; and he was confirmed in his decision by the fact that the villa was no great distance from the humble dwelling he was so reluctant to leave. They were to have possession at once; and Miss Jemima was permitted to plunge without delay into the delights of buying furniture, engaging servants, and such like fascinating concerns.

During these busy days, "Cobbler" Horn himself was absorbed in the arrangements for the rehabilitation of his old workshop. He subjected it to a complete renovation, in keeping with its character and use. A new tile floor, a better window, a fresh covering of whitewash on the walls, and a new coat of paint for the wood-work, effected a transformation as agreeable as it was complete. He kept the old stool; but procured a new and modern set of tools, and furnished himself with a stock of the best leather the market could supply.

He had no difficulty in letting his poor customers know of his charitable designs, and he soon had as much work as he could do. As his sister had warned him, he had many applications from those who were unworthy of his help. He did not like to turn any of the applicants away; but he did so remorselessly in every instance in which, after careful investigation, the case broke down, his chief regret being that his gratuitous services were rarely sought by those who needed them most. But this is to anticipate.

It was in connection with what was regarded as the *quixotic* undertaking of Miss Jemima's brother to mend, free of charge, the boots and shoes of his poor neighbours, that he soon became generally known as "Cobbler" Horn.

# CHAPTER XIV

## "THE GOLDEN SHOEMAKER"
## WAITS UPON HIS MINISTER

"Cobbler" Horn's correspondence was steadily accumulating. Every day brought fresh supplies of letters; and the humble cottage was in danger of being swamped by an epistolary inundation, which was the despair of "Cobbler" Horn, and a growing vexation to his sister's order-loving soul.

For some time "the Golden Shoemaker" persisted valiantly in his attempt to answer every letter he received. Miss Jemima's scornful disapproval was of no avail. In vain she declared her conviction that every other letter was an imposture or a hoax, and pointed out that, if people wanted their letters answered, they ought to enclose a stamp. Then, for the twentieth time, she repeated her suggestion that a secretary should be engaged. At first her brother waived this proposal aside; but at length it became imperative that help should be sought. "Cobbler" Horn was like a man who attempts, single-handed, to cut his way through a still-accumulating snow-drift. The man must perish, if help do not come; unless "Cobbler" Horn secured assistance in dealing with his letters, it was impossible to tell what his fate might be. It was now simply a question by what means the needed help might best be obtained; and both "Cobbler" Horn and his sister agreed that the wisest thing would be to consult the minister of their church. This, accordingly, "Cobbler" Horn resolved to do.

"Cobbler" Horn's minister officiated in a sanctuary such as was formerly called a "chapel," but is now, more frequently designated a "church." His name was Durnford; and he was a man of strongly-marked individuality—a godly, earnest, shrewd, and somewhat eccentric, minister of the Gospel. He was always accessible to his people in their trouble or perplexity, and they came to him without reserve. But surely his advice had never been sought concerning difficulties so peculiar as those which were about to be laid before him by "Cobbler" Horn!

It was about ten o'clock on the Monday morning following his visit to the lawyers, that "Cobbler" Horn sat in Mr. Durnford's study, waiting for the minister to appear. He had not long to wait. The door opened, and Mr. Durnford entered. He was a middle-aged man of medium height, with keen yet kindly features, and hair and beard of iron grey. He greeted his visitor with unaffected cordiality.

"I've come to ask your advice, sir, under circumstances of some difficulty," said "Cobbler" Horn, when they were seated facing each other before a cheerful fire.

This being a kind of appeal to which he was accustomed, the minister received the announcement calmly enough.

"Glad to help you, if I can, Mr. Horn," he said.

There was a breeziness about Mr. Durnford which at once afforded preliminary refreshment to such troubled spirits as sought his counsel.

"Thank you, sir," said "Cobbler" Horn, "I'm sure you will.

You have heard of the sudden and unexpected—"

"To be sure!" broke in the minister, leaping to his feet, and grasping his visitor's hand, "Pardon me; I quite forgot. Let me congratulate you. Of course it's true?"

"Yes, sir, thank you; it's true—too true, I'm afraid."

Mr. Durnford laughed.

"How if I were to commiserate you, then?" he said.

"No, sir," said "Cobbler" Horn gravely, "not that either. It's the Lord's will after all; and it's a great joy to me to be able to do so much that I have long wished to do. It's the responsibility that I feel."

"Very good," replied the minister; "such joy is the purest pleasure wealth can give. But the responsibility of such a position as yours, is, no doubt, as you say, very great."

"Yes, sir; I feel that I hold all this wealth in trust from God; and I want to be a faithful steward. I am resolved to use my Lord's money exactly as I believe He desires that I should—in fact as He Himself would use it, if He were in my place."

"Excellent, Mr. Horn!" exclaimed the minister; "you have spoken like a Christian."

"Thank you, sir. But there's another thing; it seems so dreadful that one man should have so much money. Do you know, sir, I'm almost a millionaire?"

He made this announcement in very much the same tone in which he would have informed the minister that he was stricken with some dire disease.

"Is your trouble so great as that?" asked Mr. Durnford, in mock dismay.

"Yes, sir; and it's a very serious matter indeed. It doesn't seem right for me to be so rich, while so many have too little, and not a few nothing at all."

"That can soon be rectified," said Mr. Durnford.

"Perhaps so, sir; though it may not be so easy as you suppose. But there's another matter that troubles me. I can't think that this great wealth has been all acquired by fair means. Indeed I have only too much reason to suspect that it was not. I feel ashamed that some of the money which my uncle made should have become mine. I feel as though a curse were on it."

"Ah!" exclaimed the minister, with a long-drawn sigh, "such feelings do you credit, Mr. Horn; but don't you see that God means you to turn that curse into a blessing?"

"Yes; and yet I am almost inclined to wish my uncle had taken his money with him."

"Scarcely a charitable wish, from any point of view," said Mr. Durnford, smiling. "It seems to me that nothing could have been better than the arrangement as it stands."

"Well, at any rate, I wish it were possible to restore their money to any persons who may have been wronged."

"A laudible, but impossible wish, my dear sir; but, though you cannot restore your uncle's wealth to those from whom it may have been wrongfully acquired, you can, in some measure, make atonement for the evil involved in its acquisition, by employing it for the benefit of those in general who suffer and are in need."

"Yes," assented "Cobbler" Horn, with emphasis; "if I thought otherwise, every coin of the money that I handled would scorch my fingers to the bone."

After this there was a brief silence, and the minister sat back in his chair, with closed eyes, smiling gently.

"I beg your pardon," he said, in another moment, starting forward, "I have been thinking of all the good that might be done, if every rich man were like you. But you came to ask my advice?"

"Yes, sir," replied "Cobbler" Horn; "and I am keeping you too long."

"Not at all, my dear sir! Your visit has refreshed me greatly. Your talk is like a cool breeze on a hot day. It is not often that a millionaire comes to discuss with me the responsibilities of wealth. But let me hear what the peculiar difficulty is of which you spoke."

"Well, sir, there is a serious inconvenience involved in my new position, with which I am quite unable to grapple."

"Ah," said the minister, raising his eye-brows, "what is that?"

"Why it is just the number of letters I receive."

"Of course!" cried the minister, with twinkling eyes. "The birds of prey will be upon you from every side; and your being a religious man will, by no means, mitigate the evil."

"Ah, I have no doubt you are right, sir! And it's a sort of compliment to religion, isn't it?"

"Of course it is," said Mr. Durnford; "and a very beautiful way of looking at it too."

"Thank you, sir. Well, there are two sides to my difficulty. First I wish to answer every letter I receive; but I cannot possibly do it myself."

"No," said the minister. "But surely many of them need not be answered at all."

"Yes, sir, by your leave. My sister says that many of the letters are probably impostures. But you see I cannot tell certainly which are of that kind. She also points out that very few of them contain stamps for reply. But I tell her that a few stamps, more or less, are of no moment to me now."

"I don't know," broke in the minister, "which more to admire—your sister's wisdom or your own goodness."

"Cobbler" Horn deprecatingly waved his hand.

"Now, sir," he resumed, "Jemima advises me to engage a secretary."

"Obviously," assented the minister, "that is your best course."

"I suppose it is, sir; but I am all at sea, and want your help."

"And you shall have it," said the minister heartily. "There are scores of young men—and young women too—who would jump at the chance of such a post as that of your secretary would probably be."

"Thank you, sir; but you said young *women*?"

"Precisely. Young women often accept, and very efficiently fill, such posts."

"Indeed? I don't know how my sister—"

"Of course not. But suppose we look for a moment at the other side of your difficulty."

"Very well, sir; the other trouble is that I find it hard to decide what answers to send to a good many of the letters. They are mostly applications for money; and it's not easy to tell whether they are genuine. Then there are a great many appeals on behalf of all sorts of good objects. May I venture to hope, sir, that you will give me your advice in these matters?"

"With pleasure!" replied Mr. Durnford, with sparkling eyes.

"Thank you, sir; thank you very much indeed," said "Cobbler" Horn, greatly relieved. "And will it be too much if I ask you to advise me, in due course, as to the best way of making this money of my uncle's do as much good as possible, in a general way?"

"By no means," protested Mr. Durnford, "I am entirely at your service, my dear sir. But now," he added, after a pause, "I've been considering, and I think I can find you a secretary."

"Ah! who is he, sir?"

"It is she, not he."

"But, sir!"

"Yes, I know; but this is an exceptional young lady."

"A *young* lady?"

"Yes, a capable, well-behaved, Christian young lady. I have known her for a good many years, and would recommend her to anybody. I know she is looking out for such a situation as this. She would serve you well—better than any young man, I know—and would be a most agreeable addition to your family circle. Besides, by engaging my friend, Miss Owen, you would be affording help in a case of real need and sterling merit. The girl has no parents, and has been brought up by some kind friends. But they are not rich, and she will have to make her own way. Now, look here; suppose the young lady were to run down and see you? She lives in Birmingham."

"Do you really think it would be advisable?"

"Indeed I do. She'll disarm Miss Horn at once. It'll be a case of love at first sight."

"Well, sir, let it be as you say."

"Then I may write to her without delay?"

"If you please, sir."

"Pray for me, Mr. Durnford," said "Cobbler" Horn, as he took his leave.

"I will, my friend," was the hearty response.

"It's not often," resumed "Cobbler" Horn, "that a Christian man is placed in circumstances of such difficulty as mine."

The minister laughed heartily and long.

"I really mean it, sir," persisted "Cobbler" Horn, with a deprecatory smile. "When I think of all that my having this money involves, I almost wish the Lord had been pleased to leave me in my contented poverty."

"My dear friend," said the minister, "that will not do at all. Depend upon it, the joy of using your wealth for the Lord, and for His 'little ones,' will far more than make up for the vanished delights of your departed poverty."

J. W. Keyworth

# CHAPTER XV

## "COBBLER" HORN ENGAGES A SECRETARY

On his way home from the minister's house, "Cobbler" Horn was somewhat exercised in his mind as to how he should tell his sister what he had done. He could inform her, without hesitation, that the minister had recommended a secretary; but how should he make known the fact that the commended secretary was a lady? He was not afraid of his sister; but he preferred that she should approve of his doings, and he wished to render his approaching announcement as little distasteful to her as might be. But the difficulty of doing this would be great. It would have been hard to imagine a communication likely to prove more unwelcome to Miss Jemima than the announcement that her brother contemplated the employment of a lady secretary. Nor was the difficulty of the situation relieved by the fact that the lady was young, and possibly attractive. It would have been as easy to impart a delectable flavour to a dose of castor-oil, as to render agreeable to his sister the announcement he must immediately make. Long before he reached home, he relinquished all attempt to settle the difficulty which was agitating his mind. He would begin by telling his sister that the minister had recommended a secretary, and then trust to the inspiration of the moment for the rest.

Miss Jemima, encompassed with a comprehensive brown apron, stood at the table peeling the potatoes for dinner.

"You've been a long time gone, Thomas," she said complacently—for Miss Jemima was in one of her most amiable moods.

"Yes; we found many things to talk about."

"Well, what did he say on the secretary question?"

"Oh, he has recommended one to me who, he thinks, will do first-rate."

"Ah! and who is the young man? For of course he is young; all secretaries are."

"The person lives in Birmingham," was the guarded reply, "and goes by the name of Owen."

Miss Jemima felt by instinct that her brother was keeping something back. She shot at him a keen, swift glance, and then resumed the peeling of the potato just then in hand, which operation she effected with such extreme care, that it was a very attenuated strip of peeling which fell curling from her knife into the brown water in the bowl beneath.

"What is this young man's other name?" she calmly asked.

"Well, now, I don't know," said "Cobbler" Horn, with a shrewd smile.

"Just like you men!" whipped out Miss Jemima, pausing in her work; "but I suppose, as the minister recommends him, it will be all right."

There was nothing for it now but a straightforward declaration of the dreadful truth.

"Jemima," said "Cobbler" Horn, "I mustn't mislead you. It's not a young man at all."

Miss Jemima let fall into the water, with a sudden flop, the potato she was peeling, and faced her brother, knife in hand, with a look of wild astonishment in her eyes.

"Not a young man!" she almost shrieked, "What then?"

Her brother's emphasis had been on the word *man*, and not on the word *young*.

"Well, my dear," he replied, "a young—in fact, a young lady."

Up went Miss Jemima's hands.

"Thomas!"

"Yes, Jemima; such is the minister's suggestion."

Miss Jemima, who had resumed her work, proceeded to dig out the eye of a potato with unwonted prodigality.

"Mr. Durnford," resumed "Cobbler" Horn, "tells me it is a common thing for young ladies to be secretaries now-a-days; and he very highly recommended this one in particular."

Miss Jemima knew, that if her brother's mind was made up, it would be useless to withstand his will.

"When is she coming?" was all she said.

"I don't know. Mr. Durnford promised to write and ask her to come and see us first. You shall talk with her yourself, Jemima; and, believe me, if there is any good reason to object to the arrangement, she shall not be engaged."

Miss Jemima permitted herself just one other word.

"I am surprised at Mr. Durnford!" she said; and then the matter dropped.

Two days later, in prompt response to the minister's letter, Miss Owen duly arrived. Mr. Durnford met her at the station, and conducted her to the house of "Cobbler" Horn. He had sent her, in his letter, all needful information concerning "Cobbler" Horn, and the circumstances which rendered it necessary for him to engage a secretary.

"They reside at present," he said during the walk from the station, "in a small house, but will soon remove to a larger one."

"Cobbler" Horn was busy in his workshop when they arrived; but Miss Jemima was awaiting them in solitary state, in the front-room. The good lady had meant to be forbidding and severe in her reception of the "forward minx," whom she had settled it in her mind the prospective secretary would prove to be. But the moment her eyes beheld Miss Owen she was disarmed. The dark-eyed, black-haired, modestly-attired, and even sober-looking girl, who put out her hand with a very simple movement, and spoke, with considerable self-possession truly, but certainly not with an impudent air, bore but scant resemblance to the "brazen hussey" who had haunted Miss Jemima's mind for the past two days.

"Cobbler" Horn came in from his workshop, and greeted the young girl with an honest heartiness which placed her at her

J. W. Keyworth

ease at once.

With almost a cordial air, Miss Jemima invited the visitors to sit down. As Miss Owen glanced a second time around the room, a look of perplexity came into her face.

"Do you know, Miss Horn," she said, "your house seems quite familiar to me. I almost feel as if I had been here before. Of course I never have. It's just one of those queer feelings everybody has sometimes, as if what you are going through at the time had all taken place before."

She spoke out the thought of her mind with a simple impulsiveness which had its own charm.

"No doubt," said Miss Jemima, with a start; but she was deterred from further remark by Mr. Durnford's rising from his seat.

"I think I'll leave you," he said, "and call for Miss Owen in— say a quarter of an hour. With your permission, Mr. Horn, she will sleep at our house to-night."

"Don't go, sir," said "Cobbler" Horn. "Your presence will be a help to us on both sides."

It needed no further pursuasion to induce the minister to remain: with his assistance, "Cobbler" Horn soon came to terms with the young lady; and, as, upon a hint conveyed in the letter she had received from the minister, she had come to Cottonborough prepared, if necessary, to remain, it was arranged that she should commence her duties on the following day.

"And would it not be as well for her to come to us to-night?" asked "Cobbler" Horn. "The sooner she begins to get used to us the better. And she can still spend the evening with you, Mr. Durnford."

The minister looked enquiringly at Miss Owen,

"What do you say, my dear?"

"I am entirely in your hands, sir, and those of Mr. Horn."

"Well," said Mr. Durnford, "if you really wish it. Mr. Horn, Miss Owen shall come to you to-night."

And thus it was arranged.

# CHAPTER XVI

## THE ATTACK ON THE CORRESPONDENCE

When "Cobbler" Horn's secretary awoke next morning, she experienced a return of the feeling of familiarity with her surroundings of which she had been conscious on first entering the house. The little white-washed bedroom, with its simple furniture, seemed like a vision of the past. She had a dreamy impression that she had slept in this little white room many times before. There was, in particular, a startling appearance of familiarity in a certain picture which hung upon the wall, beyond the foot of the bed. It was an old-fashioned coloured print, in a black frame, and represented Jacob's dream. For a long time she gazed at the picture. Then she gave herself a shake, and sighed, and laughed a low, pathetic little laugh.

"What nonsense!" she thought. "As if I could ever have been here before, or set eyes on the picture! Though I may have seen one like it somewhere else, to be sure."

Then she roused herself, and got out of bed. But when, having dressed, she went downstairs, the same sense of familiarity with her surroundings surged over her again. The boxed-up staircase seemed to her a not untrodden way; and when she emerged in the kitchen at its foot, and saw the round deal table spread for breakfast with its humble array, she almost staggered at the familiarity of the scene.

"Cobbler" Horn was in his workshop, and Miss Jemima had gone into the yard; and, as the young girl gazed around the humble room it seemed, in some strange fashion, to have belonged to her past life. The very tap-tap of "Cobbler" Horn's hammer, coming cheerily from the workshop behind, awoke weird echoes in her brain, and helped to render her illusion complete.

All breakfast-time she felt like one in a dream. She seemed to be drifting into a new life, which was not new but old; and she almost felt as if she had *come home*. She was utterly unable to imagine what might be the explanation of this strange experience. She had not a glimmering of the actual truth. She struggled against the feeling which possessed her, and partly overcame it; but it returned again and again during her stay in the house, though with diminished force.

After breakfast, "Cobbler" Horn invited his secretary to attack the accumulated mass of letters which waited for despatch.

"You see, Miss Owen," he said in half-apology for asking her to begin work so soon, "the pile gets larger every day; and, if we don't do something to reduce it at once, it will get altogether beyond bounds."

Miss Owen turned her sparkling dark eyes upon her employer.

"Oh, Mr. Horn," she exclaimed, as she took her seat at the table, "the sooner we get to work the better! I did not come here to play, you know."

"Cobbler" Horn poured an armful of unanswered letters down upon the table, in front of his ardent young secretary.

"There's a snow-drift for you, Miss Owen!" he said.

"Thank you, sir," was the cheery response, "we must do our best to clear it away."

Miss Owen was already beginning to feel quite at home with "Cobbler" Horn; and she even ventured at this point, to rally him on the dismay with which he regarded his piles of letters.

"Don't you think, sir," she asked, with a radiant smile, "that a little sunshine might help us?"

"Cobbler" Horn started, and glanced towards the window. The morning was dull.

"Yes," he said; "but we can't command—" Then he perceived her meaning, and broke off with a smile. "To be sure; you are right, Miss Owen. It is wrong of me to be wearing such a gloomy face. But you see this kind of thing is all so new and strange to me; and you need not wonder that I am dismayed."

"No," replied the secretary, with just the faintest little touch of patronage in her tone; "it's not surprising in your case. But I am not dismayed. Answering letters has always been my delight."

"That's well," said "Cobbler" Horn, gravely; "And I think you will have to supply a large share of the 'sunshine' too, Miss Owen."

"I'll try," she replied, simply, with a beaming smile;  and  she squared her shapely arms, and bent her dusky head, and set to work with a will, while "Cobbler" Horn, regarding her from the opposite side of the table, was divided between two mysteries, which were, how she could write so fast and well, and what it was which made him feel as if he had known her all his life?

Most of the letters contained applications for money. Some few were from the representatives of well-known philanthropic societies; many others were appeals on behalf of local charities or associations; and no small proportion were the applications of individuals, who either had great need, or were very cunning, or both.

The private appeals were of great variety. "Cobbler" Horn was amazed to find how many people were at the point of despair for want of just the help that he was able to give. It was past belief how large a number of persons he had the opportunity of saving from ruin, and with how small a sum of money, in each case, it might be done. What a manifold disclosure of human misery and despair those letters were, or seemed to be! Some of them, doubtless, had been written with breaking hearts, and punctuated with tears; but which?

"I had no idea there was so much trouble in the world!" cried "Cobbler" Horn, in dismay.

"Perhaps there is not quite so much as your letters seem to imply, sir," suggested the secretary.

"You think not?" queried "Cobbler" Horn.

"I feel sure of it," said the young girl, with a knowing shake of her head. "But we must do our best to discriminate. I should throw some of these letters into the fire at once, if I were you, Mr. Horn."

J. W. Keyworth

"But they must be answered first!"

"Must they, sir? Every one?" enquired the secretary, arching her dark eye-brows. "Why it will cost you a small fortune in stamps, Mr. Horn!"

"But you forget how rich I am, Miss Owen. And I would rather be cheated a thousand times, than withhold, in a single instance, the help I ought to give."

"Well, Mr. Horn, I'm your secretary, and must obey your commands, whether I approve of them or not."

She spoke with a merry trill of laughter; and "Cobbler" Horn, far from being offended, shot back upon her a beaming smile.

They took the letters as they came. Concerning some of the applications, "Cobbler" Horn felt quite able to decide himself. Appeals from duly-accredited philanthropic institutions received from him a liberal response, and so large were some of the amounts that the young secretary felt constrained to remonstrate.

"You forget," he replied, "how much money I've got."

"But—excuse me, sir—you seem resolved to give it all away!"

"Yes, almost," was the calm reply.

There was but little difficulty, moreover, in dealing with the applications on behalf of local interests. It was the private appeals which afforded most trouble. Every case had to be strenuously debated with Miss Owen, who maintained that not one of these importunate correspondents ought to be assisted, until "Cobbler" Horn had satisfied himself that the case was one of actual necessity, and real merit. By dint of great persistency, she succeeded in convincing her employer that many of these private appeals were not worthy of a moment's consideration. To each of the writers of these a polite note of refusal was to be despatched. With regard to the rest, it was decided that an application for references should be made.

"I shall have to be your *woman* of business, Mr. Horn," said Miss Owen, "as well as your secretary; and, between us, I think we can manage."

She felt that there was a true Christian work for her in doing what she could to help this poor embarrassed Christian man of wealth.

"Cobbler" Horn was enraptured with his secretary. She seemed to be fitting herself into a vacant place in his life. It appeared the most natural thing in the world that she should be there writing his letters. If his little Marian had not gone from him years ago, she might have been his secretary now. He sighed at the thought; and then, as he looked across at the animated face of Miss Owen, as she bent over her work, and swept the table with her abundant tresses, he was comforted in no small degree.

Miss Jemima's respect for the proprieties, rendered her reluctant to absent herself much from the room where her brother and his engaging young secretary sat together at their interesting work; and she manifested, from time to time, a lively interest in the progress of their task.

# CHAPTER XVII

## A PARTING GIFT FOR
## "THE LITTLE TWIN BRETHREN"

The honest joy of "the little twin brethren" at the sudden enrichment of their friend, "Cobbler" Horn, was dashed with a deep regret. It was excellent that he had been made a wealthy man. As Tommy Dudgeon expressed it, "Providence had not made a mistake this time, anyhow." But, in common with the rest of "Cobbler" Horn's neighbours, the two worthy little men bitterly deplored the inevitable departure of their friend from their midst. It was "not to be supposed," said Tommy again—it was always Tommy who said things; to John had been assigned the honour of perpetuating the family name—it was "not to be supposed that a millionaire would live in a small house, in a narrow street, remain at the cobbler's bench, or continue to associate with poor folks like themselves." The little hucksters considered it a matter of course that "Cobbler" Horn would shortly remove to another and very different abode, and they mourned over the prospect with sincere and bitter grief.

The little men had good reason for their sorrow, for to none of all his poor neighbours had "Cobbler" Horn been a better friend. And their regret in view of his approaching removal was fully reciprocated by "Cobbler" Horn himself. Of all the friends, in the network of streets surrounding his humble abode, whom he had fastened to his heart with the golden hooks of love, there were none whom he held more closely there than the two little tradesmen across the way. His intercourse with them had been one of the chief refreshments of his life; and he knew that he would sadly miss his humble little friends.

And now the time had come for the removal, and the evening previous to the departure from the old home, "the Golden Shoemaker" paid his last visit, in the capacity of neighbour, to the worthy little twins. He had long known that they had a constant struggle to make their way. He had often assisted them as far as his own hitherto humble means would allow; and now, he had resolved that before leaving the neighbourhood, he would make them such a present as would lift them, once for all, out of the quagmire of adversity in which they had floundered so long.

At six o'clock, on that autumn evening, it being already dusk, "Cobbler" Horn opened his front door, and stood for a moment on the step. Miss Jemima and the young secretary were both out of the way. If Miss Jemima had known where her brother was going and for what purpose, she would have held up her hands in horror and dismay, and might even, had she been present, have tried to detain him in the house by main force.

"Cobbler" Horn lingered a moment on the door-step, with the instinctive hesitation of one who is about to perform an act of unaccustomed magnitude; but his soul revelled in the thought of what he was going to do. He was about to exercise the gracious privilege of the wealthy Christian man; and, as he handled a bundle of crisp bank-notes which he held in the side pocket of his coat, his fingers positively tingled with rapture.

The street was very quiet. A milk girl was going from door to door, and the lamplighter was vanishing in the distance. Yet "Cobbler" Horn flitted furtively across the way, as though he were afraid of being seen; and, having glided with the stealth of a burglar through the doorway of the little shop, found himself face to face with Tommy Dudgeon. The smile of commercial satisfaction, which had been summoned to the face of the little man by the consciousness that some one was coming into the shop, resolved itself into an air of respectful yet genial greeting when he recognised "Cobbler" Horn.

"Ah, good evening, Mr. Horn! You said you would pay us a farewell visit, and we were expecting you. Come in, sir."

"Cobbler" Horn followed his humble conductor into the small but cosy living-room behind, which the large number of its occupants caused to appear even smaller than it was. John Dudgeon was there, and Mrs. John, and several offshoots of the Dudgeon tree. Mrs. Dudgeon was ironing at a table beneath the one small window, in the fading light. She was a staid and dapper matron, with here and there the faintest line of care upon her comely face. A couple of the children were rolling upon the hearthrug in the ruddy glow of the fire, and two or three others were doing their home-lessons by the aid of the same unsteady gleam. The father, swept to one side by the surges of his superabundant family, sat on a chair at the extreme corner of the hearthrug, with both the twins upon his knees.

"Cobbler" Horn was greeted with the cordiality due to an old family friend. Even the children clustered around him and clung to his arms and legs. Mrs. John, as she was invariably called—possibly on the assumption that Tommy Dudgeon also would, in due time, take a wife, cleared the children away from the side of the hearth opposite to her husband,

and placed a chair for the ever-welcome guest. Tommy Dudgeon, who had slipped into the shop to adjust the door-bell, so that he might have timely notice of the entrance of a customer, soon returned, and placing a chair for himself between his brother and "Cobbler" Horn, sat down with his feet amongst the children, and his gaze fixed on the fire.

For a time there was no sound in the room but the click of Mrs. John's iron, as it travelled swiftly to and fro. Even the children were preternaturally quiet. At length Tommy spoke, in sepulchral tones, with his eyes still on the fire.

"Only to think that it's the last time!"

"What's the last time, friend?" asked "Cobbler" Horn, with a start.

"Why this—that we shall see you sitting there so sociable like, Mr. Horn."

"Indeed, I hope not," was the hearty response. "You're not going to get rid of me so easily as that, old friend."

"Why," exclaimed Tommy, "I thought you were going to remove; and I'm sure no one could find fault with it."

"Yes: but you surely don't suppose I'm going to turn my back on my old neighbours altogether?"

"What you say is very kind," replied Tommy; "but, Mr. Horn, we can't expect to see you very often after this."

"Well, friend, perhaps oftener than you think." Then he told them that he had bought the house in which he had lived amongst them, and meant to keep it up, and come there almost every day to mend boots and shoes, without charge for his poor customers.

"Well, to be sure!" exclaimed Tommy Dudgeon, while John chuckled exultantly to the twins, and Mrs. John moved her iron more vigorously to and fro, and hastily raised her hand to brush away a grateful and admiring tear.

Meanwhile "Cobbler" Horn was considering how he might most delicately disclose the special purpose of his visit.

"But after all," he said at length, "this is a farewell visit. I'm going away, and, after to-morrow, I shall not be your neighbour any more."

For some moments his hand had been once more in his pocket, fingering the bank-notes. He now drew them forth very much in the way in which a man entrapped into a den of robbers might draw a pocket-pistol, and smoothed them out upon his knee.

"I thought, old friend," he said, turning to Tommy Dudgeon, "that perhaps you might be willing to accept a trifling memento of our long acquaintance. And, indeed, you mustn't say no."

John Dudgeon was too deeply engaged with the twins to note what was said; Tommy but dimly perceived the drift of his friend; but upon Mrs. John the full truth flashed with the clearness of noon.

The next moment the notes were being transferred to the hands of the astonished Tommy. John was still absorbed with his couple of babies. Mrs. John was ironing more furiously than ever. Tommy felt, with his finger and thumb, that there were many of the notes; and he perceived that he and his were being made the recipients of an act of stupendous generosity. Tears trickled down his cheeks; his throat and tongue were parched. He tried to thrust the bank-notes back into the hand of his friend.

"Mr. Horn, you must not beggar yourself on our account."

"Cobbler" laughed. In truth, he was much relieved. It seemed that his humble friend objected to his gift only because he thought it was too large.

"'Beggar' myself, Tommy?" he cried. "I should have to be a very reckless spendthrift indeed to do that. You forget how dreadfully rich I am. Why these paltry notes are a mere nothing to such a wealth-encumbered unfortunate as I. But I thought the money would be a help to you. And you must take it, Tommy, you must indeed. The Lord told me to give it to you; and what shall I say to Him, if I allow you to refuse His gift?"

And so the generous will of "the Golden Shoemaker" prevailed; and if he could have heard and seen all that took place by that humble fireside, after he was gone, he would have been assured that at least one small portion of his uncle's wealth had been well-bestowed.

# CHAPTER XVIII

## THE NEW HOUSE

"Cobbler" Horn's new house, which was situated, as we have seen, on one of the chief roads leading out of the town, marked almost the verge, in that direction, of the straggling fringe of urban outskirts. Beyond it there was only the small cottage in which had lived, and still resided, the woman who had seen Marian as she trotted so eagerly away into the great pitiless world. "Cobbler" Horn had not deliberately set himself to seek a house upon this road. But, when he found there a residence to let which seemed to be almost exactly the kind of dwelling he required, the fact that it was situated in a locality so tenderly associated with the memory of his lost child, in no degree diminished his desire to make it his abode.

"It was here that she went by," he said softly to himself, at the close of their visit of inspection, as he stood with Miss Jemima at the gate; "and it was yonder that she was last seen."

What were Miss Jemima's thoughts, as she followed, with her eyes, the direction of her brother's gaze, may not be known; for an unwonted silence had fallen on her usually ready tongue.

It was a good house, with a pleasant lawn in front, and a yard, containing coach-house and stables, behind. The house itself was well-built, commodious, and fitted with all the conveniences of the day. As most of the furniture was new, the removal of the family was not a very elaborate process. In this, as in all other things, "Cobbler" Horn found that his money secured him the minimum of trouble. He had simply given a few orders—which his sister, it is true, had supplemented with a great many more—; and, when the day of removal came, they found themselves duly installed in a house furnished with a completeness which left nothing to be desired.

On their arrival, they were received in the hall by three smiling maids, a coachman, and a boy in buttons. "The Golden Shoemaker" almost staggered, as the members of his domestic staff paid due homage to their master. He half-turned to his sister, and saw that, she, unlike himself, was not taken by surprise. Then he hastily returned the respectful salutations of the beaming group, and passed into the house.

It was afternoon when the removal took place, and the remainder of the day was spent in inspecting the premises, and settling down. With the aid of his indefatigable secretary, "Cobbler" Horn had disposed of his morning's letters before leaving the old house, and, as it happened, the later mails were small that day. Miss Jemima stepped into her new position as mistress of a large establishment with ease and grace; and, assisted by the young secretary, who was fast gaining the goodwill of her employer's sister, was already giving to the house, by means of a few slight touches here and there, that indescribable air of homeliness which money cannot buy, and no skill of builder or upholsterer can impart.

To "Cobbler" Horn himself that evening was a restless time.

He felt himself to be strangely out of place; and he was almost afraid to tread upon the thick soft carpets, or to sit upon the luxurious chairs. And yet he smiled to himself, as he contrasted his own uneasiness with the complacency with which his sister was fitting herself into her place in their new sphere.

Under the guidance of the coachman, "Cobbler" Horn inspected the horses and carriages. The coachman, who was the most highly-finished specimen of his kind who could be obtained for money, treated his new master with an oppressive air of respect. "Cobbler" Horn would have preferred a more familiar bearing on the part of his gorgeously-attired servant; but Bounder was obdurate, for he knew his place. His only recognition of the somewhat unusual sociability of his master, was to touch his hat with a more impressive action, and to impart a still deeper note of respect to the tones of his voice. His bearing implied a solemn rebuke. It was as though he said, "If you, sir, don't know your place, I know mine."

"The Golden Shoemaker," having completed his survey of his new abode and its surroundings, realized more fuller than hitherto the change his circumstances had undergone. The old life was now indeed past, and he was fairly launched upon the new. Well, by the help of God, he had tried to do his duty in the humble sphere of poverty; and he would attempt the same in the infinitely more difficult position in which he was now placed.

Entering the house by the back way, he paused and lingered regretfully for a moment at the kitchen door. One of the maids perceived his hesitation, and wondered if master was of the interfering kind. He dispelled her alarm by passing slowly on.

After supper, in the dining-room, Miss Jemima handed the old family Bible to her brother, and he took it with a loving grasp. Here, at least, was a part of the old life still.

"Shall I ring for the servants?" asked Miss Jemima.

"By all means," said her brother, with a slight start.

Miss Jemima touched the electric bell, with the air of one who had been in the habit of ringing for servants all her life. In quick response, the door was opened; and the maids, the coachman, and the boy, who had all been well schooled by Miss Jemima, filed gravely in.

The ordeal through which "Cobbler" Horn had now to pass was very unlike the homely family prayer of the old life. He performed his task, however, with a simplicity and fervour with which the domestics were duly impressed; and when it was over he made them a genial yet dignified little speech, and wished them all a hearty good night.

"Brother," Miss Jemima ventured to remark, when the servants were gone, "I am afraid you lean too much to the side of familiarity with the servants."

"Sister," was the mildly sarcastic response, "you are quite able to adjust the balance."

Amongst the few things which were transferred from the old house to the new, was a small tin trunk, the conveyance of which Miss Jemima was at great pains personally to superintend. It contained the tiny wardrobe of the long lost child, which the sorrowing, and still self-accusing, lady had continued to preserve.

It is doubtful whether "Cobbler" Horn was aware of his

sister's pathetic hoard; but there were two mementos of his lost darling which he himself preserved. For the custody of papers, deeds, and other valuables, he had placed in the room set apart as his office, a brand new safe. In one of its most secure recesses he deposited, with gentle care, a tiny parcel done up in much soft paper. It contained a mud-soiled print bonnet-string, and a little dust-stained shoe.

"They will never be of any more use to her," he had said to himself; "but they may help to find her some day."

# CHAPTER XIX

## A TALK WITH THE MINISTER ABOUT MONEY

"Cobbler" Horn knew his minister to be a man of strict integrity and sound judgment; and it was with complete confidence that he sought Mr. Durnford's advice with regard to those of his letters with which his secretary and himself were unable satisfactorily to deal. The morning after the removal to the new house, he hastened to the residence of the minister with a bundle of such letters in his pocket. Mr. Durnford read the letters carefully through, and gave him in each case suitable advice; and then "Cobbler" Horn had a question to ask.

"Will you tell me, sir, why you have not yet asked me for anything towards any of our own church funds?"

"Well," replied the minister, with a shrewd twinkle in his eye, "you see, Mr. Horn, I thought I might safely leave the matter to your generosity and good sense."

"Thank you, sir. Well, I am anxious that my own church should have its full share of what I have to give. Will you, sir," he added diffidently, "kindly tell me what funds there are, and how much I ought to give to each."

As he spoke, he extracted from his pocket, with some difficulty, a bulky cheque-book, and flattened it out on the table with almost reverent fingers; for he had not yet come to regard the possession of a cheque-book as a commonplace circumstance of his life.

"That's just like you, Mr. Horn," said the minister, with glistening eyes.

He was a straightforward man, and transparent as glass. He would not manifest false delicacy, or make an insincere demur.

"There are plenty of ways for your money, with us, Mr. Horn," he added. "But what is your wish? Shall I make a list of the various funds?"

Mr. Durnford drew his chair to his writing-table, as he spoke, and took up his pen.

"If you please, sir," said "Cobbler" Horn.

No sooner said than done; and in a few moments the half-sheet of large manuscript paper which the minister had placed before him was filled from top to bottom with a list of the designations of various religious funds.

"Thank you, sir," said "Cobbler" Horn, glancing at the paper. "Will you, now, kindly set down in order how much you think I ought to give in each case."

With the very slightest hesitation, and in perfect silence, Mr. Durnford undertook this second task; and, in a few minutes, having jotted down a specific amount opposite to each of the lines in the list, he handed the paper again to "Cobbler" Horn.

Mr. Durnford's estimate of his visitor's liberality had not erred by excess of modesty; and he was startled when he mentally reckoned up the sum of the various amounts he had set down. But "Cobbler" Horn's reception of the list startled him still more.

"My dear sir," said "the Golden Shoemaker," with a smile, "I'm afraid you do not realize how very rich I am. This list will not help me much in getting rid of the amount of money of which I shall have to dispose, for the Lord, every year. Try your hand again."

Mr. Durnford asked pardon for the modesty of his suggestions, and promptly revised the list.

"Ah, that is better," said "Cobbler" Horn. "The subscriptions you have set down may stand, as far as the ordinary funds are concerned; but now about the debt fund? What is the amount of the debt?"

"Two thousand pounds."

"Well, I will pay off half of it at once; and, when you have raised two-thirds of the rest, let me know."

"Thank you, sir, indeed!" exclaimed the minister, almost smacking his lips, as he dipped his pen in the ink, and added this munificent promise to the already long list.

"It is a mere nothing," said "Cobbler" Horn. "It is but a trifling instalment of the debt I owe to God on account of this church, and its minister. But you are beginning to find, Mr. Durnford, that I am rather eccentric in money matters?"

"Delightfully so!" exclaimed the minister.

"Well, the right use of money has always been a point with me. Even in the days when I had very little money through my hands, I tried to remember that I was the steward of my Lord. It was difficult, then, to carry out the idea, because it often seemed as though I could not spare what I really thought I ought to give. My present difficulty is to dispose of even a small part of what I can easily spare."

"Ah!" exclaimed the minister, in whose face there was an expression of deep interest.

"Now," resumed "Cobbler" Horn, "will you, Mr. Durnford, help me in this matter? Will you let me know of any suitable channels for my money of which you may, from time to time, be aware?"

"You may depend upon me in that, my dear sir," said the minister, with gusto.

"Thank you, sir!" exclaimed "the Golden Shoemaker," as fervently as though his minister had promised to make him acquainted with chances of gaining money, instead of letting him know of opportunities of giving it away. "And now I think of it, Mr. Durnford, I should like to place in your hands a sum for use at your own discretion. You must meet with many cases of necessity which you would not care to mention to the authorities of the church; and it would be a distinct advantage to you to have a sum of money for use in such instances absolutely at your own command. Now I am going to write you a cheque for fifty pounds to be used as you think fit; and when it is done, you shall have more."

"Mr. Horn!" exclaimed the startled minister.

"Yes, yes, it's all right. All the money I've promised you this morning is a mere trifle to me. And now, with your permission, I'll write the cheques."

Why "Cobbler" Horn should not have included the whole amount of his gifts in one cheque it is difficult to say. Perhaps he thought that, by writing a separate cheque for the last fifty pounds, he would more effectually ensure Mr. Durnford's having the absolute disposal of that amount.

The writing of the cheques was a work of time.

"There, sir," said "Cobbler" Horn, at last, as he handed the two precious slips of paper across the table, "I hope you will find them all right."

"Thank you, Mr. Horn, again and again," said the minister, as he folded up the cheques and placed them in his pocket-book; "they are perfectly right, I am sure."

"Has it occurred to you," he continued, "that it would be well if you were systematic in your giving?"

"Yes; and I intend systematically to give away as much as I can."

"But have you thought of fixing what proportion of your income you will give? Not," added the minister, laughing, "that I am afraid lest you should not give away enough."

"Oh yes," responded "Cobbler" Horn, laughing in his turn; "I have decided to give proportionately; and the proportion I mean to give is almost all I've got."

"I see you are incorrigible," laughed Mr. Durnford.

"You'll find that I am. But now—" and "Cobbler" Horn regarded his minister with an expression of modest, friendly interest in his face—"I'm going to write another cheque."

"You must be fond of the occupation, Mr. Horn."

"Cobbler" Horn's enrichment had not, in any degree, caused the cordiality of his relations with his minister to decline. There was nothing in "Cobbler" Horn to encourage sycophancy; and there was not in Mr. Durnford a particle of the sycophant.

"I believe I don't altogether dislike it, sir," assented "Cobbler" Horn in response to the minister's last remark. "But," he added, handing to him the cheque he had now finished writing, "will you, my dear sir, accept that for yourself? Your stipend is far too small; and I know Mrs. Durnford's illness in the spring must have been very expensive. Don't say no, I beg of you; but take it—as a favour to me."

He had risen from his seat, and the next moment, with a hurried "good morning," he was gone, leaving the astonished minister in possession of a cheque for one hundred pounds!

# CHAPTER XX

## "COBBLER" HORN'S VILLAGE

It was the custom of "Cobbler" Horn to spend the first hour of every morning, after breakfast, in the office, with his secretary. They would go through the letters which required attention; and, after he had given Miss Owen specific directions with regard to some of them, he would leave her to use her own discretion with reference to the rest. Amongst the former, there were frequently a few which he reserved for the judgment of Mr. Durnford. It was the duty of the young secretary to scan the letters which came by the later posts; but none of them were to be submitted to "Cobbler" Horn until the next morning, unless they were of urgent importance.

One morning, about a week after the removal to the new house, the office door suddenly opened, and "Cobbler" Horn emerged into the hall in a state of great excitement, holding an open letter in his hand.

"Jemima!" he shouted.

The only response was a sound of angry voices from the region of the kitchen, amidst which he recognised his sister's familiar tones. Surely Jemima was not having trouble with the servants! Approaching the kitchen door, he pushed it slightly open, and peeped into the room. Miss Jemima was emphatically laying down the law to the young and comely cook, who stood back against the table, facing her mistress, with the rolling-pin in her hand, and rebellion in every curve of her figure and in every feature of her face.

"You are a saucy minx," Miss Jemima was saying, in her sharpest tones.

"'Minx' yourself," was the pert reply. "No mistress shan't interfere with me and my work, as you've done this last week. If you was a real lady, you wouldn't do it."

"You rude girl, I'll teach you to keep your place."

"Keep your own," rapped out the girl; "and it 'ull be the better for all parties. As for me, I shan't keep this place, and I give you warning from now, so there!"

At this moment, the girl caught sight of her master's face at the door, and flinging herself around to the table, resumed her work. Miss Jemima, in her great anger, advanced a pace or two, with uplifted hand, towards the broad back of her rebellious cook: "Cobbler" Horn, observing the position of affairs, spoke in emphatic tones.

"Jemima, I want you at once."

Miss Jemima started, and then, without a word, followed her brother to the dining-room.

"Brother," she said, snatching, in her anger, the first word, "that girl has insulted me grossly."

"Yes, Jemima, I heard; but try to forget it for a moment. I

have great news for you. This letter is about cousin Jack."

In a moment Miss Jemima had forgotten her insubordinate cook.

"So the poor creature is found!" she said when she had taken, and read, the letter.

"Yes, and he proves to be in a condition which will render doubly welcome the good news he will shortly receive."

"Then you persist in your intention to hand over to him a share of uncle's money?"

"To be sure I do!"

"Well," retorted Miss Jemima, somewhat acrimoniously, "it's a pity. That portion of the money will be dispersed in a worse manner even than it was gathered."

"Don't say that, Jemima," said her brother gravely.

"Well," asked Miss Jemima, dispensing with further protest, "what are you going to do?"

"The first thing is to see Messrs. Tongs and Ball. You see they ask me to do so. I can't get away to-day. To-morrow I am to visit our village, you know; and, as it is on the way to London, the best plan will be to go on when I am so far."

So it was settled, and Miss Owen was instructed to write the lawyers, saying that Mr. Horn would wait upon them on the morning of the third day from that time.

The next morning, "Cobbler" Horn, having invested his young secretary with full powers in regard to his correspondence, during his absence, set off by an early train for Daisy Lane, en route for London. He had but a vague idea as to the village of which he was the chief proprietor. He was aware, however, that his property there, including the old hall itself, was, to quote Mr. Ball, "somewhat out of repair"; and he rejoiced in the prospect of the opportunity its dilapidation might present of turning to good account some considerable portion of his immense wealth.

It was almost noon when the train stopped at the small station at which he was to alight. He was the only passenger who left the train at that station; and, almost before his feet had touched the platform, he was greeted by a plain, middle-aged man, of medium height and broad of build, whose hair was reddish-brown and his whiskers brownish-red, while his tanned and glowing face bore ample evidence of an out-door life. He had the appearance of a good-natured, intelligent, and trustworthy man. This was John Gray, the agent of the property; and "Cobbler" Horn liked him from the first.

"It's only a mile and a half to the village sir," said the man, as they mounted the trap which was waiting outside the station; "and we shall soon run along."

The trap was a nondescript and dilapidated vehicle, and the horse was by no means a thoroughbred. But the whole turn-out was faultlessly clean.

"It's rather a crazy concern, sir," said Mr. Gray candidly. "But you needn't be afraid. It will hold together for this time, I think."

"Cobbler" Horn smiled somewhat sadly, as he mounted to his seat. Here was probably an instalment of much with which he was destined to meet that day.

"Wake up, Jack!" said Mr. Gray, shaking the reins. The appearance of the animal indicated that it was necessary for him to take his master's injunction in a literal sense. He awoke with a start, and set off at a walking pace, from which, by dint of much persuasion on the part of his driver, he was induced to pass into a gentle trot.

"He never goes any faster than that," said the agent.

"Ah!" ejaculated "Cobbler" Horn. "But we must try to get you something better to drive about in than this, Mr. Gray."

"Thank you, sir. It will be a good thing."

As they slowly progressed along the pleasant country road, the agent gave his new employer sundry particulars concerning the property of which he had become possessed.

"Nearly all the village belongs to you, sir. There's only the church and vicarage, and one farm-house, with a couple of cottages attached, that are not yours. But you'll find your property in an awful state. I've done what I could to patch it up; but what can you do without money?"

"I hope, Mr. Gray," said the new proprietor, "that we shall soon rectify all that."

"Of course you will, sir," said the candid agent. "It's very painful," he added, "to hear the complaints the people make."

"No doubt. You must take me to see some of my tenants; but you must not tell them who I am."

"There's a decent house!" he remarked presently, as they came in sight of a comfortable-looking residence, which stood on their left, at the entrance of the village.

"Ah, that's the vicarage," replied the agent, "and the church is a little beyond, and along there, on the other side of the road, is the farm-house which does not belong to you."

They were now entering the village, the long, straggling street of which soon afforded "the Golden Shoemaker" evidence enough of his deceased uncle's parsimonious ideas. Half-ruined cottages and tumbledown houses were dispersed around; here and there along the main street, were two or three melancholy shops; and in the centre of the village stood a disreputable-looking public-house.

"I could wish," said "Cobbler" Horn, as they passed the last-mentioned building, "that my village did not contain any place of that kind."

"There's no reason," responded the agent, with a quiet smile, "why you should have a public-house in the place, if you don't want one."

"Couldn't we have a public-house without strong drink?"

"No doubt we could, sir; but it wouldn't pay."

"You mean as a matter of money, of course. But that is nothing to me, and the scheme would pay in other respects. I leave it to you, Mr. Gray, to get rid of the present occupant of the house as soon as it can be done without injustice, and to convert the establishment into a public-house without the drink—a place which will afford suitable accommodation for travellers, and be a pleasant meeting place, of an evening, for the men and boys of the village."

"Thank you, sir," said the agent, with huge delight. "Have I carte blanche?"

"'Carte blanche'?" queried "Cobbler" Horn, with a puzzled air. "Let me see; that's—what? Ah, I know—a free hand, isn't it?"

"Yes, sir," replied the agent gravely.

"Then that's just what I mean."

As they drove on, "Cobbler" Horn observed that most of the gardens attached to the cottages were in good order, and that some of the people had been at great pains to conceal the mouldering walls of their wretched huts with roses, honeysuckle, and various climbing plants. Glowing with honest shame, he became restlessly eager to wave his golden wand over this desolate scene.

"This is my place, sir," said the agent, as they stopped at the gate of a dingy, double-fronted house. "You'll have a bit of dinner with us in our humble way?"

"Thank you," said "the Golden Shoemaker," "I shall be very glad."

# CHAPTER XXI

## IN NEED OF REPAIRS

After dinner, "Cobbler" Horn set out with his agent on a tour of inspection through the village.

"We'll take this row first, sir, if you please," said Mr. Gray. "One of the people has sent for me to call."

So saying he led the way towards a row of decrepit cottages which, with their dingy walls and black thatch, looked like a group of fungi, rather than a row of habitations erected by the hand of man.

At the crazy door of the first cottage they were confronted by a stout, red-faced woman with bare beefy arms, who, on seeing "Cobbler" Horn, dropped a curtsey, and suppressed the angry salutation which she had prepared for Mr. Gray.

"A friend of mine, Mrs. Blobs," said the agent.

"Glad to see you, sir," said the woman to "Cobbler" Horn. "Will you please to walk in, gentlemen."

"Just cast your eye up there, Mr. Gray," she added when they were inside. "It's come through at last."

Sure enough it had. Above their heads was a vast hole in the ceiling, and above that a huge gap in the thatch; and at their feet lay a heap of bricks, mortar, and fragments of rotten wood.

"Why the chimney has come through!" exclaimed Mr. Gray.

"Little doubt of that," said Mrs. Blobs.

"Was anybody hurt?"

"No, but they might ha' bin. It was this very morning. The master was at his work, and the children away at school; but, if I hadn't just stepped out to have a few words with a neighbour, I might ha' bin just under the very place. Isn't it disgraceful, sir," she added, turning to "Cobbler" Horn, "that human beings should be made to live in such tumbledown places? I believe Mr. Gray, here, would have put things right long ago; but he's been kept that tight by the old skin-flint what's just died. They do say as now the property have got into better hands; but—"

"Well, well, Mrs. Blobs" interposed the agent; "we shall soon see a change now I hope."

"Yes," assented "Cobbler" Horn, "we'll have—that is, I'm sure Mr. Gray will soon make you snug, ma'am."

"We must call at every house, sir," said Mr. Gray, as they passed to the next door. "There isn't one of the lot but wants patching up almost every day."

"Cheer up, Mr. Gray," said "the Golden Shoemaker." "There shall be no more patching after this."

In each of the miserable cottages they met with a repetition of their experience in the first. If the reproaches of the living could bring back the dead, old Jacob Horn should have formed one of the group in those mouldy and rotting cottages, to listen to the reiteration of the shameful story of his criminal neglect. Here the windows were bursting from their setting, like the bulging eyes of suffocating men; and here the door-frame was in a state of collapse. In one cottage the ceiling was depositing itself, by frequent instalments, on the floor; and in another the floor itself was rotting away. In every case, Mr. Gray made bold to promise the speedy rectification of everything that was wrong; and "Cobbler" Horn confirmed his promises in a manner so authoritative that it would have been a wonder if his discontented tenants had not caught some glimmering of the truth as to who he was.

On leaving the cottages, Mr. Gray took his employer to one of the farm-houses which his property comprised. They found the farmer, a burly, red-faced, ultra-choleric man, excited over some recently-consummated dilapidations on his premises. He conducted his visitors over his house and farm-buildings, grumbling like an ungreased wagon. His abuse of "Cobbler" Horn's dead uncle was unstinted, and almost every other word was a rumbling oath. Mr. Gray assured him that all would be put right now in a very short time; and "Cobbler" Horn said, "Yes, he was sure it would."

The farmer stared in surprise; but his blunter perception proved less penetrative than the keen insight of the women, and he simply wondered what this rather rough looking stranger could know about it, anyhow. He expressed a hope that it might be as Mr. Gray said. For himself he hadn't much faith. But, if there wasn't something done soon, the new landlord had better not show himself there, that was all; and the aggrieved farmer clenched his implied threat with the most emphatic oath he was able to produce.

Their inspection of the remainder of the village revealed, on every side, the same condition of ruin and decay; and it was with a sad and indignant heart that "Cobbler" Horn at length sat down, in Mrs. Gray's front parlour, to a late but welcome cup of tea.

"To-morrow," he said, "we'll have a look at the old hall."

"The Golden Shoemaker" spent the evening in close consultation with his agent. The state of the property was thoroughly discussed, and Mr. Gray was invested with full power to renovate and renew. His employer enjoined him to make complete work. He was to exceed, rather than stop short of, what was necessary, and to do even more than the tenants asked.

"You will understand, Mr. Gray," said "Cobbler" Horn, "that I want all my property in this village to be put into such thorough repair that, as far as the comfort and convenience of my tenants are concerned, nothing shall remain to be desired. So set to work with all your might; and we shall not quarrel about the bill—if you only make it large enough."

Mr. Gray's big heart bounded within him, as he received this generous commission.

"And don't forget your own house," added his employer. "I think you had better build yourself a new one while you are about it; and let it be a house fit to live in."

Mr. Gray warmly expressed his thanks, and they proceeded to the consideration of the numberless matters which it was necessary to discuss.

In the morning, under the guidance of the agent, "Cobbler" Horn paid his promised visit to the old Hall. It was a venerable Elizabethan mansion, and, like everything else in the village that belonged to him, was sadly out of repair. As he entered the ancient pile, and passed from room to room, a purpose with regard to the old Hall which already vaguely occupied his mind, took definite shape; and he seemed to hear, in the empty rooms, the glad ring of children's laughter and the patter of children's feet. In memory of his long-lost Marian, and for the glory of the Divine Friend of children, the old Hall should be transformed into a Home for little ones who were homeless and without a friend.

As they drove to the station, a little later, he announced his attention, with regard to the Hall, to Mr. Gray.

"I shall leave the business in your hands, Mr. Gray. You must consult those who understand such things, and visit similar institutions, and turn the old place into the best 'Children's Home' that can be produced."

"Very well, sir; but the children?"

"That matter I will arrange myself."

The agent was getting used to surprises; but the next that came almost took his breath away.

"I believe," said "Cobbler" Horn, at the end of a brief silence, "that your salary, Mr. Gray, is L150 a year?"

"Yes, sir."

"Well, I wish to increase the amount. Pray consider that you will receive, from this time, at the rate of L500 a year."

"Mr. Horn!" cried the startled agent, "such generosity!"

"Not at all; I mean you to earn it, you know. But let your horse move on, or I shall miss my train. And, by the way, will you oblige me, Mr. Gray, by procuring for yourself a horse and trap better calculated to serve the interests of my property than this sorry turn-out. Get the best equipment which can be obtained for money."

The agent, not knowing whether he was touched the more by the kindness of the injunction, or by the delicacy with which it had been expressed, murmured incoherent thanks, and promised speedy compliance with his employer's commands.

# CHAPTER XXII

## "THE GOLDEN SHOEMAKER"
## INSTRUCTS HIS LAWYERS

"Cobbler" Horn reached London early the same evening, and the following morning, at the appointed hour, duly presented himself at the office of Messrs. Tongs and Ball. He was received with enthusiasm by the men of law. Long Mr. Ball was, as usual, the chief speaker; and round Mr. Tongs yielded meek and monosyllabic assent to all his partner's words.

"And how are you by this time, my dear sir?" asked Mr. Ball, almost affectionately, when they had taken their seats.

"Cobbler" Horn had a vague impression that the lawyer was asking his question on behalf of his partner as well as of himself.

"Thank you, gentlemen," was his cordial reply. "I am thankful to say I never was better in my life; and I hope I find you the same?"

"Thank you, my dear sir," answered Mr. Ball, "speaking for self and partner, I think I may say that we are well."

"Yes," said Mr. Tongs.

"But," resumed Mr. Ball, turning to the table, "your time is precious, Mr. Horn. Shall we proceed?"

"If you please, gentlemen."

"Very well," said the lawyer, taking up a bundle of papers; "these are the letters relating to the case of your unfortunate cousin. Shall I give you their contents in due order, Mr. Horn?"

"If you please," and "Cobbler" Horn composed himself to listen, with a grave face.

The letters were from the agents of Messrs. Tongs and Ball in New York; and the information they conveyed was to the effect that "Cobbler" Horn's scapegrace cousin had been traced to a poor lodging-house in that city, where he was slowly dying of consumption. He might last for months, but it was possible he would not linger more than a few weeks.

"Cobbler" Horn listened to the reading of the letters with head down-bent. When it was finished, he looked up.

"Thank you, gentlemen," he said; "have you done anything?"

Mr. Ball gazed at his client through his spectacles, over the top of the last of the letters, which he still held open in his hand, and there was gentle expostulation in his eye.

"Our instructions, Mr. Horn, were to find your cousin."

"I see," said "Cobbler" Horn, with a smile; "and you have done that. Well now, gentlemen, will you be kind enough to do something more?"

"We will attend to your commands, Mr. Horn," was the deferential response. "That is our business."

"Yes," was the emphatic assent of Mr. Tongs.

"The Golden Shoemaker" was becoming accustomed to the readiness of all with whom he had to do to wait upon his will.

"Well, gentlemen," he said, "I wish everything to be done to relieve my poor cousin's distress, and even, if possible, to save his life. Be good enough to telegraph directions for him to be removed without delay to some place where he will receive the best care that money can procure. If his life cannot be saved, he may at least be kept alive till I can reach his bedside."

"Your commands shall be obeyed, sir," said Mr. Ball; "but," he added with much surprise, "is it necessary for you to go to New York yourself?"

"That you must leave to me, gentlemen," said "the Golden Shoemaker" in a tone which put an end to debate.

"Now, gentlemen," he resumed, "kindly hand me those letters; and let me know how soon, after to-morrow, I can set out."

"You don't mean to lose any time, sir," said Mr. Ball, handing the bundle of letters to his client.

In a few moments, the lawyers were able to supply the information that a berth could be secured in a first-class steamer which would leave Liverpool for New York in two days' time; and it was arranged that a passage should be booked.

"We await your further orders, Mr. Horn," said Mr. Ball, rubbing his hands together, as he perceived that his client still retained his seat.

"I'm afraid I detain you, gentlemen."

"By no means, my dear sir," protested Mr. Ball.

"No," echoed Mr. Tongs.

"I am glad of that," said "Cobbler" Horn. "I should be sorry to waste your valuable time."

More than once a clerk had come to the door to announce that so-and-so or so-and-so, awaited the leisure of his employers; and, in every case, the answer had been, "let them wait."

The time of Messrs. Tongs and Ball was indeed valuable, and no portion of it was likely to prove more so than that bestowed on the affairs of "Cobbler" Horn.

Both the lawyers smiled amiably.

"You could not waste our time, Mr. Horn," said Mr. Ball.

"No," echoed Mr. Tongs.

"That's very good of you, gentlemen. But at any rate I really have some business of the gravest importance still to discuss with you."

"By all means, my dear sir," said Mr. Ball with gusto, settling himself in an attitude of attention, while Mr. Tongs also prepared himself to listen.

"I wish, gentlemen," announced "the Golden Shoemaker," "to make my will."

"To be sure," said Mr. Ball.

"You see," continued "Cobbler" Horn, "a journey to America is attended with some risk."

"Precisely," assented Mr. Ball. "And a man of your wealth, Mr. Horn, should not, in any case, postpone the making of his will. It was our intention to speak to you about the matter to-day."

"To be sure," said "Cobbler" Horn. "Can it be done at once?"

"Certainly," responded the lawyer, drawing his chair to the table, and preparing, pen in hand, to receive the instructions of his client.

"You have no children, I think, Mr. Horn?"

"Cobbler" Horn's cheeks blanched, and his lips quivered; but he instantly regained his self-control.

"That is my difficulty," he said. "I had a child, but—"

"Ah!" interrupted Mr. Ball, "I understand. Very sad."

"No, sir," said "Cobbler" Horn sternly, "you do not understand. It is not as you think. But can I make my will in favour of a person who may, or may not, be alive?"

Mr. Ball was in no wise abashed.

"Do I take you, my dear sir? You—"

"The person," interposed "Cobbler" Horn, "to whom I wish to leave my property is my little daughter, Marian, who wandered away twelve years ago, and has never been heard of since. Can I do it, gentlemen?"

"I think you can, Mr. Horn," replied Mr. Ball. "In the absence of any proof of death, your daughter may be considered to be still alive. What do you say, Mr. Tongs?"

"Oh yes; to be sure; certainly," exclaimed Mr. Tongs, who seemed to have been aroused from a reverie, and for whom it was enough that he was required to confirm some dictum of his partner.

"Thank you, gentlemen. Then please to note that I wish my property to pass, at my death, to my daughter, Marian Horn."

"Very good, sir," said Mr. Ball, making a note on a sheet of paper. "But," he added, with an enquiring glance towards his client, "in the event—that is to say, supposing your daughter were not to reappear, Mr. Horn?"

"I am coming to that," was the calm reply. "If my daughter does not come back before my death, I wish everything to go to my sister, Jemima Horn, on the condition that she gives it up to my daughter when she does return."

"Ah!" ejaculated Mr. Ball. "And may I ask, my dear sir?—If Miss Horn should die, say shortly after your own decease, what then?"

"I have thought of that too. Would it be in order, to appoint a trustee, to hold the property, in such a case, for my child?"

"Yes, quite in order. Have you the name ready, my dear sir?"

"I will give you that of Rev. George Durnford, of Cottonborough."

"And, for how long, Mr. Horn," asked Mr. Ball, when he had written down Mr. Durnford's name and address, "must the property be thus held?"

"Till my daughter comes to claim it."

"But, but, my dear sir—"

"Very well," said "Cobbler" Horn, breaking in upon the lawyer's incipient protest; "put it like this. Say that, in the event of my sister's death, everything is to go into the hands of Mr. Durnford, to be held by him in trust for my daughter, and to be dealt with according to his own discretion."

"That is all on that subject, gentlemen," he added, in a tone of finality; and, having summarily dismissed one matter of business, he as summarily introduced another. "And now," he said, "having made provision for my daughter in the event of my death, I wish also to provide for her in case she should come back during my life. I desire the sum of L50,000 to be set aside and invested in such a manner, that my daughter may have it—principal and interest—as her own private fortune during my life."

Mr. Ball regarded his singular client with a doubtful look.

"Is it necessary to do that, my dear sir? With your wealth, you will be able, at any time, to do for your daughter what you please."

"Yes," said Mr. Tongs, who seemed to think it time to put in his word.

"Gentlemen," said "Cobbler" Horn. "You must let me have my own way. It is my intention to turn my money to the best account, according to my light; and I wish to have the L50,000 secured to my child, lest, when she comes back, there should be nothing left for her."

"Well, Mr. Horn, of course your wishes shall be obeyed," said Mr. Ball, with a sigh; "but it is not an arrangement which I should advise."

With this final protest the subject was dismissed; but, for many days, the L50,000 to be invested for the missing daughter of his eccentric client remained a burden on the mind of Mr. Ball.

"And now," said "the Golden Shoemaker," "there is just another thing before I go. I have been to see my village. I found it, as you warned me, in a sadly dilapidated condition; and I have desired Mr. Gray to make all the necessary repairs. Will you, gentlemen, give him all the help you can, and see that he doesn't want for money?"

"We shall be delighted, my dear sir, as a matter of course."

"Thank you: Mr. Gray will probably apply to you on various points; and I wish you to know that he has my authority for all he does."

"Very good, sir," said Mr. Ball, in a respectful tone.

"Then, while I was at Daisy Lane, I paid a visit to the old Hall."

"Ah!" exclaimed Mr. Ball, "a splendid family mansion, Mr. Horn?"

"Yes; I have desired Mr. Gray to have it renovated and furnished."

"As a residence for yourself, of course?"

"No; I have other designs."

Then, in the deeply-attentive ears of the two men of law, "the Golden Shoemaker" recited his plans with regard to the old Hall.

It would be a mild statement to say that Messrs. Tongs and Ball were taken by surprise; but their client afforded them slight opportunity to interpose even a comment on his scheme.

"You must help Mr. Gray in this matter especially, gentlemen, if you please. Do all you can for him. I want it to be the best 'Children's Home' in the country. Don't spare expense. I wish everything to be provided that is good for little children. My friend, Mr. Durnford will, perhaps, help me to find a 'father and mother' for the 'Home;' you, gentlemen, shall assist me in the engagement of skilful nurses and trustworthy servants. In order that we may make the place as nearly perfect as possible, I have requested Mr. Gray to visit similar institutions in various parts of the country. He will look to you for advice; and I should be obliged, gentlemen, if you would put him on the right track."

Then he paused, and looked at his lawyers with a glowing face.

"It's for the sake," he said, and there was a catch in his voice, "of my little Marian, who went from me a wanderer upon the face of the earth."

Then, having arranged to call in the morning, for the purpose of signing his will, previous to his departure from town, he took his leave.

J. W. Keyworth

# CHAPTER XXIII

## MEMORIES

The following morning "Cobbler" Horn called at the office of Messrs. Tongs and Ball at the appointed time. The will was ready, and, having signed it, he said "good day" to the lawyers, and took the next train to Cottonborough, where he arrived early in the afternoon.

Subsequently, at the dinner-table, he answered freely the questions of Miss Jemima concerning his doings during his absence. Nor did he feel the presence of his young secretary to be, in any degree, a restraint. Already she was as one of the family, and was almost as much in the confidence of "the Golden Shoemaker" as was Miss Jemima herself. "Cobbler" Horn told of the dilapidated condition in which he had found the village, and of the instructions he had given to the agent. At the recital of the latter, Miss Jemima held up her hands in dismay, while the eyes of the secretary glistened with unconcealed delight. But the climax was reached when "Cobbler" Horn spoke of his intentions with regard to the old Hall. Miss Jemima uttered a positive shriek, and shook her head till her straight, stiff side-curls quivered again.

"Thomas," she cried, "you must be mad! It will cost you thousands of pounds!"

"Yes, Jemima," was the quiet reply; "and surely they could not be better spent! And then there'll still be a few thousands left," he added with a smile. "It's a way of spending the Lord's money of which I'm sure He will approve. What do you say, Miss Owen?"

"I think it's just splendid of you, Mr. Horn!"

To do Miss Jemima justice, her annoyance arose quite as much from the annihilation of her dearly cherished hopes of becoming the mistress of an ideal country mansion, and filling the place of lady magnificent of her brother's village, as from the thought of the gigantic extravagance which his designs with regard to the old Hall would involve.

But the poor lady was to be yet further astonished.

"Oh, I forgot to tell you, Jemima," said her brother, after a brief pause, and speaking with a whimsical air of apology, "that I am to start for America to-morrow."

He spoke as though he were announcing a trip into the next county; and Miss Jemima could scarcely have shown greater amazement, if he had declared his intention of starting for the moon.

The good lady almost bounced from her seat.

"Thomas!"

She had not breath for more than that.

In truth the announcement "the Golden Shoemaker" had made was startling enough. Even Miss Owen looked up in intense surprise; and the servant girl, who was in the act of taking away the meat, was so startled that she almost let it fall into her master's lap.

"Cobbler" Horn alone was unmoved.

"You see," he said calmly, "when I considered the sad plight of our poor cousin, I thought it would be best for me to go and see to him myself. There are the letters," he added, taking them from his pocket, and handing them to his sister. "You will see, Jemima, that the poor fellow is in sore straits—ill, and destitute in a low lodging-house in New York, Miss Owen! He will be informed, by now, of his change of fortune, and everything possible is to be done for him. But I feel that I can't leave him to strangers. And then there may be a chance of leading him to the Saviour, who can tell? Besides, Jemima, a journey to America is not so much of an undertaking now-a-days, you know; and I sha'n't be many weeks away."

By this time, Miss Jemima had managed to recover her breath, and, in part, her wits.

"But I can't get you ready by to-morrow, Thomas!"

"My dear Jemima, that doesn't matter at all: whether you can get me ready or not, I must go. The lawyers will have taken my passage by this time."

"But—but you can never take care of yourself in America, Thomas. It's such a large country, and so dreadful; and the Americans are such strange people."

"Never mind, Jemima," was the pleasant reply, "Messrs. Tongs and Ball have sent a cablegram to their agent in New York, instructing him to look after me. And, besides, I've made my will."

"What?" shouted Miss Jemima, "made your will?"

To Miss Jemima it seemed a dreadful thing to make one's will. It was a last desperate resort. It was in view of death that people made their wills. It was evident her brother did not expect to get safely back.

"Yes," repeated "Cobbler" Horn, with a quiet smile, "I've made my will. But, don't be alarmed, Jemima; I sha'n't die any the sooner for that. I did it as a wise precaution, with the approval of the lawyers. Even if I had not been going to America, I should have had to make my will sooner or later. Cheer up, Jemima! Our Heavenly Father bears rule in America, and on the sea, as well as here at home."

Miss Jemima had relapsed into silence. She was beginning to realize the fact that her brother had made his will, which, after all, was not so very strange a thing. But what was the nature of the will? She did not desire to inherit her brother's property herself. She was rich enough already. But she was apprehensive that he might have made some foolish disposition of his money of which she would not be able to approve. To whom, or to what she would have desired him to leave his wealth, she could not, perhaps, have told; but she would not be easy till she knew the contents of his will. And yet she could not question her brother on the subject in the presence of his secretary. The girl might be very well, but must not be allowed to know too much.

"If I don't come back, Jemima," said "Cobbler" Horn, as though he had read his sister's thoughts, "you will know what my will contains soon enough. If I do—of which I have little doubt—I will tell you all about it myself."

After dinner, "Cobbler" Horn retired, with his secretary, to the office, for the purpose of dealing with the letters which had accumulated during his absence from home. As they proceeded with their work, Miss Owen learnt that, while her employer was away in America, she was to have discretionary powers with regard to the whole of the correspondence. With all her self-confidence, the young secretary was rather staggered by this announcement; but she could obtain no release from the firm decree.

"You see, I have perfect confidence in you, Miss Owen," explained "Cobbler" Horn, simply; "and besides, you know very well that, in most cases, you are better able to decide what to do than I am myself. But, if there are any of the letters that you would rather not deal with till I come back, just let them wait."

This matter had been arranged during the first half-hour, in the course of a dropping conversation, carried on in the pauses of their work. They had put in a few words here and there in the crannies and crevices of their business so to speak. In the same manner, "Cobbler" Horn now proceeded to tell his secretary of his interview with his lawyers, and of the making of his will.

"The Golden Shoemaker" had already become wonderfully attached to his young secretary. She had exercised no arts; she had practised no wiles. She was a sincere, guileless, Christian girl. Shrewd enough she was, indeed, but utterly incapable of scheming for any manner of selfish or sordid end. With her divine endowment of good looks and her consecrated good nature, she could not fail to captivate; and there is small room for wonder that she had made large inroads upon "Cobbler" Horn's big heart.

The degree to which his engaging young secretary had won the confidence of "Cobbler" Horn will appear from the fact that he was about to reveal to her, this afternoon, those particulars with regard to his recently-made will the communication of which to his sister he had avowedly postponed. It was not his intention to treat Miss Jemima with disrespect. He felt that he could freely talk to Miss Owen; with his sister it would be a matter of greater delicacy to deal. He often fancied that his young secretary was just such as his darling Marian would have been; and quite naturally, and very simply, he told her about his will, and even spoke of the money that was to be invested for his lost child. He was quite able now to talk calmly of the great sorrow of his life. The gentle and continued rubbing of the hand of time had allayed its sharper pang.

"What do you think of it all, Miss Owen?"

"I think, Mr. Horn," said the secretary, with the end of her penholder between her ruby lips, and a wistful look in her dark eyes, "that your daughter would be a very fortunate young lady, if she only knew it; and that there are not many fathers like you."

"Then you think I have done well?"

"I think, sir, that you have done better than well."

After another spell of work, Miss Owen looked up again with an eager face.

"What was your little Marian like, Mr. Horn?" she asked, in a tender and subdued tone.

"Well, she was—" But the ardent girl took him up before he could proceed.

"Would she have grown to be anything like me? I suppose she would be about my age."

She was leaning forward now, with her elbows on the table, and her hands supporting her chin. Her richly-tinted cheeks glowed with interest; her large, dark eyes shone like two bright stars. The question she had asked could not be to her more than a subject of amiable curiosity; but no doubt the enthusiastic nature of the girl fully accounted for the eagerness with which she had spoken. Her sudden enquiry wafted "Cobbler" Horn back into the past; and there rose before him the vision of a bonny little nut-brown damsel of five summers, with eyes like sloes, and a mass of dusky hair. For an instant he caught his breath. He was startled to see, in the face of his young secretary what he would probably never have detected, if her question had not pointed it out.

"Well, really, Miss Owen," he said, simply, "now you speak of it, you are something like what my little Marian may have grown to be by this time."

"How delicious!" exclaimed Miss Owen.

"Cobbler" Horn was gazing intently at his young secretary. What vague surmisings, like shadows on a window-blind— were flitting through his brain? What dim rays of hope were struggling to penetrate the gloom? Suddenly he started, and shook himself, with a sigh. Of course it could only be a fancy. How strange the frequent inability to perceive the significance of circumstances plainly suggestive of the fulfilment of some long-cherished hope! The joy, deferred so long comes, at last, in an hour when we are not aware, only to find us utterly oblivious that it is so near!

"Well, Miss Owen," said "Cobbler" Horn, rising to his feet, "I must be going to my cobbling. If you want me, you will know where to come."

"Yes, Mr. Horn."

She was aware of his custom of resorting now and then to his old workshop. When he was gone, she paused for a moment, with her penholder once more between her lips.

"How nice to think that I am like what that dear little Marian would have been! I wonder whether we should have been friends, if she had lived? Poor little thing, she's almost sure to be dead! Though, perhaps not—who can tell? How queer that Mr. Horn should have lost a little girl, just as I must have been lost, and about the same time too! As for my being like her—perhaps, after all, that's only a fancy of his. Well, at any rate, I must comfort and help him all I can. I can't step into his daughter's place exactly; but God has put it into my power to be to him, in many things, what little Marian would have been if he had not lost her; and for Christ's sake—"

At this point, the young secretary's thoughts became too sacred for prying eyes. Very soon she turned to her writing again. Half an hour later, the afternoon post arrived, bringing, amongst other letters, one or two which necessitated an immediate interview with "Cobbler" Horn. To trip up to her bedroom and dress herself for going out was the work of a very few moments; and in a short time she was entering the street where "Cobbler" Horn and his sister had lived so long, and whence the hapless little Marian had so heedlessly set out into the great world, on that bright May morning so many years ago.

As Miss Owen entered the narrow street, she involuntarily raised her hand to her forehead. The weird feeling of familiarity with the old house and its vicinity, of which she had already been conscious more than once, had crept over her again.

"How very strange!" she said to herself. "But there can't be anything in it!"

As she approached the house, she became aware of the unconcealed scrutiny of a little man who was standing in the doorway of a shop on the other side of the street.

It was Tommy Dudgeon, who had just then come to the door to show a customer out, a civility which he was wont to bestow, if possible, upon every one who came to the shop. Lingering for a moment, in the hope of descrying another customer, he saw Miss Owen coming down the street. Tommy knew about "Cobbler" Horn's secretary; but he had not, as yet, had a fair view of the young lady. He had not even thought much about her, and he did not suspect that it was she who was now coming along the street, until she passed into the old house. But, as he saw her now, with her black hair and dark glowing face, walking along the pavement in her decided way, he felt, as he afterwards said, "quite all-overish like." It was, at first, the vaguest of impressions that he received. Then, as he gazed, he began to think that he had seen that figure before—though he continued to assure himself that he had not; and then, as Miss Owen drew nearer, he concluded that there must be some one of whom she reminded him—some one whom he had known long ago. Then, with a flash, came back to him the scene—never to be forgotten—on that long-ago May morning; and Tommy Dudgeon heaved a sigh, for he had obtained his clue.

"What a rude little man!" thought Miss Owen. "And yet he looks harmless enough. Why he must be one of the little twin shopkeepers of whom I have heard Mr. Horn speak. That will account for his interest in me."

The absorption of the young secretary in the duties of her office, during her stay in the old house, no doubt fully accounted for the fact that she had not become more familiar with the appearance of Tommy Dudgeon.

By this time Tommy had withdrawn into his shop. But he continued to watch. Standing partly concealed behind some of the merchandise displayed in the shop window, he saw Miss Owen enter "Cobbler" Horn's former abode, and then waited for her once more to emerge.

In ten minutes the young secretary again appeared. Pausing on the door-step, she looked this way and that, and then, with emphatic tread, stepped out in the very track of the little twinkling feet which Tommy had watched in their last departure on that ill-fated spring morning so long ago. The little man craned his neck to see the better through the window, and then, unable to restrain himself, he hurried to the doorway of the shop once more, and, with enlightened eyes, watched the figure of the girl till it passed out of sight. Then he turned, and rushed into the kitchen behind the shop. His brother was trying to put one of the twins to sleep by carrying it to and fro; his brother's wife was making bread. He raised his hands.

"She's come back!" he cried. Then, recollecting himself, he said, more quietly, "I mean I've seen the sec'tary."

# CHAPTER XXIV

## ON THE OCEAN

The evening of the next day saw "the Golden Shoemaker" steaming out of the Mersey, on board the first-rate Atlantic liner on which his passage had been taken by Messrs. Tongs and Ball. Miss Jemima had bidden her brother a reluctant farewell. In her secret soul, she nursed a doubt, of which, indeed, she was half-ashamed, as to the prospect of his safe return; and she endeavoured to fortify her timorous heart by the utterance of sundry sharp speeches concerning the folly of his enterprise.

The voyage across the great ocean, in the splendid *floating hotel* in which he had embarked was a new and delightful experience to "Cobbler" Horn. But his peace of mind sustained brief disturbance on his being shown to his quarters on board the vessel. His lawyers had, as a matter of course, taken for their wealthy client a first-class passage. It had not occurred to him to give them any instructions on the point, and they had taken it for granted that they were doing what he would desire. Perhaps, if they had asked him, he might, in his ignorance of such matters, have said, "Oh yes, first-class, by all means." But when he saw the splendid accommodation which his money had procured, he started back, and said to the attendant:

"This is much too grand for me. Can't I make a change?"

The attendant stared in surprise.

"'Fraid not sir," he said, "every second-class berth is taken."

"I don't mind about the money," said "Cobbler" Horn hastily. "But I should be more comfortable in a plainer cabin," and he looked around uneasily at the luxurious and splendid appointments of the quarters which had been assigned to him, as his home, for the next few days.

The attendant, regarding with a critical eye the modest attire and unassuming demeanour of "Cobbler" Horn, inwardly agreed with what this somewhat eccentric passenger had said.

"The only way, sir," said the man, at length, "is to get some one to change with you."

"Ah, the very thing! How can it be managed?"

The attendant mused with hand on chin.

"Well, sir," he said, gliding into an interrogative tone, "if you really mean it—?"

"Most certainly I do."

"Then I think I can arrange it for you, sir. There is one second-class passenger who would probably jump at such a chance. He is an invalid; and it would be a great comfort to him to get into such quarters as these. I've heard a good bit about him since he came on board."

"Then he's our man," said "Cobbler" Horn; and then, he

added hesitatingly, "there'll be a sovereign for you, if you manage it at once. I'll wait here till you let me know."

The attendant sped on his errand, and, before night, the desired exchange had been duly made—"Cobbler" Horn was established in the comfortable and congenial accommodation afforded by a second-class cabin, and the invalid passenger was blessing his unknown benefactor, as he sank to rest amidst the luxury of his new surroundings.

It was late autumn, and the sea, though not stormy, was sufficiently restless to make the commencement of the passage unpleasant for all who were not good sailors. "Cobbler" Horn was not one of these; and, when, upon the second day out, he observed the deserted appearance of the decks and saloons, and, on making enquiry of an official, learnt that most of the passengers were sick, he realized with a healthy and grateful thrill of pleasure, that he was blessed with immunity from the almost universal tribulation which waylays the landsman who ventures on the treacherous deep.

It will, therefore, be readily believed that "the Golden Shoemaker" keenly enjoyed the whole of the voyage. He breathed the fresh, briny air with much relish; the wonders of the sea furnished him with many instructive and pious thoughts; and the ship itself supplied him with an inexhaustible fund of interest. In particular, he paid frequent visits to the steerage, where large numbers of emigrants were bestowed. He spent many hours amongst these poor people; and, by entering into conversation with such of them as were disposed to talk, he became acquainted with many cases of necessity, which he was not slow to relieve. Nor did the gifts of money, which he bestowed with his usual large generosity, constitute the only form of help he gave. In a thousand nameless ways he ministered to the wants and relieved the difficulties of his humble fellow-passengers, who quickly came to look upon him as the good genius of the ship. As a matter of course, the whisper soon went round, "Who is he?" And when, in some inscrutable way, the truth leaked out, the poor people regarded him with a kind of awe. Some, indeed, criticised, and said he did not look much like a millionaire; but there were many in that motley crowd in whose hearts, during those few brief days on the ocean, "Cobbler" Horn made for himself a very sacred place.

In the course of a day or two, the decks and saloons began to assume a more animated appearance. Hitherto "Cobbler" Horn had not greatly attracted the attention of the passengers with whom he was more immediately associated; but now that they were in a condition to think of something other than their own concerns, their interest in him began to awake. Who had not heard of "the Golden Shoemaker"—"The Millionaire Cordwainer"—"The Lucky Son of Crispin"—as he had been variously designated in the newspapers of the day? When it became known that so great a celebrity was on board, there was a general desire to make his acquaintance. Some vainly asked the captain to give them an introduction; some boldly introduced themselves.

"Cobbler" Horn was courteous to all, in his homely way; but he showed no anxiety to become further acquainted with these obtrusive persons. The simplicity of his manners and the plainness of his dress caused much surprise; and the public interest concerning him sensibly quickened when whispers floated forth of the giving up of his berth to the invalid passenger, and of his charitable doings amongst the poor emigrants.

During the voyage, "the Golden Shoemaker" spent much time in close and prayerful study of his Bible, which had ever been, and still was, his dearest, and well nigh his only, book. He was induced to do this not only by his love of the

J. W. Keyworth

Book itself, but also by a definite desire to absorb, and transfuse into his own experience, all those teachings of the Word of God which bore upon the new position in which he had been so strangely placed.

First of all, he turned to certain notable passages of Scripture which shot up before his memory like well-known beacon-lights along a rocky coast. There glared upon him, first of all, the lurid denunciation which opens the fifth chapter of the Epistle of James, commencing, "Go to now, ye rich men, weep and howl for your miseries that shall come upon you!" "God forbid," he cried, "that my 'gold and silver' should ever become 'cankered!' It would be a terrible thing for their 'rust' to 'witness against me,' and eat my 'flesh as it were fire'; and it would be yet more dreadful for the money which has such power for good to be itself given up to canker and rust!" Then he would meditate on the uncompromising declarations of Christ—"How hardly shall they that have riches enter into the Kingdom of God!" "It is easier for a camel to go through the eye of a needle, than for a rich man to enter into the Kingdom of God." He trembled as he read; but, pondering, he took heart again. Though hard, it was not impossible, for a man of wealth to enter into the Kingdom of God. "Camel!" "Eye of a Needle!" He did not know exactly what this strange saying meant; but he thought he had heard the minister say that it was intended to show the great difficulty involved in the salvation of a rich man. Then he read further, "How hard is it for them that trust in riches to enter into the Kingdom of God," and that seemed to make the matter plain. "Ah," he thought, "may I be saved from ever trusting in my riches!"

He plucked an ear of wholesome admonition from the parable of the Sower. "The deceitfulness of riches!" he murmured. "How true!" And he subjected himself to the most vigilant scrutiny, lest he should be beguiled by the unlimited possibilities of self-indulgence which his wealth supplied. He turned frequently to the emphatic declaration of Paul to Timothy. "They that will be rich," it runs, "fall into temptation and a snare, and into many foolish and hurtful lusts, which drown men in destruction and perdition. For the love of money is the root of all evil: which while some coveted after, they have erred from the faith, and pierced themselves through with many sorrows." "Ah!" he would exclaim, "I didn't want to be rich. At the very most Agur's prayer would have been mine: 'Give me neither poverty nor riches.' But it's quite true that riches bring 'temptations' and are a 'snare,' whether people 'will' be rich or become rich against their will; and I must be on the watch. And then there's that about 'the love of money' being 'the root of all evil!'" As he spoke, he drew a handful of coins from his pocket, and eyed them askance. "Queer things to love!" he mused. And then, as he thought of his balance at the bank, his large rent-roll, and his many profitable investments, his face grew very grave. "Ah," he sighed, letting copper, silver, and gold, slide jingling back into his pocket, "I think I have an idea how some people get to love their money. Lord save *me*."

He was very fond of the book of Proverbs. Its short, sententious sentences were altogether to his mind. "There is that scattereth," he read, "and yet increaseth; and there is that withholdeth more than is meet, but it tendeth to poverty." "I scatter," he said; "but I don't want to increase. Lord, spare me the consequences of my scattering! 'Withholdeth more than is meet'! Lord, by Thy grace, that will not I! I have no objection to poverty; but I would not have it come in that way!"

"There is that maketh himself rich," he read again, "Yet hath nothing; there is that maketh himself poor, yet hath great riches." "Ah," he sighed, "to possess such riches, I would gladly make myself poor!" But there was one text in the book of Proverbs which "Cobbler" Horn could never read without a smile. "The poor," it ran "is hated even of his own neighbour; but the rich hath many friends." He thought of his daily shoals of letters, of the numerous visiting cards which had been left at the door of his new abode, and of the obsequious attentions he had begun to receive from the office-bearers and leading members of his church; and he called to mind the eagerness of his fellow-voyagers to make his acquaintance. "Ah" he mused shrewdly, "friends, like most good things, are chiefly to be had when you don't need them!"

In these sacred studies, the days passed swiftly for "the Golden Shoemaker." Very different were the methods by which the majority of his fellow-passengers endeavoured to beguile the time. Amongst the least objectionable of these were concerts, theatricals, billiards, and all kinds of games. Much time was spent by the ladies in idle chat, to which the gentlemen added the seductions of cigar and pipe. There were not a few of the passengers, moreover, who resorted to the vicious excitement of betting; and "Cobbler" Horn marked with amazement and horror the eagerness with which they staked their money on a variety of unutterably trivial questions. The disposition of really large sums of money was made to depend, on whether a certain cloud would obscure the sun or not; whether a large bird, seen as they neared the land, would sweep by on one side of the ship or the other; whether the pilot would prove to be tall or short; and upon a multitude of other matters so utterly unimportant, that "the Golden Shoemaker" began to think he was voyaging with a company of escaped lunatics.

To one gentleman, who proposed to take a bet with him as to the nationality of the next vessel they might happen to meet, he gave a characteristic reply.

"Thank you," he said gravely, "I am not anxious on that subject; and, if I were, I should wait for the appearance of the vessel itself. Besides, I cannot think it right to risk my money in the way you propose. I dare not throw away upon a mere frivolity what God has given me to use for the good of my fellows. And then, if we were to bet, as you suggest, the one who happened to win would be receiving what he had no moral right to possess. I don't—"

Thus far the would-be better had listened patiently. But it was a bet he wanted, and not a sermon.

"I beg your pardon," he therefore said, at this point, "I see I have made a mistake;" and with a polite bow, he moved hastily away.

One fine evening, towards the end of the voyage, as "Cobbler" Horn was taking the air on deck, he was accosted by the attendant who had arranged the transfer of his berth from first to second-class.

"The gentleman, sir," he said, touching his cap, "who took your cabin—he—"

"Yes," interrupted "Cobbler" Horn; "how is he? Better, I hope."

"Much better, sir; and he thought, perhaps you would see him."

"Do you know what he wants?" asked "Cobbler" Horn, in a hesitating tone.

"Well, sir," replied the man, "he didn't exactly say; but I rather suspect it's a little matter of thanks. And, begging your pardon, sir, it's very natural."

"Cobbler" Horn was not offended at the man's freedom of address, as another in his place might have been.

"If that is all, then," he said, "I think he must excuse me. I deserve no thanks. I consulted my own inclination, as much as his comfort. I am glad he is better. Tell him he is heartily welcome, and ask him if there is anything more I can do."

The next morning, as "Cobbler" Horn stood talking, for a minute or so, to the captain, the obsequious attendant once more appeared. Touching his cap with double emphasis, in honour of the captain, he handed a letter to "Cobbler" Horn.

"From the gentleman in your cabin, sir. No answer, sir—I was told to say," and, once more touching his cap, the polite functionary marched sedately away.

"I must leave you to read your letter, Mr. Horn," said the captain; and, with the word, he withdrew to attend to his duties in another part of the ship.

"Cobbler" Horn's letter was brief, and ran as follows:

"DEAR SIR,

"Though I may not in person express my gratitude for your great kindness, I have that to tell which you ought to know. Poverty, sickness, loss of dear ones, perfidy of professed friends, and ills of all imaginable kinds, have fallen to my lot. I am an American. I have a young wife, and a dear little girl in New York. I have been to Europe upon what has turned out a most disastrous business trip. I came on board this vessel a battered, broken man, not knowing, and scarcely caring, whether I should live to reach the other side. Faith in Christianity, in religion, in God Himself, I had utterly renounced. But I want to tell you that all that is changed. I now wish, and hope, to live; my health is vastly improved; and—will you let me say it without offence?—I find myself able once more to believe in God, and in such religion as yours. I will not again ask you to see me; but if, after reading this letter, you should feel inclined to pay me a visit, I need not tell you how delighted I should be.

"I am,

"Dear Sir,

"Yours gratefully,

"THADDEUS P. WALDRON."

"Cobbler" Horn read this gratifying letter over and over again, with a secret joy. But it was not till the next day that he could bring himself to comply with the invitation of its closing sentence, and pay a visit to the writer. He found the young man, who was far on his way to recovery, full of thankfulness to him and of gratitude to God. It seemed that, previous to the accumulation of troubles beneath which his faith had given away, the young fellow had been a zealous Christian. "Cobbler" Horn found him sincerely penitent; and, during this, and succeeding interviews, he had the joy of leading him back to the Saviour.

# CHAPTER XXV

## COUSIN JACK

As "Cobbler" Horn was leaving the vessel at New York, he witnessed the meeting of Thaddeus P. Waldron and his wife. Mrs. Waldron had come on board the steamer. She was a wholesome, glowing little woman, encumbered with no inconvenient quantity of reserve. She flung her arms impulsively around her husband's neck, and kissed him with a smack like the report of a pistol.

"Why, Thad," she cried, "do tell! You've completely taken me in! I expected a scarecrow. What for did you frighten me with that letter I got last week? It might have been my death!"

Then, with a little trill of a laugh, the happy woman hugged once more the equally delighted "Thad," and gave him another resounding kiss.

By this time the attention of those who were passing to and fro around them began to be attracted; and, amongst the rest, "Cobbler" Horn, who was held for a few moments in the crowd, was watching them with deep interest.

"Hold hard, little woman," exclaimed Thaddeus, "or I guess I sha'n't have breath left to tell you my news! And," he added, "it's better even than you think."

"Oh, Thad, do tell!" she cried, still regarding her husband with admiring eyes.

"Well, my health has been fixed up by the sea air, and the comfort and attention I've had during the voyage, which is all through the goodness of one man. I calculate that man 'ull have to show up before we leave this vessel. He wasn't out of sight five minutes ago."

As he spoke, he looked round, and saw the figure of "Cobbler" Horn, who, evidently in dread of a demonstration on the part of his grateful friend, was modestly moving away amongst the crowd. One stride of Thaddeus P. Waldron's long legs, and he had his benefactor by the arm.

"Here, stranger—no, darn it all, you aren't a stranger, no how you fix it—this way sir, if *you* please."

"Now, little woman," he exclaimed, triumphantly dragging his reluctant captive towards his wife, "this is the man you have to thank—this man and God! He gave up—"

"Oh," interrupted "Cobbler" Horn, "you mustn't allow him to thank me for that, ma-am. I did it quite as much for my own sake."

"Hear him!" exclaimed Thaddeus, with incredulous admiration. "Anyhow he made me think, little wife, that there was some genuine religion in the world after all. And that helped me to get better too. And the long and short of it is, I've been made a new man of, inside and out; and we're going to have some real good times! And now, old girl, you've just got to give the man whose done it all a hug and a buss, and then we'll come along."

"Cobbler" Horn started back in dismay. But Mrs. Thaddeus was thoroughly of her husband's mind. What he had been, as she knew from his letters, and what she found him now, passed through her mind in a flash. She was modest enough, but not squeamish; and the honest face of "Cobbler" Horn was one which no woman, under the circumstances, need have hesitated to kiss. So, in a moment, to the amusement of the crowd, to the huge delight of the grateful Thaddeus, and to the confusion of "the Golden Shoemaker" himself, the thing was done.

The next minute, the happy and grateful couple were gone, and "Cobbler" Horn had scarcely time to recover his composure before he found himself greeted by the agent of Messrs. Tongs and Ball, who, having been furnished by those gentlemen with a particular description of the personal appearance of their eccentric client, had experienced but little difficulty in singling him out. From this gentleman "Cobbler" Horn learnt that his ill-fated cousin had been removed from the wretched lodgings where he was found to the best private hospital in New York, where he was receiving every possible care. The agent had also engaged apartments for "Cobbler" Horn himself in a first-class hotel in the neighbourhood of the hospital. It was a great relief to "Cobbler" Horn that his conductor had undertaken the care of his luggage, and the management of everything connected with his debarkation. He was realizing more and more the immense advantages conferred by wealth. On being shown into the splendid apartments which had been engaged for him in the hotel, he shrank back as he had done from the first-class accommodation assigned to him on board the steam-boat. But this time he was obliged to submit. Wealth has its penalties, as well as its advantages.

It was early in the forenoon when the vessel arrived; and, when "the Golden Shoemaker" was duly installed in his luxurious quarters at the hotel, the agent left him, having first promised to come back at three o'clock, and conduct him to the bedside of his cousin.

At the appointed time the agent returned.

"Cobbler" Horn was eager to be going, and they at once set out. A few minutes brought them to the hospital where his cousin lay. They were immediately shown in, and "Cobbler" Horn found himself entering a bright and airy chamber, where he presently stood beside his cousin's bed.

The sick man had been apprised of the approaching visit of his generous relative from over the water, and he regarded "Cobbler" Horn now with a kind of dull wonder in his hollow eyes. At the same time he held out a hand which was wasted almost to transparency. "Cobbler" Horn took the thin fingers in his strong grasp; and, as he looked, with a great pity, on the sunken cheeks, the protruding mouth, the dark gleaming eyes, and the contracted forehead with its setting of black damp hair, he thought that, if ever he had seen the stamp of death upon a human face, he saw it now.

"Well, cousin Jack," he said sadly, "it grieves me that our first meeting should be like this."

Cousin Jack, struggling with strong emotion, regarded his visitor with a fixed look. His mouth worked convulsively, and it was some moments before he could speak. At length he found utterance, in hollow tones, and with laboured breath.

"Have you—come all this way—across the water—on purpose to see me?"

"Yes," replied "Cobbler" Horn, simply, "of course I have. I wanted you to know that you are to have your honest share of our poor uncle's money. And because I was determined to make sure that everything was done for you that could be done, and because I wished to do some little for you myself, I did not send, but came."

"Uncle's money! Ah, yes, they told me about it. Well, you might have kept it all; and it's very good of you—very. But money won't be much use to me very long. It's your coming that I take so kindly. You see, I hadn't a friend; and it seemed so dreadful to die like that. Oh, it was good of you to come!"

In his wonder at the loving solicitude which had brought his cousin across the water to his dying bed, he almost seemed to undervalue the act of rare unselfishness by which so much money had been relinquished which might have been kept without fear of reproach. "Cobbler" Horn was not hurt by the seeming insensibility of his poor cousin to the great sacrifice he had made on his behalf. He did not desire, nor did he think that he deserved, any credit for what he had done. He had simply done his duty, as a matter of course. But he was much gratified that his poor cousin was so grateful for his coming. He sat down, with shining eyes, by the bedside, and took the wasted hand in his once more.

"Cousin," he asked, "have they cared for you in every way?"

"Yes, cousin, they have done what they could, thanks to your goodness!"

"Not at all. Your own money will pay the bill, you know."

For a moment cousin Jack was perplexed. His own money? He had not a cent. in the world! He had actually forgotten that his cousin had made him rich.

"My own money?"

"Yes; the third part of what uncle left you know."

A slight flush mantled the hollow cheeks.

"Oh yes; what a dunce I am! I'm afraid I'm very ungrateful. But you see I seem to have done with such things. And yet the money is going to be of some use to me after all."

"Yes, that it is! It shall bring you comfort, ease, and, if possible, health and life."

The sick man shook his head.

"No," he said, wistfully; "a little of the first two, perhaps, but none of the last. I know I can't live many weeks; and it's no use deceiving myself with false hopes."

As "Cobbler" Horn looked at his cousin, he knew that he was not mistaken in his forecast.

"Cobbler" Horn did not remain long with his sick cousin at this time.

"There is one thing I should like," he said gravely, as he rose from his seat.

"There is not much that I can deny you," replied Jack; "what is it?"

He spoke without much show of interest.

"I should like to pray with you before I go."

Cousin Jack started, and again his pale face flushed.

"Certainly," he said, "if you wish it; but it will be of no use. Nothing is of any use now."

"The Golden Shoemaker" knelt down beside the bed, and prayed for his dying cousin, in his own simple, fervent way. Then, with a promise to come again on the following day, he passed out of the room.

The prayer had been brief, and poor Jack had listened to it with heedless resignation; but it had struck a chord in his bruised heart which continued to vibrate long after his visitor was gone.

The next day "Cobbler" Horn found his cousin in a more serious mood. The poor young man told him something of his sad history; and "Cobbler" Horn spoke many earnest and faithful words. It became increasingly evident to "Cobbler" Horn, day by day, that life was ebbing fast within his cousin's shattered frame; and he grew ever more anxious to bring the poor young fellow to the Saviour. But somehow the work seemed to drag. Jack would express a desire for salvation; and yet, somehow he seemed to be holding back. The hindrance was revealed, one day, by a stray question asked by "Cobbler" Horn.

"How about your will, Jack?"

Jack stared blankly.

"My will? Why should I make a will?"

"Because you have some money to leave."

"Ah! Whose will it be, if I die without a will?"

"Mine, I suppose," said "Cobbler" Horn reluctantly, after a

moment's thought.

"Well, then, let it be; nothing could be better."

"But is there no one to whom you would like to leave your money?"

Jack looked fixedly at the already beloved face of his cousin. Then his own face worked convulsively, and he covered it with his wasted fingers.

"Yes, yes," he said, in tones of distress; "there is some one. That is—You are sure the money is really my own?"

He seemed all eagerness now to possess his share of the money.

"To be sure it is," responded "Cobbler" Horn. "That is quite settled."

"Well, then, there is a poor girl who would have given her life for mine; but I have behaved to her like a brute. She shall have every penny of it."

"Cobbler" Horn listened with intense interest, and at once gave expression to a burning apprehension which had instantly pierced his mind.

"Behaved like a brute!" he exclaimed. "Not in the worst way of all, I hope, Jack?"

"No, no, not that!" cried Jack, in horror.

"Thank God! But now, do you know where this poor girl is to be found?"

"I think so. Her name is Bertha Norman, and her parents live in a village only a few miles from here. When I gave her up, I believe she left her situation, here in the city, and went home with a broken heart."

"Well, Jack, your decision will meet with the approval of God. But, in the meantime, we must try to find this poor girl."

"If you only would!"

"Of course. But, with regard to the other matter—you would like to have the thing done at once?"

"The thing?"

"The will."

"Oh yes; it would be better so."

"Then we'll arrange, if possible, for this afternoon. Perhaps you know a lawyer?"

"No. Amongst all my follies, I have kept out of the hands of the lawyers. But there is the gentleman who rescued me from that den, where I should have been dead by now. Perhaps he would do?"

"Ah, the agent of my lawyers in London! Well, I'll see him at once."

So the thing was done. That afternoon the lawyer came to receive instructions, and the next morning the will was presented and duly signed.

When the lawyer was gone, Jack turned feebly to "Cobbler" Horn.

"There's just one thing more," he said. "I must see her, and tell her about it myself."

"Would she come" asked "Cobbler" Horn. "And do you think it would be well?"

"'Come'? She would come, if I were dying at North Pole. And there will be no peace for me, till I have heard from her own lips that she has forgiven me."

"Ah!" ejaculated "Cobbler" Horn. "Do you say so?"

"Yes, cousin; I feel that it's no use to ask pardon of God, till Bertha has forgiven me. You know what I mean."

"Yes," said "Cobbler" Horn gently; "I know what you mean, and I'll do what I can."

"Thank you!" said Jack, fervently. "But it mustn't be by letter. You must go and see her yourself, if you will; and I don't think you will refuse."

"Cobbler" Horn shrank, at first, from so delicate and difficult a mission, for which he pronounced himself utterly unfit. But the pathetic appeal of the dark, hollow eyes, which gleamed upon him from the pillow, ultimately prevailed.

"Tell her," said Jack, as "Cobbler" Horn wished him good night, "that I dare not ask pardon of God, till I have her forgiveness from her own lips."

In a village almost English in its rural loveliness "Cobbler" Horn found himself, the next morning, face to face, in the little front-room of a humble cottage, with a pale, sorrowful maiden, on whose pensively-beautiful face hope and fear mingled their lights and shadows while he delivered his tender message.

"Would she go with him?"

"Go?" she exclaimed, with trembling eagerness, "of course I will! But how good it is of you, sir—a stranger, to come like this!"

So Bertha Norman came back with "Cobbler" Horn to the private hospital in New York. He put her into her cousin's room, closed the door, and then quietly came downstairs. Bertha did not notice that her conductor had withdrawn. She flew to the bedside. The dying man put out a trembling hand.

"Forgive—" he began in broken tones.

But she stifled his words with gentle kisses, and, sitting down by the bed, clasped his poor thin hand.

"Ask God to forgive you, dear Jack. I've never stopped loving you a bit!"

"Yes, I will ask God that," he said. "I can now. But I want to tell you something first, Bertha. I am a rich man."

Then he told her the wonderful story.

"Ah!" she exclaimed, "that was your friend who brought me here. I felt that he was good."

"He is," said Jack. "And now Bertha, it's all yours. I've made my will, and the money is to come to you when I'm gone. You know I'm going, Bertha?"

She tightened the grasp of her hand on his with a convulsive movement, but did not speak.

"It 'ull be your very own, Bertha," he said.

"Yes, thank you, dear Jack. But forgive me, if I don't think much about that just now."

Then there was a brief silence, which was presently broken by Jack.

"You won't leave me, yet, Bertha? You'll stay with me a little while?"

"Jack I shall never leave you any more!" and there was a world of love in her gentle eyes.

"Thank God!" murmured the dying man. "Till—till—you mean?"

"Yes; but, Jack, you must come back to God!"

"Yes, I will. But call cousin Thomas in."

She found "the Golden Shoemaker" in a small sitting-room downstairs; and, having brought him up to the sick-chamber, stood before him in the middle of the room, and, taking his big hand, gently lifted it, with both her tiny white ones, to her lips.

"In the presence of my dear Jack," she said, "I thank you. But, dear friend, I think you should take the money back when he is gone."

"My dear young lady," protested "Cobbler" Horn, with uplifted hand, "how can I take it, seeing it is not mine? But," he added softly, "we will not speak of it now."

True to her promise, Bertha did not leave her beloved Jack

until the end; and the regular attendants, supplied by the house, so far from regarding her presence as an intrusion, were easily induced to look upon her as one of themselves. "Cobbler" Horn was rarely absent during the day-time; and, in the brief remaining space of poor Jack's chequered life, his gentle lover, and his high-souled cousin, had the great joy of leading him to entertain a genuine trust in the Saviour. The end came so suddenly, that they had no time for parting words; but they had good hope, as they reverently closed his eyes. When all was over, and he had been laid to rest in the cemetery, "Cobbler" Horn took Bertha back to her village home, and then set his face once more towards England, bearing in his heart a chastened memory, and the image of a sweet, pensive face.

# CHAPTER XXVI

## HOME AGAIN

It was with feelings of deep gratitude to God that "Cobbler" Horn set foot once more upon his native land. After having been away no longer than four weeks, he landed at Liverpool on a bright winter's morning, and, taking an early train, reached Cottonborough about mid-day. He had telegraphed the time of his arrival, and Bounder, the coachman, was at the station to meet him with the dog-cart. He had sent his message for the purpose of preparing his sister for his arrival; for he knew she preferred not to be taken unawares by such events. If he had given the matter a thought, he would have told them not to send to meet him at the station. He would much rather have walked, than ridden, a distance so short. And then he shrank, at all times, from the idea of making a public parade of his newly-acquired state. And, if all the truth must be told, he was—not awed, but mildly irritated, by the imposing presence, and reproachful civility, of the ideal Bounder.

Here was Bounder now, with his dignified salute. "Cobbler" Horn yearned to give the man a hearty shake of the hand, and ask him sociably how he had been getting on. This was obviously out of the question; but, just then, little Tommy Dudgeon happened to come up, on his way into the station.

J. W. Keyworth

Here was an opportunity not to be let slip, and "Cobbler" Horn seized with avidity on his humble little friend, and gave him the hearty hand-shake which he would fain have bestowed upon the high and mighty Bounder. It was a means of grace to "the Golden Shoemaker" once more to clasp the hand of a compatriot and a friend. He stood talking to Tommy for a few minutes, while Bounder waited in his seat with an expression of very slightly veiled scorn on his majestic face.

At length, quite oblivious of the contemptuous disapproval of his coachman, and greatly refreshed in spirit, "Cobbler" Horn bade his little friend "good day," and mounted to his seat.

They drove off in silence. "Cobbler" Horn scarcely knew whether his exacting coachman would think it proper for his master to enter into conversation with him; and the coachman, on his part, would not be guilty of such a breach of decorum as to speak to his master when his master had not first spoken to him.

Miss Jemima was standing in the doorway to receive her brother; and behind her, with a radiant face, modestly waited the young secretary. Miss Jemima presented her cheek, as though for the performance of a surgical operation, and "Cobbler" Horn kissed it with a hearty smack. At the same time he grasped her hand.

"Well, Jemima," he exclaimed, "I'm back again safe and sound, you see!"

"Yes," was the solemn response, "I'm thankful to see you, brother,—and relieved."

"Cobbler" Horn laughed heartily, and kissed her on the other cheek.

"Thankful enough, Jemima, let us be. But 'relieved'! well, I had no fear. You see, my dear sister, the whole round world lies in the hand of God. And, then, I didn't understand the way the Lord has been dealing with me of late to mean that he was going to allow me to be cut off quite so soon as that."

This was said cheerily, and not at all in a preaching tone; and having said it, "Cobbler" Horn turned, with genuine pleasure, to exchange a genial greeting with his young secretary, who had remained sedately in the background.

"Dinner is almost ready," said Miss Jemima, as they entered the house; "so you must not spend long in your room."

"I promise you," said her brother, from the stairs, "that I shall be at the table almost as soon as the dinner itself."

During dinner, "Cobbler" Horn talked much about his voyage to and fro, and his impressions of America. He had sent, by letter, during his absence, a regular report, from time to time, of the progress of the sorrowful business which had taken him across the sea; and with regard to that neither he nor his sister was now inclined to speak at large.

After dinner, "Cobbler" Horn, somewhat to his sister's mortification, retired to the office, for the purpose of receiving, from his secretary, a report of the correspondence which had passed through her hands during his absence.

Let it not be supposed that Miss Jemima was capable of entertaining suspicion with regard to her brother. She would frown upon his doings and disapprove of his opinions, with complete unreserve; but she would not admit concerning him a shadow of mistrust. When, therefore, it is recorded that his frequent and close intercourse with his young secretary occasioned his sister uneasiness of mind, it must not be supposed that any evil imagining intruded upon her thoughts. Miss Jemima was simply fearful lest this young girl should, perhaps inadvertently, steal into the place in her brother's heart which belonged to her. As "Cobbler" Horn and his secretary sat in counsel, from time to time, in their respective arm-chairs, at the opposite ends of the office table, neither of them had any suspicion of Miss Jemima's jealous fears.

Miss Owen had dealt diligently, and with much shrewdness, with the ever-inflowing tide of letters. Her labour was much lightened now by reason of "Cobbler" Horn's having provided her with the best type-writer that could be obtained for money. With regard to some of the letters, she had ventured to avail herself of the advice of the minister; and she had also, with great tact, consulted Miss Jemima on points with reference to which the opinion of that lady was likely to be sound and safe. The consequence was that the letters which remained to be considered were comparatively few.

First, Miss Owen gave her employer an account of the letters of which she had disposed; then she unfolded such matters as were still the subjects of correspondence; and lastly she laid before him the letters with which she had not been able to deal.

The most important of all the letters were two long ones from Messrs. Tongs and Ball and Mr. Gray, respectively, relating to the improvements in progress at Daisy Lane in general, and in particular to the work of altering and fitting up the old Hall for the great and gracious purpose on which its owner had resolved. "The Golden Shoemaker" was gratified to learn, from these letters, that the work of renovating his dilapidated property had been so well begun, and that already, amongst his long-suffering tenants, great satisfaction was beginning to prevail. The remaining letters were passed under review, and then "Cobbler" Horn lingered for a few moment's chat.

"I mean to take my sister and you to see the village and the Hall one day soon, Miss Owen," he said.

"Oh, thank you, Mr. Horn!" enthusiastically exclaimed the young secretary.

"You would like to go?"

"I should love it dearly! I can't tell you, Mr. Horn, how much I am interested in that kind and generous scheme of yours for the old Hall."

In her intercourse with her employer, "Cobbler" Horn's secretary was quite free and unreserved, as indeed he wished her to be.

"It's to be a home for orphans, isn't it?" she asked.

"Not for orphans only," he replied, tenderly, as he thought of his own lost little one. "It's for children who have no home, whether orphans or not,—little waifs, you know, and strays—children who have no one to care for them."

"I'm doing it," he added, simply, "for the sake of my little Marian."

"Oh, how good of you! And, do you know, Mr. Horn, its being for waifs and strays makes me like it all the more; because I was a waif and stray once myself."

She was leaning forward, with her elbows on the table, and her pretty but decided chin resting on her doubled hands. As she spoke, her somewhat startling announcement presented itself to her in a serio-comic light, and a whimsical twinkle came into her eyes. The same impression was shared by "Cobbler" Horn; and, regarding his young secretary, with her neatly-clothed person, her well-arranged hair, and her capable-looking face, he found it difficult to regard as anything but a joke the announcement that she had once been, as she expressed it, "a waif and stray."

"You!" he exclaimed, with an indulgent smile.

"Yes, Mr. Horn, I was indeed a little outcast girl. Did not Mr. Durnford tell you that the dear friends who have brought me up are not my actual parents?"

"Yes," replied "Cobbler" Horn, slowly, "he certainly did. But I did not suspect—"

"Of course not!" laughed the young girl. "You would never dream of insulting me by supposing that I had once been a little tramp!"

"No, of course not," agreed "Cobbler" Horn, with a perplexed smile.

"It's true, nevertheless," affirmed Miss Owen. "Mr. and Mrs. Burton have been like parents to me almost ever since I can remember, and I always call them 'father' and 'mother'; but they are no more relations to me than are you and Miss Horn. They found me in the road, a poor little ragged mite; and they took me home, and I've been just like their own ever since. I remember something of it, in a vague sort of way."

"Cobbler" Horn was regarding his secretary with a bewildered gaze.

"You may well be astonished, Mr. Horn. But, do you know, sometimes I almost feel glad that I don't know my real father and mother. They must have been dreadful people. But, whatever they were, they could never have been better to me than Mr. and Mrs. Burton have been. They have treated me exactly as if I had been their own child."

Many confused thoughts were working in the brain of "Cobbler" Horn.

"But," said Miss Owen, resuming her work, "I must tell you about it another time."

"Yes, you shall," said "Cobbler" Horn, rousing himself. "I shall want to hear it all."

So saying, he left the room, and betook himself to his old workshop for an hour or two on his beloved cobbler's bench. He had placed the old house under the care of a widow, whom he permitted to live there rent free, and to have the use of the furniture which remained in the house, and to whom, in addition, he paid a small weekly fee.

As he walked along the street, he could not fail to think of what his secretary had just said with reference to her early life. His thoughts were full of pathetic interest. Then she too had been a little homeless one! The fact endeared to him, more than ever, the bright young girl who had come like a stream of sunshine into his life. For to "Cobbler" Horn his young secretary was indeed becoming very dear. It could not be otherwise. She was just filling his life with the gentle and considerate helpfulness which he had often thought would have been afforded to him by his little Marian. And now, it seemed to draw this young girl closer to him still, when he learnt that she had once been homeless and friendless, as he had too much reason to fear that his own little one had become. He had a feeling also that the coincidence therein involved was strange.

# CHAPTER XXVII

## COMING INTO COLLISION
## WITH THE PROPRIETIES

It is not surprising that, in his new station, "Cobbler" Horn should have committed an occasional breach of etiquette. It was unlikely that he would ever be guilty of real impropriety; but it was inevitable that he should, now and again, set at nought the so-called "proprieties" of fashionable life. In the genuine sense of the word, "Cobbler" Horn was a Christian gentleman; and he would have sustained the character in any position in which he might have been placed. But he had a feeling akin to contempt for the punctilious and conventional squeamishness of polite society.

It was, no doubt, largely for this reason that "society" did not receive "the Golden Shoemaker" within its sacred enclosure. Not that it rejected him. He had too much money for that; half his wealth would have procured him the entree to the most select circles. But the attitude he assumed towards the fashionable world rendered impossible his admission to its charmed precincts. He made it evident that he would not, and could not, conform to its customs or observe its rules. The world, indeed, courted him, at first, and would gladly have taken him within its arms. Fashion set to work to woo him, as it would have wooed an ogre possessed of his glittering credentials. But he repelled its advances with an amused indifference verging on contempt.

"Cobbler" Horn foiled, by dint of sheer unresponsiveness, the first attempt to introduce itself to him made by the world. On his return from America, one of the first things which attracted his attention was a pile of visiting cards on a silver salver which stood on the hall table. Some of these bore the most distinguished names which Cottonborough or its vicinity could boast. There were municipal personages of the utmost dignity, and the representatives of county families of the first water. It had taken the world some little time to awake to a sense of its "duty" with regard to the "Cobbler" who had suddenly acceded to so high a position in the aristocracy of wealth. But when, at length, it realized that "the Golden Shoemaker" was indeed a fact, it set itself to bestow upon him as full and free a recognition as though the blood in his veins had been of the most immaculate blue.

It was during his absence in America that the great rush of the fashionable world to his door had actually set in. But Miss Jemima had not been taken unawares. She had supplied herself betimes with a manual of etiquette, which she had studied with the assiduity of a diligent school-girl. She had also, though not without trepidation, ordered a quantity of visiting cards, and had them inscribed respectively with her own and her brother's names. And thus, when Society made its first advances, it did not find Miss Jemima unprepared.

When "Cobbler" Horn espied the visiting cards on his hall table, he said to his sister:

"What, more of these, Jemima?"

"Yes, Thomas," she responded, with evident pride; "and some of them belong to the best people in the neighbourhood!"

J. W. Keyworth

"And have all these people been here?" he asked, taking up a bunch of the cards between his finger and thumb, and regarding them with a mingling of curiosity and amusement.

"Yes," replied Miss Jemima, in exultant tones, "they have all been here; but a good many of them happened to come when I was out."

"Cobbler" Horn sighed.

"Well," he said, "I suppose this is another of 'the penalties of wealth!'"

"Say rather *privileges*, Thomas," Miss Jemima ventured delicately to suggest.

"No, Jemima. It may appear to you in that light; but I am not able to regard as a privilege the coming to us of all these grand people. How much better it would be, if they would leave us to live our life in our own way! Do you suppose they would ever have taken any notice of us at all, if it had not been for this money?"

Miss Jemima was unable to reply; for it was impossible to gainsay her brother's words. And yet it was sweet to her soul to have all the best people in the neighbourhood calling and leaving their cards. For the present, she let the matter rest. But, a day or two afterwards, the course of events brought the question to the surface again. Miss Jemima was brushing her brother's coat, in the dining-room, after dinner, previous to his setting out for his old workshop, when they saw a carriage drive up to the gate.

"Here are some more of your grand friends, Jemima," said "Cobbler" Horn, with a sigh. "How ever am I to get out?"

Miss Jemima was peeping out from behind the window-curtain, with the eagerness of a girl.

"Why," she exclaimed, as the occupants of the carriage began to alight, "it's Mr. and Mrs. Brownlow, the retired b—." "Brewer" she was going to say but checked herself. "Surely you will not think of going out now, Thomas?"

"Cobbler" Horn knew Mr. and Mrs. Brownlow very well by sight. He had known them before they rode in their carriage, and when they were much less splendid people than they had latterly become. He had never greatly desired their acquaintance when it was unattainable; and, now that it was being thrust upon him, he desired it even less than before. There was no reason why he should be intimate with this man. On what grounds had he called? "Cobbler" Horn could not refrain from regarding the visit as being an impertinence.

"My dear Jemima," he said, "I must be going at once. These people cannot have any business with me; and I have a good deal of work to do. You have received the other people; and you can manage these. But, Jemima, do not encourage them to come again!"

So saying, he moved towards the door; but Miss Jemima placed an agitated hand upon his arm.

"Thomas," she cried, "what shall I say to them?"

"Tell them I am obliged to go out. Do you think it would be right to keep my poor people waiting for their boots and shoes, while I spent the time in idle ceremony?"

Miss Jemima ceased to remonstrate, and her brother again moved towards the door. But, before he reached it, a servant appeared with the cards of Mr. and Mrs. Brownlow, who were by this time installed in the drawing-room. Miss Jemima took the cards, and "Cobbler" Horn made for the front-door.

"Not that way, Thomas!" she cried after him. "They'll see you!"

"Cobbler" Horn looked around in surprise.

"Why not, my dear? They will thus perceive that I have really gone out."

The next moment he was gone, and Miss Jemima was left to face the visitors with the best excuses she could frame.

The question of returning the numerous calls they had received occasioned much perplexity to Miss Jemima's mind. Nothing would induce her brother to accompany her on any expedition of the kind. While, therefore, in some cases, she was able to go by herself, in others she was obliged to refrain from going altogether, and, as a matter of course, offence was given. The natural consequence was that the number of callers rapidly diminished, and "the Golden Shoemaker's" reputation for eccentricity was thoroughly established.

"Cobbler" Horn very rarely consented to see any company who came merely to pay a call. But one afternoon, when his sister was out, he went into the drawing-room to excuse her absence, and, in fact, to dismiss the callers.

"My sister is not at home, ma'am," he said, addressing the buxom and magnificent lady, who, with her two slender and humble-looking sons, had awaited his coming.

Having delivered his announcement, he stood at the open door, as though to show his visitors out. The lady, however, quite unabashed, retained her seat.

"May I venture to say," she asked, "that, inasmuch as the absence of Miss Horn has procured us the pleasure of making the acquaintance of her brother, it is not entirely a matter of regret?"

"Cobbler" Horn bowed gravely.

"It is very good of you to say that, ma'am; but I'm afraid I must ask you to excuse me too. I'm very busy; and, besides, these ceremonies are not at all in my way."

The lady, who bore a title, changed countenance, and rose to her feet. She was conscious that she had been dismissed.

"Certainly, sir," she said, in accents of freezing politeness; "no doubt you have many concerns. We will retire at once."

The lady's sons also rose, moving as she moved, like the satellites of a planet.

"There is no need for you to go, ma'am," "Cobbler" Horn hastened to say, quite unaware that he had committed a grave breach of etiquette. "If you will only excuse me, and stay here by yourselves, for a little while, no doubt my sister will soon be back; and I'm sure she will be glad to see you."

"Thank you," was the haughty response of the angered dame; "we have already remained too long. Be good enough, sir, to have us shown out."

"Cobbler" Horn rang the bell; and, as the lady, followed by her sons, swept past him with a stately and disdainful bow, he felt that, in some way, he had grievously transgressed.

Miss Jemima, on her return, a few moments later, heard, with great consternation, what had taken place.

"I asked the good lady to wait till you came, Jemima; but she insisted on going away at once."

"Oh, Thomas, what have you done!" cried Miss Jemima, in piteous tones.

"What could I do?" was the reply. "You see, I could not think of wasting my time; and I thought they would not mind staying by themselves, for a few minutes, till you came in."

"Oh, dear," cried Miss Jemima, "I'm afraid she'll never come again!"

"Well, never mind, Jemima," said her brother; "I don't suppose it will matter very much."

The foreboding of Miss Jemima was fulfilled; the outraged lady returned no more. And there were many others, who, when they found that the master of the house had little taste for fashionable company, discontinued their calls. Some few of her new-made acquaintances only Miss Jemima was able, by dint of her own careful and eager politeness, to retain.

There were also other points at which "Cobbler" Horn came into collision with the customs of society. He persisted in habitually going out with his hands ungloved. He possessed a hardy frame, and, even in winter, he had rarely worn either gloves or overcoat; and now, as ever, almost his only preparation for going out was to take his hat down from its peg, and put it on his head. Miss Jemima pathetically entreated that he would at least wear gloves. But he was obdurate. His hands, he said, were always warm enough when he was out of doors; and he would try to keep them clean.

Another of the whims of "Cobbler" Horn was his fondness for doing what his sister called "common" work. One morning, for example, on coming down to breakfast, the good lady, looking through the window, saw her brother, in his shirt sleeves, engaged in trimming the grass of the lawn. With a little scream, she ran out at the front-door, and caught him by the arm.

"Thomas! Thomas!" she cried, "if you don't care about yourself, have a little thought for me!"

"What is it, Jemima?" he asked straightening himself. "Is breakfast ready? I'm very sorry to have kept you waiting. I'll come at once."

"No, no," exclaimed Miss Jemima; "it's not that! But for a man in your position to be working like a common gardener—it's shameful! Pray come in at once, before you are seen by any one going by! Without your coat too, on a sharp winter's morning like this!"

"My dear Jemima," said "Cobbler" Horn, as he turned with her towards the house, "if I *were* a common gardener, there would be no disgrace, any more than in my present position. There's no shame in a bit of honest work, anyhow, Jemima; and it's a great treat to me."

Miss Jemima's chief concern was to get her unmanageable brother into the house as quickly as possible, and she paid little heed to what he said.

# CHAPTER XXVIII

## BOUNDER GIVES WARNING

There was another personage to whom the unconventional ways of "the Golden Shoemaker" gave great offence; and that was Mr. Bounder, the coachman. As a coachman, Bounder was faultless. His native genius had been developed and matured by a long course of first-class experience. In matters of etiquette, within his province, Bounder was precise. Right behaviour between master and coachman was, in his opinion, "the whole duty of man." He held in equal contempt a presuming coachman and a master who did not keep his place.

Bounder soon discovered that, in "Cobbler" Horn, he had a master of whom it was impossible to approve. Bounder "see'd from the fust as Mr. Horn warn't no gentleman." It was always the way with "them as was made rich all of a suddint like." And Bounder puffed out his red cheeks till they looked like two toy balloons. It was "bad enough to be kept waiting outside the station, while your master stood talking to a little feller as looked as like a rag and bone man as anythink; but when you was required to stop the kerridge and pick up every tramp as you overtook on the road, it was coming it a little too strong." This last was a slight exaggeration on the part of Bounder. The exact truth was that, on one occasion, his master had stopped the carriage for the purpose of giving a lift to a respectable, though not well-to-do, pedestrian, and in another instance, a working-class woman and her tired little one had been invited to take their seats on Bounder's sacred cushions, Bounder's master himself alighting to lift the bedusted child to her place.

But this was not the worst. The woman who lived in the little cottage past which Marian had trotted so eagerly, on the morning of her disappearance so long ago, had a daughter who was a cripple from disease of the spine. She was the only daughter, and, being well up in her teens, would have been a great help to her mother if she had been well. "Cobbler" Horn was deeply moved by the pale cheeks and frail bent form of the invalid girl. He induced his sister to call at the cottage, and they took the poor suffering creature under their care. It was not unnatural that the young secretary should also be enlisted in this kindly service. First she was sent to the cottage with delicacies to tempt the appetite of the sick girl; and then she began to go there of her own accord. During one of her visits, the mother happened to say:

"You see, miss, what she wants is fresh air. But how's she to get it? She can't walk only a few yards at a time; and even a mild winter's not the time for sitting out."

The woman spoke without any special design; but her words suggested to the mind of Miss Owen a happy thought. The young secretary was so firmly established, by this time, in the regard of her employer that she was able to approach him with the least degree of reserve. So she spoke out her thought to him with the frankness of a favourite daughter. An actual daughter would have thrown her arms around his neck, and emphasized her suggestion with a kiss. Miss Owen did not do this; but the tone of respectful yet affectionate confidence in which she spoke served her purpose just as well.

"Mr. Horn"—they were in the midst of their daily grapple with the correspondence—"the doctor says poor Susie Martin ought to have a great deal of fresh air. Don't you think a carriage drive now and then would be a good thing?"

Her knowledge of "Cobbler" Horn assured her that her suggestion would be adopted. Otherwise she would have hesitated to throw it out.

"Cobbler" Horn laid down the pen with which he had been making some jottings for the guidance of his secretary, and regarded her steadfastly for a moment or two. Then his face lighted up with a sudden glow.

"To be sure! Why didn't I think of that? My dear young lady, you are my good angel!"

That evening Miss Owen was desired to take a message to the cottage; and the next day Bounder was confounded by being ordered to convey Miss Owen and the invalid girl for a country drive, in the pony carriage. Bounder stared, became apoplectic in appearance, and stutteringly asked to have the order repeated. His master complied with his request; and Bounder turned away, with haughty mien, to do as he was bid. He was consumed with fierce mortification. He would bear it this time, but not again. He was like the proverbial camel, which succumbs beneath the last straw. Very soon the point would be reached at which long-suffering endurance must give way.

It was a deep grievance with Bounder that he was seldom ordered to drive to big houses. He was required to turn the heads of his horses into many strange ways. He was almost daily ordered to drive down streets where he was ashamed to be seen, and to stop at doors at which he felt it to be an indignity to be compelled to pull up his prancing steeds.

Bounder hailed with relief the occasions on which he was required to take Miss Jemima out. Then he was sure of not receiving an order to obey which would be beneath the dignity of a coachman who, until now, had known no service but of the highest class. Such occasions supplied salve to his wounded spirit. But his wound was reopened every day by some fresh insult at the hands of his master. He had submitted to the odious necessity of driving out in his carriage the crippled girl, and that not only once or twice. But the tide of rebellion was rising higher and higher in his breast, and gathering strength from day to day; and, at length, Bounder resolved to give his master "warning," and remove himself from so uncongenial a sphere. He did not quite like to make his master's kindness to the poor invalid girl his ostensible reason for desiring a change; and, while he was looking around for a plausible pretext, the course of events supplied him with exactly such an occasion as he sought.

Bounder had not as yet become aware of the daily visits of his master to his old workshop. He had been kept in ignorance of the matter merely because there was no special reason why he should be informed. One afternoon, on leaving home, "Cobbler" Horn had left word with Miss Jemima for the coachman to come to the old house, with the dog-cart, at three o'clock. Bounder received the order with a feeling of apathetic wonder as to what new freak he was expected to countenance and aid. At the entrance of the street in which the old house stood, he involuntarily pulled up his horse. Then, with an air of ineffable disdain, he drove slowly on, and proceeded to the number at which he had been directed to call.

Summoning a passing boy, he ordered him to knock at the door. The boy contemplated disobedience; but a glance at Bounder's whip induced him to change his mind, and he gave the door a sounding rap. The door speedily opened, and

J. W. Keyworth

Bounder's master appeared. But such was his disguise that Bounder was necessitated to rub his eyes. Divested of his coat, and enfolded in a leathern apron, "the Golden Shoemaker" stood in the doorway, with bare arms, holding out a pair of newly-mended hob-nailed boots.

"That's right," he said; "I'm glad you're punctual. Will you kindly take these boots to No. 17, Drake Street, round the corner; and then come back here;" and, stepping out upon the pavement, he placed the boots on the vacant cushion of the dog-cart, close to Bounder's magnificent person.

Bounder touched his hat as usual; but there was an evil fire in his heart, and, as he drove slowly away, a lava-tide of fierce thought coursed through his mind. That he, Bounder, "what had drove real gentlemen and ladies, such as a member of Parliament and a *barrow-knight*," should have been ordered to drive home a pair of labourer's boots! This was "the last straw," indeed!

Arrived at No. 17, Drake Street, Bounder altogether declined to touch the offending boots. He simply indicated them with his whip to the woman who had come to the door in some surprise, and ignoring her expression of thanks, turned the head of his horse, and drove gloomily away.

That night, "Cobbler" Horn's outraged coachman sought speech with his master.

"I wish to give you warning, sir," he said, touching his hat, and speaking in tones of perfect respect.

Bounder's master started. He had intended to make the best of his coachman.

"Why so, Bounder?" he asked. "Don't I give you money

enough, or what?"

"Oh," replied Bounder, "the money's all right; but, to make a clean breast of it, the service ain't ezactly what I've been used to. I ain't been accustomed to drive about in back streets, and stop at cottages and such; and to take up every tramp as you meets; and to carry labourer's boots on the seat of the dog-cart."

"I'm afraid, Mr. Bounder," said "Cobbler" Horn, with a broad smile, "that I've hurt your dignity."

"Well, as to that, sir," said the coachman, uneasily, "all as I wishes to say is that I've been used to a 'igh class service; and I took this place under a mis-happrehension."

"Very well, Bounder," rejoined "Cobbler" Horn, more gravely, "then we had better part. For I can't promise you any different class of service, seeing it is my intention to use my carriages quite as much for the benefit of other people as for my own; and it is not at all likely that I shall drive about much amongst fashionable folks. When do you wish to go, Mr. Bounder?"

This was business-like indeed. Bounder was in no haste to reply.

"Because," resumed his master, "I will release you next week, if you wish."

"Well, sir," replied Bounder slowly, "I shouldn't wish to go under the month."

"Very well. But, you must know, Bounder, that I have no fault to find with you. It's you who have given me notice, you know."

Bounder drew himself up to his full height. "Fault to find" with him! The mere suggestion was an insult. But Bounder put it into his pocket.

"If you are in want of a character, now," resumed "Cobbler" Horn, "I shall—"

"Thank you, sir," interposed Bounder with hauteur, "I am provided as to that. There's more than one gentleman who will speak for me," and Bounder faced about, and marched away with his nose turned towards the stars.

# CHAPTER XXIX

## VAGUE SURMISINGS

The feeling of familiarity with the previous abode of her
employer, and its surroundings, of which Miss Owen had
been conscious at first, had become modified as the weeks
went by. The removal to the new house had, no doubt, in part
contributed to this result; and, very soon, if she did not forget
the impression of revived remembrance of which she had
been aware at first, she ceased to be conscious that any trace
of it remained. She did not, indeed, forget that it had been;
she remembered vividly the fact that, when she first entered
the old house, she had almost felt as if she had come home.
That feeling had now almost passed away. But she was
beginning to ponder certain things which seemed to be
connected with it in some vague way.

Though she had often been told of the circumstances under
which she had been rescued from a life of poverty and
possible shame, her own recollection of the matter was very
dim. She seemed to remember a time of great trouble, and
then a sudden change, since which all had been happy and
bright; and certainly, if she had not been definitely informed
of the fact, she would never have suspected that the kind
friends to whom she owed so much were not her actual
parents. That vague reminiscence of early distress would

J. W. Keyworth

have lingered with her as the memory of a troubled dream, and nothing more.

Hitherto she had not been anxious for further information concerning her parentage and early life. There were times when she felt some small measure of dissatisfaction at the thought that she did not know who she really was. But this feeling was held in check by the consideration that, if her parents had been good and kind, she would probably not have been in a position to need the loving service which had been rendered to her by Mr. and Mrs. Burton; and she felt that she would a thousand times rather have them for her father and mother, than be compelled to give those dear names to such persons as it was more than likely her actual parents had been. For the most part, therefore, she had feared, rather than hoped, that her real father and mother might appear.

Now, however, vague surmisings were being awakened in the mind of the young secretary. Her kind employer had mysteriously lost a little girl. This suggested to her a new set of possibilities as to her own past. It came to her mind that perhaps she also had been lost, and that the misery she vaguely remembered, had been inflicted by other hands than those of her parents. If, like little Marian, she had actually wandered away, it was probably no fault of theirs, and perhaps they had been mourning for her all these years. Then, almost for the first time, she was conscious of an ardent desire to know who her parents had been. Over this question she pondered often and long. She could do nothing more—except pray. And pray she did. She asked that, if it were right and best, the cloud of obscurity might be lifted from her earlier years. And yet, as day by day she persisted in this prayer, she had a feeling that the prayer itself, and the desire from which it proceeded, might, perhaps, constitute a species of disloyalty to the only parents she seemed ever to have known. To this feeling her great love and strong conscientiousness gave birth. Yet she could neither repress her desire nor refrain from her prayer.

But there was another thing which "Cobbler" Horn had said. When his secretary asked him what little Marian would probably be like, if she were still alive, he, in all simplicity, and without perceiving the possible direction that might be given to her thoughts, had replied that his lost child, if living, would be not unlike what his secretary actually was. He probably intended no more than that there might be a general resemblance between the two girls; and he might be mistaken even in that. Miss Owen herself took such a view of the matter at the time, and passed it lightly by. But, afterwards, in the course of her ponderings, it came back again. The unpremeditated words, in which her employer had admitted the probability of a resemblance between herself and what his own lost child might most likely have become, seemed to find their place amongst the other strange things which were perplexing her mind.

Very deeply Miss Owen pondered these many puzzling things, from day to day. A momentous possibility seemed to be dawning on her view; but she was like one who, being but half-awake, cannot decide whether the brightness of coming day may not, after all, be merely a dim dream-light which will presently fade away. It appeared to her sometimes as though she were on the verge of the momentous discovery which she had often wondered whether she would ever make. Could it be that the mystery of her parentage was about to be solved, and that with a result which would be altogether to her mind? But, as often as she reached this point, she pulled herself sharply up. Her name was Mary Ann Owen: that settled the question at once. But was it so? There came a time when she began to have doubts even as to her name. Perhaps the wish was father to the thought. At any rate, she had never liked the name by which she was known; and now she was conscious of a very definite reason for wishing that it might, in some way, turn out not to be her name after all. Was it certain that her name was Mary Ann Owen? She had a strange, weird feeling at the thought of what the question implied. And there was distinct ground for doubt. When she had been found by her adopted parents, her baby tongue, in answer to their questioning, had pronounced her name as best it could. But, as her speech was less distinct than is usually that of a child of her apparent years, they had never felt quite sure about her name. The name by which she forthwith became known to them was the best interpretation they could put upon her broken words, and it had been accepted by the child herself without objection; but in the minds of Mr. and Mrs. Burton there had always been a lingering doubt. Miss Owen had been aware of this, but had given it little heed. Now, however, the fact that there was uncertainty as to her name came vividly to her mind. And yet, if her name was not Mary Ann Owen, it might be something else quite as far from her desires. But stay, might it not be supposed that her real name, whatever it might be, was similar in sound to the name her baby tongue had been thought to pronounce? She had tried to tell her kind friends her name; and they had understood her to say that it was Mary Ann Owen. If they were mistaken, what other name was there of similar sound? Ah, there was one! Then she thrilled with almost a delirium of delight, which quickly gave place to a guilty feeling—as though she had put forth her hand towards that which was too sacred for her touch.

"What silly day-dreams have come into my head!" she cried.

"The Golden Shoemaker" too had his ponderings, in these days. Of late he had been thinking more about his little Marian than for many years past; and, if he had searched for the reason of this, he would have discovered it in the fact that his young girl secretary daily reminded him, in various ways, of his long lost child. Miss Owen was—or so he fancied— very much like what his darling would have become. There was, to be sure, not much in that, after all; and the same might have been the case with many another young girl. But the points of resemblance between the history of his young secretary and the early fate of his little Marian constituted another circumstance of strange import. Like his own child, Miss Owen had been an outcast. Kind friends had given her a home. Might it not be that similar happiness had fallen to the lot of his little Marian? If he could think so, he would almost be reconciled to the prospect of never seeing her again. And every day he felt that his young secretary was making for herself a larger place in his heart.

J. W. Keyworth

# CHAPTER XXX

## A NOVEL DIFFICULTY FOR A MAN OF WEALTH

The trouble with most people, rich and otherwise, is to know how to keep their money; how to get rid of it was the difficulty with which "the Golden Shoemaker" was beset. "Cobbler" Horn's unalterable purpose was to retain no more than a comparatively small portion of his wealth for his own use. Since he had entered upon his fortune, he had already given away a great deal of money; but it seemed to him a very trifling amount in proportion to the vast sum he possessed. He was, moreover, aware that he was getting richer every day. Since the property had come into his hands, the investments it comprised were yielding better than ever before; and he could not endure that such vast sums of money should be accumulating upon him, while there was so much misery and want in the world. He believed that his immense wealth had been given him, in trust, by God; and that it was not absolutely his own. The purpose of God, in bestowing it upon him, was that he should use it for the benefit of all who had any need which might be supplied by its means; and, by so much, it belonged, not to "Cobbler" Horn himself, but, under God, to those who possessed any such claim to its use. He was convinced that no preacher had ever been more definitely or solemnly called to the ministration of the "Word" than was he, "the Golden

Shoemaker," to the ministry of wealth. And it was a ministry after his own heart. Full of Christ-like love and pity for the needy, the sad, and the sinful, he revelled in the gracious opportunities which now crowded his life. He had few greater pleasures, in these days, than that afforded him by the signing of cheques. To negotiate a contribution from him for some worthy object was a means of grace;—so hearty and joyous was his response to the appeal, and so thankful did he seem for the opportunity it had brought.

Never, perhaps, were the functions of a Christian man of wealth more clearly comprehended, or the possibilities of blessedness involved in the possession of riches more fully realized, than by "Cobbler" Horn. He often told himself that, by making others happy with his money, he secured the highest benefit it was able to impart. Thus bestowed, his wealth afforded him infinitely greater satisfaction, than if he had devoted it entirely to his own personal ends.

But "the Golden Shoemaker" was not satisfied. His money was not going fast enough. The amounts he had already dispensed appeared but as a few splashes of foam from the sea. He wanted channels for his benevolence. His difficulty was rare. Most men of means find that they have not the wherewithal to supply the demands of their own many-handed need. He was able to satisfy almost unlimited necessities beyond his own, but was sadly troubled to know how it might be done. Yet he was determined that he would not rest, until he had found means of disposing, in his Lord's service, of every penny that remained to him, after his own modest wants had been supplied.

Actuated by this purpose, "Cobbler" Horn resolved to pay another visit to his minister. Mr. Durnford had helped him before, and would help him again. Of set purpose, he selected Monday morning for his visit. Unless his business

J. W. Keyworth

had been very urgent indeed, he would not have run the risk of disturbing Mr. Durnford at his studies by going to see him on any other morning than this. But he knew that, on Monday morning, the minister was accustomed to throw himself somewhat on the loose, and was rather glad, than otherwise, to welcome a congenial visitor at that time.

Mr. Durnford, as usual, gave his friend a cordial greeting. There was not a member of his church who occupied a higher place in his regard than did "Cobbler" Horn.

"Glad to see you, Mr. Horn!" he said, entering the dining-room, whither his visitor had been shown by the maid; and he heartily shook "the Golden Shoemaker" by the hand. "This is a regular 'Blue Monday' with me, as, indeed, most of my Mondays are; and a little brotherly chat will give me a lift. How go the millions?"

By this time they were seated opposite to each other, in two comfortable chairs, before a cheerful fire. The minister's half-joking question touched so closely the trouble just then upon "Cobbler" Horn's mind, that he took it quite seriously, and returned a very grave reply.

"The 'millions,' sir, are not going fast enough; in fact, they go very slowly indeed. And, to make a clean breast of it, that is what has brought me here this morning."

"Ah!" exclaimed Mr. Durnford, with deep interest.

"But, sir," added "Cobbler" Horn, half-rising, and putting out his hand, "don't let me hinder you. I can come another time, if you are busy just now."

"Don't speak of such a thing, my dear friend!" cried the minister, putting out his hand in turn. "Keep your seat. I'm never busy on a Monday morning—if I can help it. I am always ready, between the hours of nine and one on Monday, for any innocent diversion that may come in my way. I keep what is called 'Saint Monday'—at least in the morning. If I am disturbed on any other morning, I—well, I don't like it. But any reasonable person who finds me at home on a Monday morning—against which, I must admit, the chances are strong, for I frequently go off on some harmless jaunt—is quite welcome to me for that time."

"I had an idea of that, sir," responded "Cobbler" Horn.

"Ah, you are a most considerate man! But now, about the millions?"

"The Golden Shoemaker" smiled.

"Not 'millions,' sir—hardly one million yet—indeed a great deal less now, actually in my own hands; though I am seriously afraid of what it may become. All my investments are turning out so well, that the money is coming in much faster than I can get rid of it! It's positively dreadful! I shall have to increase my givings very largely in some way."

The minister held up his hands in mock astonishment; and there was a twinkle of honest pleasure in his keen, grey eyes.

"Mr. Horn, I believe you are the first man, since the foundation of the world, who has been troubled because his money didn't go fast enough!"

"Well, sir, that is the case."

His unwieldy wealth weighed too heavily upon his heart and conscience to permit of his adopting the half-humorous view of the situation which Mr. Durnford seemed to take.

"But surely, Mr. Horn," urged the minister, becoming serious, "there are plenty of ways for your money. To get money is often difficult; it should be easy enough to get rid of it."

"Yes, sir, there are plenty of ways. My poor, devoted secretary knows that as well as I do. But the puzzle is, to find the right ways. If I merely wanted to get rid of my money, the letters of a single week would almost enable me to do that."

"Yes, yes," said Mr. Durnford, "of course. I know exactly how it is. You could make your money up in a bag, and toss it into the sea at one throw, if that were all."

"Yes," replied "Cobbler" Horn, with a quiet smile; and he sighed faintly, as though he wished it were permissible to rid himself thus easily of his golden encumbrance.

"But that is not all, Mr. Durnford," he then said.

"No, Mr. Horn, you feel that it would not do to cast your bread on the waters in that literal sense. You are constrained to cast it, not into the sea, but, like precious seed, into the soil of human hearts and lives—soil that has been prepared by the plough of poverty and the harrow of suffering. Isn't that it, my friend?"

"Cobbler" Horn leaned forward in his chair, with glistening eyes.

"Yes, sir; go on; you are a splendid thought reader."

"You feel that merely to dispose of your money anyhow—without discrimination—would be worse than hoarding it up?"

"That I do, sir!"

"It is not your money, but the Lord's; and you wish to dispose of every penny in a way He would approve?"

"Yes, sir," was "Cobbler" Horn's emphatic confirmation; "and I'm so anxious about it that often I can't sleep at nights. I expect the Lord gave me all this money because He knew I should want to use it for Him; and I'm determined not to disappoint Him. I feel the more strongly on the subject, because there's so much of the Lord's money in the world that he never gets the benefit of at all."

The minister listened gravely.

"So you want my advice?"

"Yes, sir; and your help. My difficulty is that it is the unworthy who are most eager to ask for help. Those who are really deserving are often the last to cry out; and many of them would rather die than beg. Now, sir, I want you to help me to find out cases of real need, to tell me of any good cause that comes to your knowledge; and suggest as many ways as you can of making a good use of my money. Will you do this for me, sir? Although you have helped me so much already, I don't think you will refuse my request."

The minister listened to this appeal from "the Golden Shoemaker" with a feeling of holy joy.

"No, my dear friend," he said, "I will not refuse your request. How can I? Believing, with you, that your wealth is a Divine trust, I regard your appeal as a call from God Himself. Besides, you could not have demanded from me a more congenial service. You shall have all the help I can give; and between us," he added, with a reviving flicker of his previous facetiousness, "we shall make the millions fly."

"Thank you, heartily, sir. But I must warn you that you have undertaken no light task. We shall have to dispose of many thou—"

"We will make them vanish," broke in the minister, "like half-pence in the hands of a conjuror."

"I know," said "Cobbler" Horn, with a smile, "that you ministers are well able to dispose of the money."

"Yes, I suppose we are. But, dear friend, let it be understood, at the outset, that I can be no party to your defrauding yourself."

"It is all the Lord's money," said "the Golden Shoemaker."

"Yes; but, if you employ it for Him, He means you to have your commission."

"Oh, as to that, a very little will serve. My wants are few."

"My dear friend," remonstrated the minister, "are you not in danger of falling into a mistake? God has given you the power to acquire a great deal of the good of this world; and I don't think it would be right for you not to make a pretty complete use of your opportunities. Though you should be ever so generous to yourself, and live a very full and abundant life, you will still be able to give immense sums of money away; and such a life would fit you all the better to serve God in your new sphere."

"You think that, do you, sir?" asked "Cobbler" Horn, evidently impressed.

"I certainly do."

"Well, I will consider it; for I dare say you are right. But to return to what we were talking about just now, perhaps, sir, you could give me a hint or two, this morning, with regard to my money?"

Thus invited, Mr. Durnford ventured to mention several cases of individual necessity with which he was acquainted, and to indicate various schemes of wide-spread benevolence in which a man of wealth might embark.

"Cobbler" Horn listened attentively; and, having entered in his note-book the names Mr. Durnford had given him, promised also to consider the more general suggestions he had made.

"I am very much obliged to you, sir," he said; "and shall often come to you for advice of this kind."

"As often as you like, Mr. Horn," laughed the minister; "it doesn't cost much to give advice. It is those who follow it that have to pay."

"Yes," rejoined "Cobbler" Horn; "and that will I do most gladly."

So saying, he rose from his seat, and held out his hand.

"Good morning, sir!"

"Good morning, my dear sir!" said the minister, grasping the proffered hand. "By the way, how is Miss Owen getting on?"

"My dear sir, I owe you eternal gratitude for having made me acquainted with that young lady!"

"I'm glad of that, but not a bit surprised."

"She is a greater help to me than I can tell. And what a sad history she seems to have had—in early life, that is! Her childhood appears to have been a sad time."

"Ah, she has told you, then?"

"Yes, it came out quite by accident. She didn't obtrude it in any way."

"I am sure she wouldn't."

"And the fact that she was once a little outcast girl increases my interest in her very much."

"That," said the minister, "is a matter of course."

# CHAPTER XXXI

## "COBBLER" HORN'S CRITICS

The months passed. Christmas came, and was left behind, and now spring had fairly set in.

"The Golden Shoemaker" had become a person of great consideration to the dignitaries of his church. It is true there were those amongst its wealthy members by whom he was unsparingly criticised behind his back. But this did not deter them from paying him all manner of court to his face. He was startled at the importance which he had suddenly acquired. His acquaintance was sought on every side; and he found himself the subject of a variety of polite attentions to which he had been an entire stranger until now. Men of wealth and position who, though they were his fellow-members in the church, had never yet shaken him by the hand, suddenly discovered that he was their dear friend.

There was one rich man whose pew in the church was next to that of "Cobbler" Horn. Though this man had sat side by side with his poor brother for many years, in the house of God, he had seemed unaware of his existence. But no sooner did "Cobbler" Horn become "the Golden Shoemaker" than the attitude of his wealthy neighbour underwent a change. The first sign of recognition he bestowed upon his recently-enriched fellow-worshipper was a polite bow as they were leaving the church; next he ventured to show "Cobbler" Horn the hymn, when the latter happened to come late one day; and, at length, on a certain Sunday morning, as they were going out, he stepped into the aisle, and proffered his hand to "the Golden Shoemaker," for a friendly shake. "Cobbler" Horn started, and drew back. It was not in his nature to be malicious; and to decline the offered civility was the furthest thing from his thoughts. He was simply lost in amazement. The gentleman who was offering to shake hands with him was one of the most important men in Cottonborough. But his great astonishment arose from the fact that this mighty personage, after sitting within reach of him in the house of God for so many years, without bestowing upon him the slightest sign of recognition, should suddenly desire to shake him by the hand! The man noticed his hesitation, and was turning away with offended dignity. But "Cobbler" Horn quickly recovered himself, and, taking the hand which had been offered to him, gave it a heartier shake than it had, perhaps, ever received before.

"It was not that, Mr. Varley," he said, "I'm glad enough to shake hands with you, as I should have been long ago. But it did seem such a queer thing that we should have been sitting side by side here all these years, and you should never have thought of shaking hands with me before. I suppose the reason why you do it now is that the Lord has seen fit to make me a rich man. Now I really don't think I'm any more fit to be shaken hands with on that account. Personally, I'm very much the same as I've been any time these twenty years past; and it does seem to me a bit strange that you and others should appear to think otherwise."

"Cobbler" Horn spoke in a pleasant tone, and there was a twinkle of amusement in his eye. But Mr. Varley was not amused. Regarding "Cobbler" Horn with an expression of countenance which was very much like a scowl, he turned upon his heel and withdrew; and, during the week, he arranged for a sitting in another part of the church.

Mr. Varley was not the only rich and influential member of the church who had recently discovered in "Cobbler" Horn a suitable object of friendly regard. But the most cordial and obsequious of his wealthy fellow-members were ready enough to criticise him behind his back.

With the advice and help of the minister, he had begun to "make the millions fly," in good earnest; and his phenomenal liberality—prodigality, it was called by some—could not, in the nature of things, escape notice. It soon became, in fact, the talk of the town and of the country round. But it was by the members of his church that "Cobbler" Horn's lavish benefactions were most eagerly discussed. Various opinions were expressed, by his fellow-Christians, of "the Golden Shoemaker," and of the guineas with which he was so free. Some few saw the real man in their suddenly-enriched friend, and rejoiced. Others shook their heads, and said the "Shoemaker" would not be "Golden" long at that rate; and some scornfully curled their lips, and declared the man to be a fool. But the most bitter of "Cobbler" Horn's critics were certain of his wealthy brethren who seemed to regard his abundant liberality as a personal affront.

There were many wealthy members in Mr. Durnford's church. The minister sometimes thought, in his inmost soul, that his church would have been but little poorer, in any sense of the word, for the loss of some of the rich men whose names were on its roll. With all their wealth, many of them were not "rich towards God." But Mr. Durnford was circumspect. It was his endeavour, without failing in his duty, either to his Divine Master, or to these gilded sheep of his, to make what use of them he might in connection with

J. W. Keyworth

his sacred work.

There was little, it is true, to be got out of these wealthy men but their money, and they could not be persuaded to part with much of that; but the minister did not give them much rest.

One pleasant spring evening, Mr. Durnford set out on one of what he called his "financial tours" amongst this section of his members. The first house to which he went—and, as it proved, the last—was that of a very rich brewer, who was one of the main pillars of the Church. There were other members of Mr. Durnford's flock who were of the same trade. This was not gratifying to Mr. Durnford; but what could he do? The brewers were blameless in their personal behaviour, regular in their attendance in the sanctuary, and exact in their fulfilment of the conditions of church membership; and he could not unchurch them merely because they were brewers. If he began there, it would be difficult to tell where he ought to stop. Nor did he scorn their gifts of money to the cause of God. He was pleased that they were willing to devote some portion of their gains to so good a purpose; his regret was that the portion was so small.

Mr. Durnford did not hesitate to tell his rich members what he conceived to be the just claims of the cause of God upon their wealth; and, on the evening of which we speak, he called first, for this purpose, on the aforesaid brewer, Mr. Caske. This gentleman lived in a large, square, old-fashioned, comfortable house, surrounded with its own grounds, which were extensive and well laid out. The entire premises were encompassed with a high brick wall, which might well have been supposed to hide a workhouse or a prison, instead of the paradise it actually concealed. Perhaps Mr. Caske had selected this secluded abode from an instinctive disinclination to obtrude the abundance and comfort which he had derived from the manufacture and sale of beer; perhaps he had bought this particular house simply because it was in itself such a dwelling as he desired. At any rate, there he was, with his abundance and luxury, within his encircling wall; and one was tempted to wonder whether there was as much mystery in connection with the article of his manufacture, as seemed to be associated with his place of abode.

The minister let himself in at a small door in the boundary wall, and made his way, through the grounds, to the front-door of the house.

"Mr. Caske has company to-night, sir," said the maid who opened the door.

"Any one I know, Mary?"

"Yes, sir; Mr. Botterill and Mr. Kershaw."

"Oh, well, I want to see them too. Where are they?"

"In the smoke-room, sir."

"Well, show me in. It will be all right."

As Mr. Durnford was a frequent and privileged visitor, the girl promptly complied with his request.

The smoke-room was a good-sized, comfortable apartment, furnished with every convenience that smokers are supposed to require. It looked out, by two long windows, on a wide sweep of lawn which stretched away from the end of the house. In this room, in chairs of various luxurious styles, sat Mr. Caske and his two friends. Each of the three men was smoking a churchwarden pipe; and at the elbow of each stood a little three-legged, japanned smoker's table, on which was a stand of matches, an ash-tray, and a glass of whisky.

The three smokers slowly turned their heads, as the minister entered the room, and, on recognising him, they all rose to their feet.

"Good evening, sir," said Mr. Caske, advancing, with his pipe in his left hand, and his right hand stretched out; "you have surprised us at our devotions again."

"Which you are performing," rejoined the minister, "with an earnestness worthy of a nobler object of worship."

Mr. Caske laughed huskily; and the minister turned to greet Messrs. Botterill and Kershaw, who were waiting, pipes in hand, to resume their seats.

Mr. Botterill was a wine and spirit merchant, and Mr. Kershaw was a draper in a large way.

When they had all taken their seats, a few moments of silence ensued. This was occasioned by the necessity which arose for the three smokers vigorously to puff their pipes, which had burnt low; and perhaps there was some little reluctance, on the part of Mr. Caske and his friends, to resume the conversation which had been in progress previous to the entrance of Mr. Durnford. When the pipes had been blown up, and were once more in full blast, there was no longer any excuse for silence. Mr. Caske, being the host, was then the first to speak. He had known his minister too well to invite him to partake of the refreshment with which he was regaling his friends.

He was a small, rotund man, with shining, rosy cheeks, and a husky voice.

"All well with you, Mr. Durnford?"

"Yes, thank you, Mr. Caske; but I am afraid I intrude?"

He was conscious of some constraint on the part of the company.

"I fear," he resumed, "that I have interrupted some important business?" and he looked around with an air of enquiry.

Mr. Caske airily waved his long pipe.

"Oh no, sir," he said, lightly, "nothing of consequence"—here he glanced at his friends—"we were, ah—talking about our friend, ah—'the Golden Shoemaker.'"

Mr. Caske was secretly anxious to elicit the minister's opinion of "Cobbler" Horn.

"Ah," exclaimed Mr. Durnford, with an intonation in which sarcasm might not have been difficult to detect, "and what about 'the Golden Shoemaker'?"

Mr. Caske looked at Mr. Botterill and Mr. Kershaw; and Mr. Kershaw and Mr. Botterill looked first at each other, and then at Mr. Caske.

"Well," replied Mr. Caske, at length, "he's being more talked about than ever."

"Well, now," asked the minister, "as to what in particular?"

"Chiefly as to the way he's squandering his money."

"Oh, I wasn't aware Mr. Horn had become a spendthrift! You must have been misinformed, Mr. Caske," and Mr. Durnford looked the brewer intently in the face.

"Ah," said Mr. Caske, somewhat uneasily, "you don't take me, sir. It's not that he spends his money. It's the rate at which he gives it away. He's simply flinging it from him right and left!"

As he spoke, Mr. Caske swelled with righteous indignation. Money, in his eyes, was a sacred thing—to be guarded with care, and parted with reluctantly. No working man could have been more careful with regard to the disposal of each individual shilling of his weekly wages, than was Mr. Caske in the handling of his considerable wealth.

"He's simply tossing his money from him, sir," he reiterated, "as if it were just a heap of leaves."

"Yes," said Mr. Botterill, "and it doesn't seem right."

Mr. Botterill was a tall man, with glossy black hair and whiskers, and an inflamed face. He seemed never to be quite at ease in his mind, which, perhaps, was not matter for surprise.

Mr. Kershaw next felt that it was his turn to speak.

"Ah," he said, "this kind of thing makes a false impression, you know!"

Though a man of moderate bodily dimensions, Mr. Kershaw had a largeness of manner which seemed to magnify him far beyond his real proportions. He spread himself abroad, and made the most of himself. He had actually a large head, which was bald on the top, with dark bushy hair round about. His face, which was deeply pitted with small-pox, was adorned with mutton-chop whiskers, from between which a very prominent nose and chin thrust themselves forth.

"Yes," broke in Mr. Caske, "people will be apt to think that everybody who has a little bit of money ought to do as he does. But, if that were the case, where should I be, for instance?" and Mr. Caske swelled himself out more than ever.

Mr. Durnford had hitherto listened in silence. Though inclined to speak in very strong terms, he had restrained himself with a powerful effort. He knew that if he allowed these men to proceed, they would soon fill their cup.

"Well, gentlemen," he now remarked quietly, "there is force in what you say."

Mr. Caske and his two friends regarded their minister with a somewhat doubtful look. Mr. Caske seemed to think that Mr. Durnford's remark made it necessary for him to justify the attitude he had assumed with regard to "Cobbler" Horn.

"Perhaps, sir," he said, "you don't know in what a reckless fashion our friend is disposing of his money?"

"Well, Mr. Caske, let us hear," said the minister, settling himself to listen.

"Well, sir, you know about his having given up a great part of his fortune to some girl in America, because she was the sweetheart of a cousin of his who died."

"Yes," said Mr. Durnford, quietly, "I've heard of that."

"Well, there was a mad trick, to begin with," resumed Mr. Caske, in a severe tone. "And then there's that big house in the village which, it's said, all belongs to him. He's fitting it up to be a sort of home for street arabs and gipsy children; and it's costing him thousands of pounds that he'll never see again!"

"Yes, I know about that too."

"Then, you will, of course, be aware, sir, that he gives more to our church funds than any half-dozen of us put together."

"Yes," broke in Mr. Kershaw, with his obtrusive nose. "He thinks to shame the rest of us, no doubt. And they say now that he's going to employ two town missionaries and a Bible-woman out of his own pocket. Is it true, think you, sir?"

"It is not unlikely," was the quiet reply.

There was a note of warning in both Mr. Durnford's words and tone; but the admonitory sign passed unobserved.

"Well, then," resumed Mr. Caske, "think of the money he gave away during the winter. He seemed to want to do everything himself. There was hardly anything left for any one else to do."

Mr. Durnford smiled inwardly at the idea of Mr. Caske making a grievance of the fact that there had been left to him no occasion for benevolence.

"It was nothing but blankets, and coals, and money," continued Mr. Caske. "And then the families he has picked out of the slums and sent across the sea! And it's said he'll pay anybody's debts, and gives to any beggar, and will lend anybody as much money as they like to ask."

At this point Mr. Botterill once more put in his word.

"I heard, only the other day, that Mr. Horn had announced his intention of presenting the town with a Free Library and a Public Park."

"It's like his impudence!" exclaimed Mr. Kershaw.

"After that I can believe anything," cried Mr. Caske. "The man ought to be stopped. It's very much to be regretted that he ever came into the money. And what a fool he is from his own standpoint! When he has got rid of all his money, it will be doubly hard for him to go back to poverty again."

Mr. Caske was speaking somewhat at random.

"Don't you think, sir," he concluded, with a facetious air, "that Providence sometimes makes a mistake in these matters?"

The question was addressed to the minister.

"No, never!" exclaimed Mr. Durnford, with an emphasis which caused Mr. Caske to start so violently, that the stem of his pipe, which he had just replaced in his mouth, clattered against his teeth. "No, never! And least of all in the case of friend Horn."

The three critics of "the Golden Shoemaker" stared at the minister in amazement. They had been led to think Mr. Durnford was substantially in agreement with their views.

"No, gentlemen," he resumed, "my opinion is quite the reverse of yours. I believe this almost unlimited wealth has been given to our friend, because he is eminently fitted to be the steward of his Lord's goods."

This declaration was followed by an awkward pause, which

Mr. Caske was the first to break.

"Perhaps you think, sir," he said, in an injured tone, "that this upstart fellow is an example to us?"

"Mr. Caske," responded the minister, "you have interpreted my words to a nicety."

The three critics shuffled uneasily in their chairs.

"Yes," continued Mr. Durnford, "an example and a reproach! Mr. Horn has the true idea of the responsibilities of a Christian man of wealth; you have missed it. He is resolved to use his money for God, to whom it belongs; you spend yours on yourselves—except in as far as you hoard it up you know not for whom or what. He is never satisfied that he is giving enough away; you grumble and groan over every paltry sovereign with which you are induced to part. He will be able to give a good account of his stewardship when the Lord comes; there will be an awkward reckoning for you in that day."

The three friends had ceased to smoke, and were listening to Mr. Durnford's deliverance open-mouthed. They respected their minister, and valued his esteem. They were rather conscience-stricken, than offended now.

"But, surely, sir," said Mr. Kershaw, presently, finding breath first of the three, "you wouldn't have us fling away our money, as he does?"

"I shouldn't be in haste to forbid you, Mr. Kershaw, if you seemed inclined to take that course," said the minister, with a smile. "But, if you come within measurable distance of the example of our friend, you will do very well."

"But," pleaded Mr. Botterill, "ought we not to consider our wives and families?"

"You do, Mr. Botterill, you do," was the somewhat sharp reply. "But there still remains ample scope for the claims of God."

Upon this, there ensued a pause, which was at length broken by Mr. Caske, who, whatever might be his shortcomings, was not an ill-natured man. "Well, sir," he remarked, good-humouredly, "you've hit us hard."

"I am glad you are sensible of the fact," was the pleasant reply.

"No doubt you are!" rejoined Mr. Caske, in a somewhat jaunty tone. "And I suppose you intend now to give us an opportunity of following your advice?"

"Why, yes," said Mr. Durnford, with a smile, "I really came to ask you for the payment of certain subscriptions now due. It is time I was making up some of the quarterly payments. But, perhaps, after what has been said, you would like to take a day or two—?"

"No, for my part," interposed Mr. Caske, "I don't want any time. I'll double my subscriptions at once."

"Same here," said Mr. Kershaw, concisely.

"Thank you, gentlemen!" said Mr. Durnford, briskly, entering the amounts in his note book. "Now, Mr. Botterill."

"Well," was the reluctant response, "I suppose I shall have to follow suit."

J. W. Keyworth

Mr. Durnford smiled.

"Thank you, gentlemen, all," he said. "Keep that up, and it will afford you more pleasure than you think."

When, shortly afterwards, the minister took his departure, the three friends resumed their smoking; but they did not return to their criticism of "the Golden Shoemaker."

# CHAPTER XXXII

## "IN LABOURS MORE ABUNDANT"

Unlike many wealthy professors of religion, "the Golden Shoemaker" did not suppose that, in giving his money to the various funds of the church, he fulfilled, as far as he was concerned, all the claims of the Cause of Christ. He did not imagine that he could purchase, by means of his monetary gifts, exemption from the obligation to engage in active Christian work. He did not desire to be thus exempt. His greatest delight was to be directly and actively employed in serving his Divine Lord; and so little did he think of availing himself of the occasion of his sudden accession to wealth to withdraw from actual participation in the service of Christ, that he hailed with intense joy the richer opportunities of service with which he was thus supplied.

For some years "Cobbler" Horn had been a teacher in a small Mission Sunday School, which was carried on in a low part of the town by several members of Mr. Durnford's church. But, about a year previous to the change in his circumstances, he had been persuaded by the minister to transfer his services to the larger school. He always made the conversion of his scholars his chief aim; and very soon after he entered on his new sphere, one of the boys in his class, a bright little fellow about nine years old, named Willie Raynor, had been

J. W. Keyworth

very remarkably converted to God. The boy was promising to become a very thorough-going Christian, and no one rejoiced more than he in the good fortune of "Cobbler" Horn.

There was considerable speculation, amongst the friends and fellow-teachers of "the Golden Shoemaker," as to whether his altered circumstances would lead to the relinquishment of his work in the school. Little Willie Raynor heard some whisper of this talk, and was much distressed. His relations with his beloved teacher were very close; and, without a moment's hesitation, he went straight to "Cobbler" Horn, and asked him what he was going to do.

"Mr. Horn, you won't leave the school now you are a rich man, will you? Because I don't think we can do without you!"

"Cobbler" Horn was taken by surprise. The idea of leaving the school had never occurred to his mind. For one moment, there was a troubled look in his face.

"Who has put such nonsense into your head, laddie?"

"Oh, I've heard them talking about it. But I said I was sure they were wrong."

"Why, of course they were, dear lad. Why should I leave the school? Haven't I more reason than ever to work for the Lord?"

"Oh, I'm so glad!" And Willie went home with a bounding heart.

Meanwhile curiosity continued to be felt and expressed on every hand, as to the course "the Golden Shoemaker" would actually pursue; and no little surprise was created as, Sunday after Sunday, he was still seen sitting in the midst of his class, as quietly and modestly as though he were still the poor cobbler whom everybody had known so well.

Nor was he content simply to continue the work he had been accustomed to do for Christ during his previous life. The larger leisure which his wealth had brought, enabled him to multiply his religious and benevolent activities to an almost unlimited extent. He went about doing good from morning to night. He rejoiced to exercise for God the all but boundless influence which his money enabled him to exert. His original plan—which he persistently followed—of mending, free of charge, the boots and shoes of the poorer portion of his former customers was but one amongst many means by which he strove to benefit his necessitous fellowmen. He never gave money for the relief of distress, without ascertaining whether there was anything that he could do personally to help. He made it a point also to offer spiritual consolation to those upon whom he bestowed temporal benefactions. Hardly a day but found him in the abode of poverty, or in the sick-room; and not one of his numberless opportunities of speaking the words which "help and heal" did he let slip.

One evening, as he was passing through a poor part of the town, he came into collision with a drunken man, who was in the act of entering a low public-house. The wretched creature looked up into "Cobbler" Horn's face, and "Cobbler" Horn recognised him as a formerly respectable neighbour of his own.

"Richard," he cried, catching the man by the arm, "don't go in there!"

"Shall if I like, Thomas," said the man, thickly, recognising "Cobbler" Horn in turn. "D'yer think 'cause ye're rich, yer has

J. W. Keyworth

right t' say where I shall go in, and where I shan't go in?"

"Oh, no, Richard," said "Cobbler" Horn, with his hand still on the man's arm. "But you've had enough drink, and had better go quietly home."

As he spoke, he gradually drew his captive further away from the public-house. The man struggled furiously, talking all the time in rapid and excited tones.

"Let me a-be!" he exclaimed with a thickness of tone which was the combined result of indignation and strong drink. "You ha' no right to handle me like this! Ain't this a free country? Where's the perlice?"

"Come along, Richard; you'll thank me to-morrow," persisted "Cobbler" Horn quietly, moving his captive along another step or two. But, by this time, a crowd was beginning to gather; and it seemed likely that, although Richard himself might not be able effectually to resist his captor, "Cobbler" Horn's purpose would be frustrated in another way. In fact the crowd—a sadly dilapidated crew—had drawn so closely around the centre of interest, as to render almost impossible the further progress of the struggling pair.

At this point, some one recognised "Cobbler" Horn.

"Yah!" he cried, "it ain't a fight, after all! It's 'the Golden Shoemaker' a-collarin' a cove wot's drunk!"

At the announcement of "the Golden Shoemaker," the people crowded up more closely than ever. While all had heard of that glittering phenomenon, perhaps few had actually seen him, and the present opportunity was not to be lost.

"Cobbler" Horn grasped the situation, and resolved, under

the inspiration of the moment, to turn it to good account. He was not afraid that these people would interfere with his present purpose. He could see that they were regarding him with too much interest and respect for that. Moreover, since Richard belonged to another part of the town, his fortunes would not awaken any special sympathy in the breasts of the crowd. On the other hand, there was a possibility that the delay caused by the gathering of the crowd might enable "Cobbler" Horn to make a deeper impression on his poor degraded friend, than if he had simply dragged him home from the public-house. Exerting, therefore, all his strength, he thrust the hapless Richard forth at arm's length, and, in emphatic tones, bespoke for him the attention of the crowd.

"Look at him!" he exclaimed. "Once he was a respectable man, tidy and bright; and he wasn't ashamed to look anybody in the face. And now see what he is!"

The crowd looked, and saw a slovenly and dissipated man, who hung his head, with a dull feeling of shame. The people gazed upon the wretched man in silence. They were awed by the solemn and impressive manner in which they had been addressed.

"This man," resumed "Cobbler" Horn, "once had a thriving business and a comfortable home. Now his business has gone to the dogs, and his home has become a den. His wife and children are ragged and hungry; and I question if he has a penny piece left that he can justly call his own. The most complete ruin stares him in the face, and he probably won't last another year."

The crowd still gazed, and listened in silence.

"And, do you ask," continued "Cobbler" Horn, "what has done all this? No, you don't; you know too well. It's drink—

the stuff that many of you love so much. For there are many of you,"—and he swept the crowd with a scrutinizing glance—"who are far on the same downward way as this poor fool. He was my neighbour and friend; and he had as nice a little wife as ever brightened a home. But it would make the heart of a stone bleed to see her as I saw her but a few days ago. But, there; go home, Richard! And may God help you to become a man once more!"

So saying, he released his captive; and the wretched creature, partially sobered with astonishment and shame, crept through the crowd, which parted for him to pass, and staggered off on his way towards home.

Then, like some ancient prophet, upon whom the Spirit of the Lord had come, "the Golden Shoemaker" turned and preached, from the living text of his besotted friend, a telling impromptu Temperance sermon to the motley crowd. The whole incident was quite unpremeditated. He had never dreamt that he would do such a thing as he was doing now. But that by no means lessened the effect of his burning words, which went home to the hearts, and even to the consciences of not a few of those by whom they were heard.

When he had finished, he passed on, and left his hearers to their thoughts. But, for himself, there had been shown to him yet another way in which he might work for God; and, thereafter, "the Golden Shoemaker" was often seen at the corners of back streets, and in the recesses of the slums, preaching, to all who would hear, that glorious Gospel of which the message of mercy to the victims of strong drink is, after all, only a part.

# CHAPTER XXXIII

## TOMMY DUDGEON ON THE WATCH

It will be remembered that, after bursting into the back-room with the declaration, "She's come back!" Tommy Dudgeon had suddenly pulled himself up and substituted the commonplace statement that he had "seen the sec'tary." In fact, though, on marking the manner in which Miss Owen had stepped out of the house and walked along the street, he had, for an instant, imagined that little Marian had actually returned, the calmer moments which followed had shown him what seemed the folly of such a supposition. What real resemblance could there be between a child of five and a young woman of eighteen? He had, indeed, seemed to see, this afternoon, the very same determined look, and the pretty purposeful step, with which the little maid whom he had loved had passed out of his sight so long ago. But he now assured himself that "it was only the sec'tary after all."

The child, for whom he had not ceased to mourn, would certainly come back, but not like that. It was inevitable that unimaginative Tommy Dudgeon should at first dismiss the possibility that little wild-flower Marian should have returned in the person of the lady-secretary. But, none the less, the sight of the secretary had brought back to him the vision of little Marian as he had seen her last; and

J. W. Keyworth

thenceforth he was supplied with matter for much perplexing thought.

Fortunately the occupants of the room into which he had burst with his hasty exclamation, who consisted of his brother and his brother's wife alone, had but indistinctly caught his words. Consequently no one was any the wiser, and he was able to assure himself that his first impression with regard to the "sec'tary" was still the secret of his own breast.

It was a secret, however, which gave him no little trouble. The vanishing of the child had occasioned him bitter grief. He had not only mourned in respectful sympathy with the stricken father, but he had also sorrowed on his own account. He had very tenderly loved little Marian Horn. She had come to him like a fairy, scattering clouds of care, and diffusing joy; and, since her departure, it had seemed as though the sunshine had ceased to visit the narrow street upon which he looked out through the window, and from the doorway, of his little shop.

And Tommy's regret for the loss of the child was rendered keener by a haunting consciousness that a measure of responsibility for it belonged to himself. Might he not have prevented her departure? He could not, indeed, have been supposed to know that she was running away. But he did not allow himself to plead any excuse on that account. He ought to have known, was his continual reflection, that she would come to harm—going away by herself like that; and, at least, he might have questioned her as to where she was going. Through all the years, he had not ceased to afflict himself with such thoughts as these. Once he actually mentioned his self-accusing thoughts to "Cobbler" Horn. It was on one of the rare occasions when the afflicted father had spon-taneously spoken of his lost child to his humble friend. He gazed blankly at the little huckster, for a moment, as though he had not understood. Then, perceiving his drift, he gently answered, "My dear friend, you could not help it. Please do not speak of it again."

Tommy had always yearned for the recovery of the child; and, the wish being father to the thought, he fully shared with "Cobbler" Horn himself the expectation that she would eventually return. This expectation kept him on the alert; and there is little cause to wonder that even so slight a sign as the poise of the secretary's head, or the manner in which she walked, should have induced him to think, for some passing moments, that his long-cherished desire had been fulfilled at last.

And now, although he had dismissed that belief, it had left him more vigilant than ever. It may be questioned, indeed, whether he had actually dismissed it, or whether, having been dismissed, it had really gone away. There are visitors who will take no hint to depart. It would seem that here was such a visitor. The discarded impression that little Marian had come back in the person of "Cobbler" Horn's secretary refused to be banished from Tommy Dudgeon's mind. Henceforth he would have no peace until he had set the fateful question at rest once for all.

To this end he watched for the young secretary day by day. A hundred times a day he went to the shop-door, to gaze along the street; and at frequent intervals he craned his neck to get a better view through the window. He would leave the most profitable customer, at the sound of a footstep without, or at the shutting of a neighbouring door. He gave himself to deep ponderings, in the midst of which he became oblivious of all around. His anxiety told upon his appetite, and affected his health. His friends became alarmed; but, when they questioned him, he only shook his head. His very character seemed to be changed. Hitherto he had been the most transparent of men; now he moved about with the air of a conspirator, and bore himself like one on whose heart some mysterious secret weighed.

It was a long time before Tommy's watching and pondering produced any definite result. Miss Owen seldom visited the street in which "the little Twin Brethren" had their shop. By the desire of her employer she never came to him in his old workshop, except upon business which could not be delayed. Two or three times only, hitherto, had Tommy Dudgeon been privileged to feast his eyes on the dainty little figure, which, on his first sight of it, had awakened such tender memories in his mind. On each occasion those memories had returned as vividly as before; but the only result had been that his perplexity was sensibly increased.

All through the winter, the perturbation of the little huckster's mind remained unallayed; but there came a day in early spring which set his questionings at rest. In that joyous season there was born to Mr. and Mrs. John Dudgeon an eighth child. The fact that, this time, the arrival did not consist of twins was no less gratifying to the happy father, than to his much-enduring spouse. But the child was a fine one, and his birth almost cost his mother's life. As may be supposed, "the Golden Shoemaker" did not forget his humble friends in their trouble. He engaged for them the ablest doctor, and the most efficient nurse, that money could command. Every day he sent messages of enquiry, and the messengers were never empty-handed. Sometimes it was a servant who came; and sometimes it was the coachman—not Bounder, but his successor, who was quite a different man—with the carriage.

On the day of which we speak, the carriage had stopped at the door, and Tommy Dudgeon, on the watch as usual, observed that a young lady was sitting amongst its cushions.

It was the four-wheeler, and its fair occupant, basket in hand, alighted nimbly as soon as it stopped. Tommy vigorously rubbed his eyes. Yes, it was the "sec'tary!" Now, perhaps, his opportunity had come. As yet, he had never spoken to the "sec'tary," or heard her speak. He made his most polite bow, as she stepped into his shop. But how his heart thumped! He was shy with ladies at the best; but now, hope and fear, and a vague feeling that, with the entrance of this sprightly little lady, the past had all come back, increased his habitual nervousness a hundredfold. Surely it was not the first time that little tossing dusky head, with its black sparkling eyes, had presented itself in his doorway!

She paused a moment on the step, gazed around with a bewildered air, and shot a startled glance into the honest, eager face of the little man, who quivered from head to foot as he met her gaze. "That strange feeling again!" she thought, "I can never have been *here* before, at any rate!"

Tommy Dudgeon's own confusion prevented his perceiving the momentary discomposure of his visitor. The next minute, however, she was speaking to the little man in her cordial, unaffected way.

"You are Mr. Dudgeon, I expect," she said, holding out her neatly-gloved hand. "How are you, this afternoon? But," she continued after a pause, "which Mr. Dudgeon is it—the one with a wife, or the one without? My name," she added in her lively way, "is Owen—Mr. Horn's secretary, you know. You've heard of me, no doubt, Mr. Dudgeon?"

Tommy Dudgeon had not yet found his tongue.

"But," she broke out again, "I'm not giving you a chance to tell me who you are. Is it Mr. Dudgeon, or Mr. John? You see I know all about you."

Tommy Dudgeon was in no condition to answer Miss Owen's question, even yet, simple though it was. If the sight of her had brought back the past, what thronging memories crowded upon him at the sound of her voice—wooing, wilful, joyously insistent! But that she was so womanly and ladylike, and that he knew she was "only the sec'tary," he would have been ready to advance upon her with outstretched hands, and ask her if she had quite forgotten Tommy Dudgeon—her old friend, Tommy? As it was, he stood staring like one bewitched. Miss Owen, wondering at his silence, and his fixed gaze, repeated her question in another form.

"I don't wish to be rude; but are you the husband, or is it your brother?"

Tommy pulled himself together with a gasp.

"My name is Thomas, miss. It is my brother who is married, and whose wife is ill."

"Then, Mr. Thomas, I'm glad to make your acquaintance. How is your brother's wife to-day? I've brought a few little things from Miss Horn, with her respects."

Miss Owen herself would have said "love," rather than respects. But it was a great concession on the part of Miss Jemima to send anything at all to "those Dudgeons," with or without a message of any kind, and was quite a sign of grace.

"It's very kind of Miss Horn," said Tommy, who was still perturbed; "and of you as well, miss. Perhaps you will see my sister-in-law? She's much better, and sitting up—and able to converse."

As he spoke, he led the way into the kitchen, in the doorway of which the young girl once more paused, and looked around in the same bewildered way as before. But she instantly recovered herself; and, at the invitation of a woman who was in attendance, proceeded to mount the narrow stairs.

Miss Owen was performing a thoroughly congenial errand. It was her delight to be, in any way, the instrument of the wide-spread benevolence and varied Christian ministrations of her beloved employer. Nor was it an insignificant service which she therein performed. Her tender companionship had been of scarcely less benefit to the crippled girl than the almost daily rides which the generosity of "Cobbler" Horn enabled the poor invalid to enjoy; and her presence and sensible Christian talk were quite as helpful to Mrs. John Dudgeon, as were the delicacies from Miss Jemima's kitchen.

John Dudgeon, who was acting as temporary nurse, rose to his feet as the secretary entered, and stole modestly down-stairs. Miss Owen followed him with her eyes in renewed perplexity. What could it all mean? These dear, funny little men! Had she known them in a former state of existence, or what? She came downstairs when she was ready to leave, and in the kitchen she paused once more. On one side of the fire-place was an old arm-chair with a leather cushion. Seized with a sudden fancy, Miss Owen addressed the woman, who was waiting to see her out.

"May I sit in that chair a moment?" she asked.

"Certainly, miss," was the civil reply; and, in another moment, the young secretary had crossed the room, and seated herself in the chair.

"How strange!" she murmured. "How familiar everything is!"

At that moment, Tommy Dudgeon came in from the shop; and, on seeing Miss Owen in the old arm-chair, he stopped short, and uttered a cry.

"I beg your pardon, miss; I thought—"

It was in that very chair, standing in exactly the same spot as now, that little Marian had been accustomed to sit, when she used to come in and delight the two little bachelors with her quaint sayings, and queen it over them in her pretty wilful way. For her sake, the old chair had been carefully preserved.

"You thought I was taking a liberty, no doubt, sir," said Miss Owen, jumping to her feet, with a merry laugh; "and quite right too."

Tommy was horrified at the bare suggestion of such a thing. He begged her to sit down again, and she laughingly complied, insisting that he should sit in the opposite chair. Presently John came in, and stood looking calmly on. He was visited by no disturbing memories. Having chatted gaily, for a few minutes, with the two little men, Miss Owen took her leave.

"It's all so strange!" she thought, as the carriage bore her swiftly away.

Then she knitted her brows, and clenched her hands in her lap.

"Oh," she half-audibly exclaimed, "what if I *have* been here before? What if—" and she shivered with the excitement of the thought.

\* \* \* \* \*

As for Tommy Dudgeon, all his doubts were put to flight at last.

# CHAPTER XXXIV

## A "FATHER" AND "MOTHER" FOR THE "HOME"

About six weeks after this, the old Hall at Daisy Lane was ready for opening as a "Home" for waifs and strays. "Cobbler" Horn had visited Daisy Lane, from time to time, and he had also taken his sister and his young secretary to see the village and the old Hall. He had been much pleased with the progress of the improvements, and had marked with satisfaction the transformation which, in pursuance of his orders, was being effected in the Hall. It was clear that Mr. Gray was not only a most capable agent, but also a man after his employer's own heart; and it was evident that Messrs. Tongs and Ball had assisted the agent in every possible way.

The old Hall seemed likely to become an ideal Children's Home. The arrangements were most complete. A staff of capable nurses, and a bevy of maid-servants, had been engaged; to whom were added a porter and two boys, together with a head gardener and three assistants, to make, and keep, beautiful the spacious grounds.

A number of children had already been selected as inmates of the "Home." Setting aside the majority of the appeals, which had been many, from relatives who had children left on their hands by deceased parents, "Cobbler" Horn had

J. W. Keyworth

adhered to his original purpose of receiving chiefly stray children—little ones with no friends, and without homes. With the aid of his lawyers, and of Mr. Durnford, he had much communication with workhouse and parish authorities, and even with the police; and, as the opening day of the "Home" drew near, he had secured, as the nucleus of his little family, some dozen tiny outcasts, consisting of six or seven boys, and about as many girls.

It now remained that a "father" and "mother" should be found. On this subject "the Golden Shoemaker" had talked much with his minister. He shrank from the thought of advertising his need. He was afraid of bringing upon himself an avalanche of mercenary applications. His idea was to fix upon some excellent Christian man and woman who might be induced to accept the post as a sacred and delightful duty. They must be persons who loved children, and who were not in search of a living; and it would be none the worse if it were necessary for them to make what would be considered a sacrifice, in order to accept the post.

"Cobbler" Horn looked around. He had no acquaintances in whom it seemed likely that his ideal would be realized. He mentioned his views to his lawyers, and they smiled in their indulgent way. Messrs. Tongs and Ball had already learnt to respect their eccentric client. But it was difficult for their legal minds to regard the question of the appointment of a master and matron to the "Home" exactly in the light in which it presented itself to "Cobbler" Horn. He spoke of his cherished desire to Mr. Durnford.

"If I get the right man and woman, you know, sir, I shall be willing to pay them almost any amount of money. But I don't want them to know this beforehand. I must have a *father* and *mother* for my little family. It would be just as well," he added in faltering tones, "if they had lost a little one of their own. And I should like them to be some good Christian man and his wife, who would undertake the work without asking about salary at all, and would leave it to me to make that all right. Do you think they would trust me so far, Mr. Durnford?"

Mr. Durnford smiled in his shrewd way.

"If they knew you, Mr. Horn, they would rather trust you in the matter than suggest an amount themselves."

"No doubt," responded "the Golden Shoemaker," with a smile. "But now, Mr. Durnford," he persisted for the twentieth time, "do you know of such a couple as I want?"

They were in the minister's study. Mr. Durnford sat musing, with his arms resting upon his knees, and his hands together at the finger-tips. Suddenly he looked up.

"You want a couple who have lost a child, Mr. Horn? I can tell you of some good people who have found one."

"Cobbler" Horn gave a slight start. "Found a child! What child?" Such were the thoughts which darted, like lightning, through his brain. Then he smiled sadly to himself. Of course what he had imagined, for an instant, could not be.

"Well" he said calmly, "who are they? Let me hear!"

For one moment only, Mr. Durnford hesitated to reply.

"You will, perhaps, be startled, Mr. Horn, but must not misunderstand me, if I say that they are the excellent friends who have been as father and mother to your secretary, Miss Owen."

"Cobbler" Horn was indeed startled. His thoughts had not turned in the direction indicated by the minister's suggestion—that was all. But he was not displeased.

"Ah!" he exclaimed. "Well, if they are anything like my little secretary, they will do."

"Mr. and Mrs. Burton do not know that I have any thought of suggesting them to you, Mr. Horn. Nor have I the least idea whether or not they would accept the post. Mr. Burton holds a good position on the railway, in Birmingham, which I know he has no present intention of relinquishing. But there is not another couple of my acquaintance who would be likely to meet your wishes as well as these good friends of mine. You know, of course, that Miss Owen was found and rescued by them, when she was quite a little thing?"

"Yes," was the thoughtful reply; "and you really think they are the kind of persons I want?"

"I do, indeed."

"Well, well! But might I ask them, do you think?"

"Perhaps," said Mr. Durnford, "it would be as well to mention it to Miss Owen first."

"Might I do that, think you?"

"By all means!"

"Then I will."

He spoke to his secretary that very day. Miss Owen was delighted with the proposal, and approved of it with all her heart. She hoped Mr. and Mrs. Burton would consent, and felt almost sure that they would. After that the minister agreed to convey the request of "the Golden Shoemaker" to his good friends. For this purpose, he made a journey to Birmingham, and, on the evening of his return, called on "Cobbler" Horn.

"Well?" enquired the latter eagerly, almost before the minister had taken his seat.

"Our friends are favourably disposed," replied Mr. Durnford; "but they would like to have a personal interview first."

"By all means. When can they see me? And where?"

"Well, it would be a great convenience to Mr. Burton if you would go there. He cannot very well get away. But he could arrange to meet you at his own house."

Acting upon this suggestion, "Cobbler" Horn paid a visit to Birmingham, the outcome of which was the engagement of Mr. and Mrs. Burton as "father" and "mother" of the "home."

# CHAPTER XXXV

## THE OPENING OF THE "HOME"

At length the day arrived for the opening of the "Home." It was early in June, and the weather was superb. All the inhabitants of Daisy Lane, whether tenants of "Cobbler" Horn or not, were invited to the opening ceremony, and to the festivities which were to occupy the remainder of the day. There was to be first a brief religious service in front of the Hall, after which Miss Jemima was to unlock the great front door with a golden key. Then would follow a royal feast in a marquee on the lawn; and, during the afternoon and evening, the house and grounds would be open to all.

The religious service was to be conducted by Mr. Durnford. The parish clergyman had been invited to take part, but had declined. Many of his brother-clergymen would have hailed with joy such an opportunity of fulfilling the spirit of their religion; but the Vicar of Daisy Lane regarded the matter in a different light.

In due course "Cobbler" Horn, Miss Jemima, the young secretary, Tommy Dudgeon—to whom had been given a very pressing invitation to join the party,—and Mr. Durnford, alighted from the train at the station which served for Daisy Lane, and were met by Mr. Gray.

"Well, Mr. Gray," said "the Golden Shoemaker," who was in a buoyant, and almost boisterous mood, "How are things looking?"

"Everything promises well, sir," replied the agent, who was beaming with pleasure. "The arrangements are all complete; and everybody will be there—that is, with the exception of the vicar. Save his refusal to be present, there has not, thus far, been a single hitch."

"I wish," said "Cobbler" Horn, "that we could have got the poor man to come—for his own sake, I mean."

"Yes, sir; he will do himself no good. It's well they're not all like that."

Mr. Gray had brought his own dog-cart for the gentlemen; and he had provided for the ladies a comfortable basket-carriage, of which his son, a lad of fifteen, had charge. The dog-cart was a very different equipage from the miserable turn-out with which the agent had met his employer on the occasion of his first visit. Everything was of the best—the highly-finished trap, the shining harness, the dashing horse; and "Cobbler" Horn was thankful to mark the honest pride with which the agent handled the reins.

A few minutes brought them to Daisy Lane. Here indeed was a change! An unstinted expenditure of money, the toil of innumerable workmen, and the tireless energy and ever-ready tact of Mr. Gray, had converted the place into a model village. Instead of dropsical and rotting hovels, neat and smiling cottages were seen on every side. The vicarage, and the one farm-house not included in the property of "Cobbler" Horn, which had, aforetime, by their respectability and good repair, aggravated the untidiness and dilapidation of the rest of the village, were now rendered almost shabby by the fresh beauty of the renovated property of "the Golden Shoemaker."

On every hand there were signs of rejoicing. It was evidently a gala day at Daisy Lane. Over almost every garden gate there was an arch of flowers. Streamers and garlands were displayed at every convenient point. Such a quantity of bunting had never before fluttered in the breezes of Daisy Lane.

As they approached the farm-house which "Cobbler" Horn had inspected on the occasion of his first visit, their progress was stayed by the farmer himself, who was waiting for them at his gate, radiant and jovial, a farmer, as it seemed, without a grievance! He advanced into the road with uplifted hand, and Mr. Gray and his son reined in their horses. The farmer approached the side of the dog-cart.

"Let me have a shake of your fist, sir," he said, seizing the hand of "the Golden Shoemaker." "You're a model landlord. No offence; but it's hard to believe that you're anyways related to that 'ere old skin-flint as was owner here afore you."

The farmer wore on his breast a huge red rosette, almost as big as a pickling cabbage, as though the occasion had been that of an election day, or a royal wedding, or some other celebration equally august.

"I'm glad you're satisfied with what Mr. Gray has done, Mr. Carter," said "Cobbler" Horn.

"Satisfied! That ain't the word! And, as for Gray—well, he's a decent body enough. But it's little as he could ha' done, if you hadn't spoke the word."

Then they drove on, and the farmer followed in their wake, occupying, with the roll of his legs, and the flourish of his big stick, as much of the road as the carriages themselves.

As they proceeded, they passed several groups of villagers, in gala dress, who were making their way towards the gates of the Hall grounds.

"These are the laggards," explained the agent, "the bulk of the people are already on the ground."

"Cobbler" Horn was recognised by the people, most of whom knew him well by sight; and, while the men touched their hats, and the boys made their bows, the women curtseyed, and each girl gave a funny little bob. Of all the novel sensations which his wealth had brought to "the Golden Shoemaker," this was the most distinctly and entirely new. It had not seemed to him more strange, though it had been less agreeable, to be the object of Bounder's obsequious attentions, than it did now to receive the worship of these simple villagers.

In due course they reached the Hall gates, and entered the grounds. A large marquee, with its fluttering flags, had been erected on one side of the lawn, which was almost like a small field. The people were dispersed about the grass in gaily-coloured groups, though few of them had wandered very far from the gates. When the carriages were seen approaching, the various parties gathered more closely together; and the people arranged themselves in lines on either side of the drive. The horses were immediately brought to a walking pace; and then, a jolly young farmer leading off, the villagers rent the air with their shouts of welcome. It was the spontaneous tribute of these simple people to the man, whose coming had restored long unaccustomed comfort to their lives, and awakened new hope in their despondent breasts.

J. W. Keyworth

"The Golden Shoemaker" raised his hat and waved his hand; and, inasmuch as the acclamations of the people were evidently intended for the ladies also, the young secretary nodded around with beaming smiles, and even Miss Jemima perceptibly bent her rigid neck.

At length the joyous procession arrived in front of the Hall steps. Here Mr. and Mrs. Burton were waiting to receive them. In response to their smiling welcome, "Cobbler" Horn shook these good people heartily by the hand, and, having introduced them to Miss Jemima, turned aside for a moment, that they might greet their adopted daughter.

In a few moments, he turned to them again, and enquired if everything was to their mind.

"Everything, sir," said Mr. Burton. "The arrangements are perfect."

"And our little family are all here," added Mrs. Burton, pointing, with motherly pride, to a row of clean and radiant boys and girls, who were ranged at the top of the steps.

"Cobbler" Horn's face was illumined with a ray of pleasure, as he looked up, at Mrs. Burton's words; and yet there was a pensive shade upon his brow. Miss Jemima scrutinised the little regiment, and actually uttered a grunt of satisfaction. Miss Owen glanced from the happy child-faces to that of "Cobbler" Horn with eyes of reverent love. The children were not uniformly dressed; and they might very well have passed for the actual offspring of the kindly man and woman whom they were to know as "father" and "mother" from henceforth.

"Is everything ready, Mr. Gray?" asked "Cobbler" Horn.

"Yes, sir."

"Then let us begin."

At a signal from Mr. Gray, the people drew more closely up to the foot of the steps; and it was noticeable that Tommy Dudgeon had withdrawn to a modest position amongst the crowd. A hymn was then announced by Mr. Durnford, and sung from printed papers which had been distributed amongst the people. Then, while every head was bowed, the minister offered a brief, but fervent and appropriate prayer. Next came an address from "Cobbler" Horn, in which, after explaining the purpose to which the Hall was to be devoted, he took the opportunity of assuring those of his tenants who were present that he would, as their landlord, do his utmost to promote their welfare. His hearty words were received with great applause, which was redoubled when he led Miss Jemima to the front. The minister then stepped forward, and presented Miss Jemima with a golden key, with which she deftly unlocked the great door, and, having pushed it open, turned to the people, and bowing gravely in response to their cheers, made, for the first and last time in her life, a public speech. She had much pleasure, she said, in declaring the old Hall open for the reception of friendless children, many of whom, she trusted, would find a happy home within its walls, and be there trained for a useful life. Here Miss Jemima stopped abruptly, and looked straight before her, with a very stern face, as though angry with herself for what she had done. And then, under cover of the renewed cheers of the people, she withdrew into the background.

The simple ceremony being over, the people were invited to enter the building and pass through the rooms. This invitation was freely accepted; and soon the various apartments of the renovated Hall were filled with people, who did not hesitate to express their admiration of what they saw.

When all the visitors had passed through the rooms, and admired to their hearts' content, the ringing of a large hand-bell on the lawn announced that dinner was ready. At the four long tables which ran the whole length of the marquee there was room for all, and very soon every seat was occupied. The grace was announced by Mr. Durnford, and sung by the people, with a heartiness which might have been expected of hungry villagers, who had been summoned to an unaccustomed and sumptuous feast. Then the carvers got to work, and, as the waiters carried round the laden plates, comparative quiet reigned; but, when the plates began to reach the guests, the clatter of crockery, the rattle of knives and forks, and the babel of voices, made such a festive hubbub as was grateful to the ear.

After dinner, there was speech-making and merriment; and then the people left the tent, and dispersed about the grounds. While the former part of this process was in progress, Miss Owen heard a fragment of conversation which caused her to tingle to her finger-tips. She had just moved towards one of the tables for the purpose of helping an old woman to rise from her seat, and her presence was not perceived by the speakers, whose faces were turned the other way. They were two village gossips, a middle-aged woman and a younger one.

"Is she his daughter?" were the words that fell upon the young secretary's ears, spoken by the elder woman in a stage whisper.

"No," replied the other, in a similar tone. "He never had but one child—her as was lost. This one's the secretary, or some such."

"Well, I do say as she'd pass for his own daughter anywhere."

Miss Owen was not nervous; but her heart beat tumultuously at the thoughts which this whispered colloquy suggested to her mind. She placed her hand upon the table to steady herself, as the two women, all unconscious of the effect of their gossiping words, moved slowly away.

"The Golden Shoemaker" and his friends arrived at Cottonborough late that night. A carriage was waiting for them at the station; and, having said "good night" to Mr. Durnford and Tommy Dudgeon, they were soon driven home. They were a quiet—almost silent—party. The events of the day had supplied them with much food for thought. The image of his little lost Marian presented itself vividly to the mind of "Cobbler" Horn to-night. Miss Jemima's thoughts dwelt on what was her one tender memory—that of the tiny, dark-eyed damsel who had so mysteriously vanished from the sphere of her authority so long ago.

And Miss Owen? Well, when she had at last reached her room, her first act was to lock the door. Then she knelt before her small hair-covered travelling trunk, and, having unlocked it, she slowly raised the lid and placed it back against the wall. For a moment she hesitated, and then, plunging her arm down at one corner of the trunk, amongst its various contents, she brought up, from the hidden depths, a small tissue paper parcel. This she opened carefully, and disclosed a tiny shoe, homely but neat, a little child's chemise, and an old, faded, pink print sun-bonnet, minus a string. In the upper leather of the shoe were several cuts, the work of some wanton hand. Sitting back upon her heels, she let the open parcel fall into her lap.

"What would I not give," she sighed, "to find the fellow of this little shoe! But no doubt it has long ago rotted at the bottom of some muddy ditch!"

Then, for the hundredth time, she examined the little chemise, at one corner of which were worked, in red cotton, the letters "M.H."

"They have told me again and again that I had this chemise on when I was found. Of course that doesn't prove that it was my own, and I have never supposed that those two letters stand for my name. But now—well, may it not be so, after all? It was really no more than a guess, on the part of Mr. and Mrs. Burton, that my name was Mary Ann Owen; and, from what I can see, it's just as likely to have been anything else. Let me think; what name might 'M.H.' stand for? Mary Hall? Margaret Harper? Mari—. No, no, I dare not think that—at least, not yet!"

Once more she wrapped up her little parcel of relics, and returned it to its place at the bottom of her trunk.

"Heigho!" she exclaimed, as, having closed and locked the trunk, she sprang to her feet. "How I do wonder who I am!"

# CHAPTER XXXVI

## TOMMY DUDGEON UNDERTAKES
## A DELICATE ENTERPRISE

The time which had elapsed since the first visit of Miss Owen to the house of "the little Twin Brethren" had constituted, for Tommy Dudgeon, a period of mental unrest. If he had been perturbed before, he was twice as uneasy now. He had made the joyous discovery which he had been expecting to make almost ever since he had seen the young secretary walking in her emphatic way along the street. But, joyous as the discovery was, the making of it had actually increased the perturbation of his mind. His trouble was that he could not tell how he would ever be able to make his discovery known. He did not doubt that, to his dear friend, "Cobbler" Horn, and to the young secretary, the communication of it would impart great joy. But he was restrained by a fear, which would arise, notwithstanding his feeling of certainty, lest he should prove to be mistaken after all; and his fear was reinforced by an inward persuasion which he had that he was the most awkward person in the world by whom so delicate a communication could be made.

Yet he told himself he was quite sure that the young secretary was no other than little Marian come back. His doubts had vanished when he had seen her sitting in the old

J. W. Keyworth

arm-chair, just as when she was a child; and every time he had seen her since that day his assurance had been made more sure. But, as long as he was compelled to keep his discovery to himself, it was almost the same as though he had not made it at all.

Tommy almost wished that some one else had made the great discovery, as well as himself. His thoughts had turned to his brother John; and he had resolved to put him to the test, which he had subsequently done with considerable tact. On the evening of the day following that of the first visit of Miss Owen to their house, the brothers had been sitting by the fire before going to bed.

"John," Tommy had said, seizing his opportunity, "you saw the young lady who was here the other day?"

"Yes."

"She's the secretary, you know."

"Yes," said John again, yawning; for he was sleepy.

"Well, what did you think of her?"

John started, and regarded his brother with a stare of astonishment. It was the first time Tommy had ever asked his opinion on such a subject. Was he thinking of getting married, or what? John Dudgeon had a certain broad sense of humour which enabled him to perceive such ludicrous elements of a situation as showed themselves on the surface.

"Ah!" he exclaimed slyly; "are you there?"

Tommy put out his hands in some confusion.

"No, no," he said, "not what you think! But did you notice anything particular about the young lady?"

"Well no," replied John, "except that I thought she was a very nice young person. But, Tommy, isn't she rather too young? If you really are thinking of getting married, wouldn't it be better to choose some one a little nearer your own age?"

John would not be dissuaded from the idea that his brother was intent on matrimonial thoughts. Tommy waved his hand, in a deprecatory way, and rising from his chair, said "good night," and betook himself to bed.

It was plain that he was quite alone in his discovery. What was he to do? To speak to Miss Owen on the subject was out of the question. The only alternative was to communicate the good news to "Cobbler" Horn himself. But there seemed to be stupendous difficulties involved in such a course. He was aware that there was nothing his friend would more rejoice to know than that which he had to tell. From various hints thrown out by "Cobbler" Horn, Tommy knew that he regarded Miss Owen with much of the fondness of a father; and it was not likely that the joy of finding his lost child would be diminished in the least by the fact that she had presented herself in the person of his secretary. But this consideration did not relieve the perplexity with which the little huckster contemplated the necessity of making known his secret to "Cobbler" Horn. For, to say nothing of the initial obstacle of his own timidity, he feared it would be almost impossible to convince his friend that his strange surmise was correct. If "Cobbler" Horn had not discovered for himself the identity of his secretary with his long-lost child, was it likely that he would accept that astounding fact on the testimony of any other person?

It is needless to say that Tommy Dudgeon made his perplexity a matter of prayer. He prayed and pondered, night and day; and, at length a thought came to him which seemed to point out the way of which he was in search. Might he not give "Cobbler" Horn some covert hint which would put him on the track of making the great discovery for himself? Surely some such thing, though difficult, might be done! He must indeed be cautious, and not by any means reveal his design. The suggestion must seem to be incidental and unpremeditated. There must be no actual mention of little Marian, and no apparently intentional indication of Miss Owen. Something must be said which might induce "Cobbler" Horn to associate the idea of his little lost Marian with that of his young secretary—to place them side by side before his mind. And it must all arise in the course of conversation, the order of which—he Tommy Dudgeon, must deliberately plan. The audacity of the thought made his hair stand up.

It was a delicate undertaking indeed! The little man felt like a surgeon about to perform a critical operation upon his dearest friend. He was preparing to open an old wound in the heart of his beloved benefactor. True, he hoped so to deal with it that it should never bleed again. But what if he failed? That would be dreadful! Yet the attempt must be made. So he set himself to his task. His opportunity came on the afternoon of the day following that of the opening of the "Home." Watching from the corner of his window, as he was wont, about three o'clock, Tommy saw "the Golden Shoemaker" come along the street, and enter his old house. Then the little man turned away from the window, and became very nervous. For quite two minutes he stood back against the shelves, trying to compose himself. When he had succeeded, in some degree, in steadying his quivering nerves, he reached from under the counter a brown-paper parcel containing a pair of boots, which had, for some days, been lying in readiness for the occasion which had now arrived, and, calling John to mind the shop, slipped swiftly into the street. A minute later he was standing in the doorway of "Cobbler" Horn's workshop. "The little Twin Brethren" had, at first, been disposed to refrain from availing themselves of the gratuitous labours of their friend; but, perceiving that it would afford him pleasure, they had yielded with an easy grace, and now Tommy was glad to have so good an excuse for a visit to "the Golden Shoemaker," as was supplied by the boots in the parcel under his arm.

"Cobbler" Horn perceived the nervousness of his visitor, and thinking it strange that the bringing of a pair of boots to be mended should have occasioned his humble little friend so much trepidation, he did his best, by adopting a specially sociable tone, to put him at his ease.

"Ah, Tommy, what have we there?" he asked. "More work for the 'Cobbler,' eh?"

"Just an old pair of boots which want mending, Mr. Horn," said Tommy, in uncertain tones, as he unwrapped the boots and held them out with a shaking hand—"that is, if you are not too busy."

"Not by any means," said "Cobbler" Horn, with a smile. "Put them down."

Tommy obeyed.

There stood against the wall, a much-worn wooden chair from which the back had been sawn off close.

"I'll sit down, if you don't mind," gasped Tommy, depositing himself upon this superannuated seat.

"By all means," said "Cobbler" Horn cordially; "make

J. W. Keyworth

yourself quite at home."

"Thank you," said Tommy, drawing from his pocket a red and yellow handkerchief, with which he vigorously mopped his brow.

"Cobbler" Horn waited calmly for his perturbed visitor to become composed; and Tommy sat for some minutes, staring helplessly at "Cobbler" Horn, and still rubbing his forehead. What had become of the astute plan of operations which the little man had laid down?

"You have surely something on your mind, friend?" said "Cobbler" Horn, in an enquiring tone.

"Yes, I have," said Tommy, somewhat relieved; "it's been there for some time."

"Well, what is it? Can I help you in any way?"

"Oh, no; I don't want help."

His utterly incapacitated demeanour belied him; but he was speaking of financial help.

"I've been thinking of the past, Mr. Horn," he managed to say, making a faint effort to direct the conversation according to his original design.

"Ah!" sighed "Cobbler" Horn. "Of the past!" With the word, his thoughts darted back to that period of his own past towards which they so often sadly turned.

"I somehow can't help it," continued Tommy, gathering courage. "There seems to be something that keeps bringing it up."

"Cobbler" Horn fixed his keen eyes on the agitated face of his visitor. He knew what it was in the past to which Tommy referred, and appreciated his delicacy of expression.

"Yes, Tommy," he said, "and I, too, often think of the past. But is there anything special that brings it to your mind just now?"

Upon this, all Tommy Dudgeon's clever plans vanished into air. His scheme for leading the conversation up to the desired point utterly broke down. He cast himself on the mercy of his friend.

"Oh," he cried, in thrilling tones, "can't you see it? Can't you feel it—every day? The sec'tary! The sec'tary! If it is so plain to me, how can you be so blind?"

Then he darted from the room, and betook himself home with all speed.

J. W. Keyworth

# CHAPTER XXXVII

## BETWEEN LIFE AND DEATH

"Cobbler" Horn's first thought was that the strain of eccentricity in his humble little friend had developed into actual insanity. But, on further consideration, he was disposed to take another view. He felt bound to admit that, though there had been a strangeness in the behaviour of the little man throughout his visit, it had not afforded any actual ground for the suspicion of insanity, until he had so suddenly rushed away home. It was, therefore, possible that there might prove to be some important meaning in what he had said. At first "Cobbler" Horn had gathered nothing intelligible from the impassioned apostrophe of his excited little friend; but, by degrees, there dawned upon him some faint gleam of what its meaning might be. "The sec'tary!" That was the quaint term by which Tommy was wont to designate Miss Owen. But their conversation had been drifting in the direction of his little lost Marian. Why, then, should Miss Owen have been in Tommy's mind? Ah, he saw how it was! His humble friend had perceived that Miss Owen was a dear, good girl; and he had noticed her evident attachment to him—"Cobbler" Horn, and his fondness for her, and no doubt the little man had meant to suggest that she should take the place of the lost child. It was characteristic of his humble friend that he should seek, by such a hint, to point out a course which, no doubt, seemed to him, likely to afford satisfaction to all concerned; and "Cobbler" Horn could not help admiring the delicacy with which it had been done.

"The Golden Shoemaker" was quite persuaded that he had hit upon the right interpretation of the little huckster's words; and he was not altogether displeased with the suggestion he supposed them to convey. Of course Marian would ultimately come back; and no one else could be permitted permanently to occupy her place. But there was no reason why he should not let his young secretary take, for the time being, as far as possible, the place which would have been filled by his lost child. In fact, Miss Owen was almost like a daughter to him already; and he was learning to love her as such. Well, he would adopt the suggestion of his little friend. His secretary should fill, for the time, the vacant place in his life. Yet he would never leave off loving his precious Marian; and her own share of love, which could never be given to another, must be reserved for her against her return, when he would have two daughters instead of one.

Thus mused "the Golden Shoemaker," until, suddenly recollecting himself, he started up. He had promised to visit one of his former neighbours, who was sick, and it was already past the time at which the visit should have been made. He hastily threw off his leathern apron, and put on his coat and hat. At the same moment, he observed that heavy rain was beating against the window. It was now early summer; and, misled by the fair face of the sky, he had left home without an umbrella. What was he to do? He passed into the kitchen, and opening the front door, stood looking out upon the splashing rain. Behind him, in the room, sat, at her sewing, the good woman whom he had placed in charge of the house. She was small, and plump, and shining, the very picture of content. Her manner was respectful, and, as a rule, she did not address "Cobbler" Horn until he had spoken to her. To-day, however, she was the first to speak.

"Surely, sir, you won't go out in such a rain!"

As she spoke, the shower seemed suddenly to gather force, and the rain to descend in greater volume than ever.

"Thank you, Mrs. Bunn," replied "Cobbler" Horn, looking round. "I think I will wait for a moment or two; but I have no time to spare, and must go soon, in any case."

The rain had turned the street into a river, upon the surface of which the plumply-falling drops were producing multitudes of those peculiar gleaming white splashes which are known to childhood as "sixpences and half-crowns." All at once the downpour diminished. The sky became lighter, and the sun showed a cleared face through the thinning clouds.

"I think I may venture now," said "Cobbler" Horn.

"Better wait a little longer, sir; it 'ull come on again," said Mrs. Bunn, with the air of a person to whom the foibles of the weather were fully known. But "Cobbler" Horn was already in the street, and had not heard her words. It was some distance to the house of his sick friend, and he walked along at a rapid pace. But before he had proceeded far, the prophecy of Mrs. Bunn was fulfilled. In a moment, the sky grew black again; and, after a preliminary dash of heavy drops, the rain came down in greater abundance than before. It almost seemed as though a water-spout had burst. In two minutes, "the Golden Shoemaker" was wet to the skin. He might have returned to the house, from which he was distant no more than a few hundred yards; but he thought that, as he was already wet through, he might as well go on. Besides, "Cobbler" Horn's promise was sacred, and it had been given to his sick friend. So he plunged on through the flooded and splashing streets.

When he reached his destination, he was glad that he had not turned back. His poor friend was much worse, and it was evident that he had not many hours to live. Forgetful of his own discomfort, and heedless of danger from his wet clothes, "Cobbler" Horn took his place at the bedside, and remained for many hours with the dying man. His friend was a Christian, and did not fear to die. He had never been married, was almost without relatives, and had scarcely a friend. As, hour after hour, he held the hand of the dying man, "Cobbler" Horn whispered in his ear, from time to time, a cheering word, or breathed a fervent prayer. The feeble utterances of the dying man, which became less frequent as the hours crept away, left no doubt as to the reality of his faith in God, and, about midnight, he passed peacefully away.

"Cobbler" Horn lingered a few moments' longer, and set out for home. The rain had long ceased, and the sky was without a cloud. The semi-tropical shower had been followed by a rapid cooling of the atmosphere, and he shivered in his still damp clothes, as he hurried along.

He found Miss Jemima and the young secretary anxiously awaiting his return. They knew of his intention of visiting his sick friend, and were not much surprised that he was so late. But his sister was greatly concerned to find that he had remained so long with his clothes damp. He went at once to bed, and Miss Jemima insisted upon bringing to him there a steaming basin of gruel. He took a few spoonfuls, and then lay wearily back upon the bed. Miss Jemima shook up his pillows, arranged the bed-clothes, and reluctantly left him for the night.

In the morning it was evident that "the Golden Shoemaker" was ill. The wetting he had received, followed by the effect of the chill night air, had found out an unsuspected weakness in his constitution, and symptoms of acute bronchitis had set in. The doctor was hastily summoned, and, after the manner of his kind, gravely shook his head, by way of intimating that the case was much more serious than he was prepared verbally to admit. The condition of the patient, indeed, was such as to justify the most alarming interpretation of the doctor's manner and words.

Now followed a time of painful suspense. In spite of all that money could do, "Cobbler" Horn grew worse daily. The visits of the doctor, though repeated twice, and even three times a day, produced but little appreciable result. Could it be that this man, into whose possession such vast wealth had so recently come, was so early to be called to relinquish it again? Was it possible that all this money was so soon to drop from the hands which had seemed more fit to hold it than almost any other hands to which had ever been entrusted the disposal of money?

Miss Jemima did not ask herself such questions as these. She moved about the house, trying, in her grim way, to crush down within her heart the anguished thought that her beloved and worshipped brother lay at the point of death.

And Miss Owen—with what emotions did she contemplate the possibility of that dread event the actual occurrence of which became more probable every day? She went about her duties like one in a dream. What would it mean to her if he were to die? She would lose a great benefactor, and a dear friend; and that would be grief enough. But was there not something more that she would lose—something which had seemed almost within her grasp, which it had hitherto been the hope, and yet the fear, of her life that she might find, but which, of late, she had desired to find with an ardent and unhalting hope? It was with a sick heart that the young secretary discharged, from day to day, her now familiar duties. She was now so well acquainted with the mind of her employer, that she could deal with the correspondence almost as well without, as with, his help. But she missed him every moment, and the thought that he might never again take his place over against her at the office table filled her with bitter grief.

There were others who were anxious on account of the peril which threatened the life of "the Golden Shoemaker."

Mr. Durnford was weighted with grave concern. He called every day to see his friend; and each time he left the sick-chamber, he was uncertain whether his predominant feeling was that of sorrow for the illness and danger of so good a man, or rejoicing that, in his pain and peril, "Cobbler" Horn was so patient and resigned.

In the breasts of many who were accustomed to receive benefits at the hands of "the Golden Shoemaker," there was great distress. Every day, and almost every hour, there were callers, chiefly of the humbler classes, with anxious enquiries on their lips. Not the least solicitous of these were "the Little Twin Brethren." Tommy Dudgeon almost conti-nually haunted the house where his honoured friend lay in such dire straits. The anxiety of the little man was intensified by a burning desire to know whether his desperate appeal on the subject of the "sec'tary" had produced its designed effect on the mind of "Cobbler" Horn.

Public sympathy with "Cobbler" Horn and his anxious friends ran deep; and every one who could claim, in any degree, the privilege of a friend, made frequent enquiry as to the sufferer's state. But neither public sympathy nor private grief were of much avail; and it seemed, for a time, as though the earthly course of "the Golden Shoemaker" was almost run. There came a day when the doctors confessed that they could do no more. A few hours must decide the question of life or death. Dreadful was the suspense in the stricken house, and great the sorrow in many hearts outside. Mr. Durnford, who had been summoned early in the morning, remained to await the issue of the day. Little Tommy Dudgeon, who had been informed that the crisis was near, came, and lingered about the house, on one pretence or another, unable to tear himself away.

But how was it with "the Golden Shoemaker" himself? From the first, he had been calm and patient; and, even now, when he was confronted with the grim visage of death, he did not flinch. Long accustomed to leave the issues of his life to God, willing to live yet prepared to die, he realized his position without dismay. No doctor ever had a more tractable patient than was "Cobbler" Horn; and he yielded himself to his nurses like an infant of days. In the earlier stages of his illness, he had thought much about the mysterious words and strange behaviour of his friend Tommy Dudgeon, on the day on which he had been taken ill. Further consideration had not absolutely confirmed "Cobbler" Horn's first impression as to the meaning of the little huckster's words. Pondering them as he lay in bed, he had become less sure that his humble little friend had intended simply to suggest the admirable fitness of the young secretary to take the place of his lost child. Surely, he had thought, the impassioned exclamation of the eccentric little man must have borne some deeper significance than that! And then he had become utterly bewildered as to what meaning the singular words of Tommy Dudgeon had been intended to convey. And then there came a glimmering—nothing more— of the idea his faithful friend had wished to impart. But, just when he might have penetrated the mystery, if he could have thought it out a little more, he became too ill to think at all.

After this his mind wandered slightly, and once or twice a strange fancy beset him that his little Marian was in the room, and that she was putting her soft hands on his forehead; but, in a moment, the fancy was gone, and he was aware that the young secretary was laying her cool gentle palm upon his burning brow.

It had been a wonderful comfort to the girl that she had been permitted to take a spell of nursing now and then.

J. W. Keyworth

# CHAPTER XXXVIII

## A LITTLE SHOE

That which happens now and then occurred in the case of "Cobbler" Horn. The doctors proved to be mistaken; and thanks to a strong and unimpaired constitution, and to the blessing of God on efficient nursing and medical skill, "the Golden Shoemaker" survived the crisis of his illness, and commenced a steady return to health and strength.

Great was the joy on every side. But, perhaps, the person who rejoiced most was Miss Owen. Not even the satisfaction of Miss Jemima at the ultimate announcement of the doctors, that their patient might now do well, was greater than was that of the young secretary. Miss Owen rejoiced for very special reasons of her own. During the convalescence of "Cobbler" Horn, the young secretary was with him very much. He was glad to have her in his room; and, as his strength returned, he talked to her often about herself. He seemed anxious to know all she could tell him of her early life.

"Sit down here, by the bed," he would say eagerly, taking her plump, brown wrist in his wasted fingers, "and tell me about yourself."

She would obey him, laughing gently, less at the nature of the request, than at the eagerness with which it was made.

"Now begin," he said one evening, for the twentieth time, settling himself beneath the bed-clothes to listen, as though he had never heard the story before; "and mind you don't leave anything out."

"Well," she commenced, "I was a little wandering mite, with hardly any clothes and only one shoe. I was—"

His hand was on her arm in an instant. This was the first time she had mentioned the fact that, when she was found by the friends by whom she had been brought up, one of her feet was without a shoe.

"Only one shoe, did you say?" asked "Cobbler" Horn, in tremulous tones.

"Yes," she replied, not suspecting the tumult of thoughts her simple statement had excited in his mind.

In truth, her statement had agitated her listener in no slight degree. He did not, as yet, fully perceive its significance. But the coincidence was so very strange! One shoe! Only one shoe! His little Marian had lost one of her shoes when she strayed away. A wonderful coincidence, indeed!

"I was very dirty, and my clothes were torn," resumed Miss Owen; "and I was altogether a very forlorn little thing, I have no doubt. I don't remember much about it, myself, you know; but Mrs. Burton has often told me that I was crying at the time, and appeared to have been so engaged for some time. It was one evening in June, and getting dusk. Mr. and Mrs. Burton had been for a walk in the country, and were returning home, when they came upon me, walking very slowly, poking my fists into my eyes, and crying, as I said. When they asked me what was the matter, I couldn't tell them much. I seemed to be trying to say something about a 'bad woman,' and my 'daddy.' They couldn't even make out, with certainty, what I said my name was. Little as you might think it, Mr. Horn. I was a very bad talker in those days. 'Mary Ann Owen' was what my kind friends thought I called myself; and 'Mary Ann Owen' I have been ever since.

"Well, these dear people took me home; and, after they had washed me, and found some clothes for me which had belonged to a little girl they had lost—their only child—they gave me a good basin of bread and milk, and put me to bed.

"The next day they tried to get me to tell them something more, but it was no use; and as I couldn't tell them where I lived, and they didn't even feel sure about my name, they naturally felt themselves at a loss. But I don't think they were much troubled about that; for I believe they were quite prepared to keep me as their own child. You see they had lost a little one; and there was a vacant place that I expect they thought I might fill. They did, at first, try to find out who I was. But they altogether failed; and so, without more ado, they just made me their own little girl. They taught me to call them 'father' and 'mother'; and they have always been so good and kind!"

Though several points in Miss Owen's story had touched him keenly, "Cobbler" Horn quickly regained his composure after the first start of surprise. Feeling himself too weak to do battle with agitating thoughts, he put aside, for the time, the importunate questions which besieged his mind.

"Thank you," he said quietly, when the narrative was finished. "To-morrow we will talk about it all again. I think I can go to sleep now. But will you first, please, read a little from the dear old book."

The young girl reached a Bible which stood always on a table by the bedside, and, turning to one of his favourite places, read, in her sweet clear tones, words of comfort and strength. Then she bade him "good night," and moved towards the door. But he called her back.

"Will you take these letters?" he said, with his hand on a bundle of letters which lay on the table at his side; "and put them into the safe."

They were letters of importance, to which he had been giving, during the evening, such attention as he was able. During his illness, he had allowed his secretary to keep the key of the safe.

Miss Owen took the letters, and went downstairs. Going first into the dining-room, she told Miss Jemima that "Cobbler" Horn seemed likely to go to sleep, and then proceeded to the office. Without delay, she unlocked the safe, and was in the act of depositing the bundle of letters in its place, when, from a recess at the back, a small tissue-paper parcel, which she had never previously observed, fell down to the front, and became partially undone. As she picked it up, intending to restore it to the place from which it had fallen, her elbow struck the side of the safe, and the parcel was jerked out of her hand. In trying to save it, she retained in her grasp a corner of the paper, which unfolded itself, and there fell out upon the floor a little child's shoe, around which was wrapped a strip of stained and faded pink print. At a sight so unexpected she uttered a cry. Then she picked up the little shoe, and, having released it from its bandage, turned it over and over in her hands. Next she gave her attention to the piece of print. She was utterly dazed. Suddenly the full meaning of her discovery flashed upon her mind. She

J. W. Keyworth

dropped the simple articles by which she had been so deeply moved, and, covering her face with her hands, burst into a paroxysm of joyous tears. But her agitation was brief. Hastily drying her eyes, she picked up the little shoe. No need to wait till she had compared it with the one which lay in the corner of her box! The image of the latter was imprinted on her mind with the exactness of a photograph, with its every wrinkle and spot, and every slash it had received from that unknown, wanton hand. She *could* compare the two shoes here and now, as exactly as though she actually saw them side by side. Yes, this little shoe was indeed the fellow of her own! And the strip of print—what was it but her missing bonnet-string? She had found what she had so often longed to find. And she herself was—yes, why should she hesitate to say it?—the little Marian of whom she had so often heard!

How wonderful it was! Here was truth stranger than fiction, indeed! She laughed—a gentle, trilling laugh, low and sweet. But ah, she could not tell him! She could not say to him, "I am the daughter you lost so long ago. I have seen in your safe the fellow of the shoe I wore when I was found by my kind friends." Of course it would convince him; but she could not say it. She must wait until he found out the truth for himself. But would he ever find it out? She hoped and thought he would. Had he not marked what she said about her having had on only one shoe when she was found? And would not that lead him to think and enquire? Meanwhile, she herself knew the wonderful truth; and she could afford to wait. It would all come right, of course it would; any other thought was too ridiculous to be entertained.

Very quietly, and with almost reverent fingers, she wound the faded bonnet-string once more around the little shoe, and wrapped them up again in the much-crumpled paper.

"How often must he have unfolded it!" was the thought that nestled in her heart, as she replaced the precious parcel in the safe, and closed and locked the ponderous door.

From the office, the young secretary went directly to her own room. To open her trunk, and plunge her hand down into the corner where lay her own little parcel of relics, was the work of a moment. There was certainly no room for doubt. The little, stout, leather shoe which she had treasured so long was the fellow of the one she had just seen in the safe downstairs. There was the very same curve of the sole, made by the pressure of the little foot—her own, and similar inequalities in the upper part. With a sudden movement, she lifted the tiny shoe to her lips. And here was her funny old sun-bonnet! How often she had wondered what had become of its other string! Last of all, she took up the little chemise, which completed her simple store of relics, and gazed intently upon the red letters with which it was marked. All uncertainty as to their meaning was gone. What could "M.H." stand for but "Marian Horn"? With a grateful heart, she rolled up her treasures, and, having consigned them once more to their place in the trunk, went downstairs. Miss Jemima was indisposed; and, having seen the nurse duly installed in the sick-room, she had retired for the night. Accordingly, Miss Owen, much to her relief, had supper by herself. She felt that she did not wish to talk to any one just at present, and to Miss Jemima least of all.

When the young secretary fell asleep that night, she was lulled with the sweetness of the thought that she had not only found her father, but had discovered him in the person of the best man she had ever known. The discovery of her father might have proved a bitter disappointment; it was actually such as to fill her with unspeakable gratitude. She did not greatly regret that she had not found her mother, as well as her father. It would probably have caused her real grief, if any one had appeared to claim the place in her heart which was held by the woman from whom she had always received, in a peculiar degree, a mother's love and a mother's care. One could find room for any number of fathers—provided they were worthy. But a mother!—her place was sacred; there could be no sharing of her throne.

# CHAPTER XXXIX

## A JOYOUS DISCOVERY

It was long that night before "Cobbler" Horn fell asleep. He was free from pain, and felt better altogether than at any time since the beginning of his illness. Yet he could not sleep. The story of his young secretary, as she had told it this evening, had supplied him with thoughts calculated to banish slumber from the most drowsy eyes.

Miss Owen had told him her simple story many times before; but this evening she had introduced certain new particulars of a startling kind; and it was as the result of the thoughts thereby suggested that he was unable to sleep. The few additional details which the young secretary had included in her narrative this evening had given a new aspect to the story. There was the solitary shoe she had worn at the time when she had come into the kind hands of Mr. and Mrs. Burton, and the fact that she was a very indistinct talker at the time. The entire story, too, seemed to correspond so well—why should he not admit it?—with what might not improbably have been the history of his little Marian; and Marian would be, at that time, about the same age as was Miss Owen when she was found by the friends whose adopted child she became. But the solitary shoe! He wondered whether it was still in her possession. He would

J. W. Keyworth

ask her in the morning. And then the indistinct talk of which she had spoken! How well he remembered the pretty broken speech of his own little pet! Then there returned to him that gleam of intelligence with regard to the meaning of the strange words of Tommy Dudgeon with which he had been visited at the beginning of his illness. Surely this was what his faithful friend had meant! From the great affection of the little huckster for Marian, it was likely that he would have a vivid recollection of the child; and no doubt the little man had already discerned what the father himself was only now, after so many hints, beginning to perceive. Thus he pondered through the night. Strange to say, he felt neither sleepy nor tired. He was refreshed by the gracious prophecy of coming joy which the story of his young secretary had supplied; and when, after falling asleep in the early hours of the morning, he awoke towards eight o'clock, he felt as though he had slept all night.

It was the custom for the young secretary to pay a visit to her employer's room soon after breakfast, for the purpose of laying before him any of the morning's letters to which it was imperative that his personal attention should be given. Most frequently Miss Owen's visit was, as far as business was concerned, a mere formality, or little more. There were few of the letters with which she herself was not able to deal; and all that was necessary, as a rule, was for her to make a general report, which "Cobbler" Horn invariably received with an approving smile. Then the favoured young secretary would linger for a few moments in the room. She would hover about the bed; asking how he had passed the night; performing a variety of tender services, which, though he had not previously realized the need of them, increased his comfort to a wonderful extent; and talking, all the while, in her merry, heartsome way, like a privileged child, with now and then a gentle, cooing little laugh.

There was nothing, in the whole course of the day, that "the Golden Shoemaker" enjoyed so much as the morning visit of his fresh young secretary. But he had never before anticipated it as eagerly as he did this morning. He had long looked upon this young girl rather in the light of a devoted daughter, than of a paid secretary. What if, unconsciously to them both, she had thus grown into her rightful place! As the time approached for her appearance, he had insensibly brought himself to face more fully the wonderful possibility which had been presenting itself to his mind during the last few hours. The nurse was surprised that, though he seemed to be even better than usual, he could scarcely eat any breakfast. All the time, he was watching the door, and listening for the slightest sound. He wondered whether Miss Owen still had in her possession the little shoe of which she had spoken. He must ask her that at once. And how he yearned to search her face, with one long, scrutinising gaze!

At last she came, radiant, as usual! Did he notice that a slight shyness veiled her face, and that there was an unusual tremor in her voice as she wished him "good morning"? If "Cobbler" Horn perceived these signs, he paid them but scant regard. He was too much absorbed in his own thoughts, to consider what those of his young secretary might be; and he was too busily engaged in scrutinising the permanent features of her face, to give much heed to its transient expression. What he saw did not greatly assist in the settlement of the question which occupied his mind. And small wonder that it should be so; for, when he had last seen his Marian, she was a little girl of five.

No less eagerly than "Cobbler" Horn scanned the countenance of his young secretary, did her eyes, that morning, seek his face. She too had passed a broken night. But it had not seemed wearisome or long. Happy thoughts had rendered sleep an impertinence at first; and, when healthy youthful nature had, at length, asserted itself, the young girl had slept only in pleasant snatches, waking every now and then from some delicious dream, to assure herself that the sweetest dream could not be half so delightful as the glad reality which had come into her life.

If these two people could have read each other's thoughts— But that might not be. She wished him "good morning," in her own bright way; and he responded with his usual benignant smile. Then they proceeded to business. There was one very important letter, which demanded some expenditure of time. The secretary was not altogether herself. Her hand trembled a little, and there was a slight quaver in her voice. Her employer noticed these signs of discomposure, and spoke of them in his kindly way.

"Surely you are not well this morning!" he said, placing his hand lightly on her wrist.

His secretary was usually so self-possessed.

"Oh yes," she said, with a start, "I am quite well—quite."

She smiled at the very idea of her not being well, knowing what she did.

"Come and sit down beside me for a little while," said "Cobbler" Horn, when their business was finished; "and let us have some talk."

It was the ordinary invitation; but there was something unusual in the tone of his voice. As the young girl took her seat at the bedside, her previous agitation in some degree returned. "Cobbler" Horn's fingers closed upon her hand, with a gentle pressure.

"My dear young lady, there is something that I wish to ask you."

There was just the slightest tremor in his voice; and the young secretary was distinctly conscious of the beating of her heart.

"Yes, sir," she said, faintly, trembling a little.

"Don't be agitated," he continued, for it was impossible to overlook the fact of her excitement. "It's a very simple matter."

He did not know—how could he?—that her thoughts were running in the same direction as his own.

"You said," he pursued, "that, when you were found by your good friends, you were wearing only one shoe. Did you— have you that shoe still?"

It was evident that he was agitated now. Miss Owen started, and he could feel her hand quiver within his grasp, like a frightened bird.

"Yes," she answered in a whisper, above which she felt powerless to raise her voice, "I have kept it ever since."

"Then," he resumed, having now quite recovered his self-possession, "would you mind letting me see it?"

With a strong effort, she succeeded in maintaining her self-control.

"Oh no, not at all, sir!" she said, rising, and moving towards the door; "I'll fetch it at once. But it isn't much to look at now," she added over her shoulder, as she left the room.

"'Not much to look at'!" laughed "the Golden Shoemaker" softly to himself. There was nothing that he had ever been half so anxious to see!

Five minutes later he was sitting up in bed, turning over and over in his hands the fellow of the little shoe which he had cherished for so many years as the dearest memento of his lost child. Could there be any doubt? Was it not his own handiwork? It had evidently received several random slashes with a knife, and it still bore traces of mud. But he knew his own work too well; and had he not looked upon the fellow of this shoe every day for the last twelve years?

Strange to say, so completely absorbed was "Cobbler" Horn in contemplating the shoe which his Marian had worn, that, for the moment, he did not think of Marian herself. At length he looked up. But he was alone. Discretion, and the tumult of her emotions, had constrained the young secretary to withdraw from the room. Putting a strong hand upon herself, she had retired to the office, where she was, at that moment, diligently at work.

"Cobbler" Horn sighed. But perhaps it was better that the young girl had withdrawn. There was little room for doubt; but he must make assurance doubly sure. He touched the electric bell at the head of the bed, and the nurse immediately appeared.

"Will you be so good as to tell Miss Horn I should like to see her at once."

The nurse, marking the eagerness with which the request was uttered, and observing the little shoe on the counterpane, perceived that the occasion was urgent, and departed on her errand with all speed.

"I don't think he is any worse this morning," she said to Miss Jemima when she had delivered her message. "Indeed he seems, quite unaccountably, to be very much better. But it is evident something has happened."

Without waiting to hear more, Miss Jemima hurried to her brother's room. Sitting up in bed, with a happy face, he was holding in his hand a dilapidated child's shoe, which he placed in his sister's hands as soon as she approached the bed.

"Jemima, look at that!" he said joyously.

Thinking it was the shoe which her brother had always preserved with so much care, she took it, and examined it with much concern.

"Whoever can have cut it about like that?" she cried.

"Cobbler" Horn hastened to rectify her mistake.

"No, Jemima," he said, in a tone of reverent exultation; "it's the other shoe—the one we've been wanting to find all these years!"

The first thought of Miss Jemima was that her brother had gone mad. Then she examined the shoe more closely.

"To be sure!" she said. "How foolish of me! Those cuts were made long ago."

As she spoke, she put her hand on the table at the bedside, to steady herself.

"Brother," she demanded, in trembling tones, "where did you get this shoe? Did it come by the morning post?"

"Cobbler" Horn answered deliberately. He would give his sister time to take in the meaning of his words.

"It has been in the possession of Miss Owen. She brought it to me just now."

"Miss Owen?"

Miss Jemima's first impulse was towards indignation. What had Miss Owen been doing with the shoe? But the next moment, she reflected that there must be some reasonable explanation of the fact that the shoe had been in the possession of her brother's secretary—though what that explanation might be Miss Jemima could not, as yet, divine.

"She has had it," resumed "Cobbler" Horn, in the same quiet tone as before, "ever since she was a little girl. She was wearing it when she was found by the good people by whom she was adopted."

Then light came to Miss Jemima, clear and full. She grasped her brother's shoulder, and remembered his weakness only just in time to refrain from giving him a vigorous shake.

"Brother, brother," she cried, "do you understand what your words may mean?"

"Yes, Jemima—in part, at least. But we must make sure. First we will put the two shoes together, and see that they really are the same."

"Why, surely, Thomas, you have no doubt?"

"There seems little room for it, indeed; but we cannot make too sure!"

He wanted to give himself time to become accustomed to the great joy which was dawning on his life.

"You know where the other shoe is, Jemima?"

"Yes, in the safe."

"Yes; and you know that, while I have been up here, Miss Owen has kept the key of the safe?"

"Yes."

Miss Jemima had undergone much mental chafing by reason of that knowledge.

"Well, will you go to her in the office, and say I wish you to bring me something out of the safe? She will not know what you bring. She will just hand you the key, and go on with her work."

"Yes, I will go, brother. But are you sure she knows or suspects nothing? She may have seen the shoe."

"Oh no; it is well wrapped up, and I am sure she would not touch the parcel. I can trust my secretary," he added, with a new-born pride.

As Miss Jemima went down stairs, she wondered she had not long ago lighted on the discovery which her brother had now made. It explained many things. The tones and gestures which had so often startled her by their familiarity; the vague feeling that, at some time, she must have known this young girl before; the growing resemblance—evident to Miss Jemima's eyes, at least—of the young secretary to "Cobbler" Horn—these things, which, with many kindred signs, Miss Jemima had hidden in her heart, had their explanation in the discovery which had just been made.

Miss Owen yielded the key of the safe without question. Though she appeared to take no notice of Miss Jemima's doings, she knew, as by instinct, what Miss Jemima was taking out of the safe; and she told herself that she must not, and would not, let it appear that she supposed anything unusual was going on. She went on quietly with her work; but it was by dint of such an effort of self-control, as few human beings have ever found it necessary to make, or could have made.

As the result of the young secretary's effort of self-repression, there appeared in her face, at the moment when Miss Jemima turned to leave the room, an expression so much like that assumed by the countenance of "Cobbler" Horn at times when he was very firm, that the heart of Miss Jemima gave a mighty bound.

Meanwhile Miss Jemima's brother was eagerly awaiting her return. She had been absent less than five minutes, when she once more entered his room.

"There," she said, holding the two little shoes out towards her brother, side by side, "there can be no doubt about the shoes, at any rate. They are a pair, sure enough. Why," she continued, turning up the shoe that Miss Owen had produced, "I remember noticing, that very morning, that half the leather was torn away from the heel of one of the child's shoes, just like that."

As she spoke, she held out the shoe, and showed her brother that its heel had been damaged exactly as she had described. Then a strange thing happened to Miss Jemima. She dropped the little shoes upon the bed, and, covering her face with her hands, cried gently for a few moments. "The Golden

Shoemaker" gazed at his sister in some wonder; and then two large tears gathered in his own eyes, and rolled down his cheeks.

All at once Miss Jemima almost fiercely dashed her hand across her eyes.

"Brother," she cried, "I've often heard of tears of joy; but I didn't think I should live to say they were the only ones I had shed since I was a little child! But there's no mistake about those shoes. And there's no doubt about anything else either."

"Cobbler" Horn was, perhaps, quite as confident as his sister; but he was a little more cautious.

"Yes, Jemima," he said; "but we must be careful. A mistake would be dreadful—both on our own account, and on that of—of Miss Owen. We must send for Mr. and Mrs. Burton at once. Mr. Durnford will telegraph. It will be necessary, of course, to tell him of our discovery; but he may be trusted not to breathe it to any one else."

Miss Jemima readily assented to her brother's proposal. Mr. Durnford was sent for, and came without delay. His astonishment on hearing the wonderful news his friends had to tell was hardly as great as they expected. It is possible that this arose from the fact that he was acquainted with the story of Miss Owen, and that his eyes and ears had been open during the last few months. It was, however, with no lack of heartiness that he complied with the request to send a telegram summoning Mr. and Mrs. Burton to "Cobbler" Horn's bedside.

## CHAPTER XL

## TOMMY DUDGEON'S CONTRIBUTION

After the despatch of the telegram, the words of Tommy Dudgeon, with reference to the young secretary, recurred once more to the mind of "Cobbler" Horn, and he mentioned them to his sister.

"This must have been what the good fellow meant," he said. "You remember, Jemima, how fond they were of each other—Tommy and the child?"

"Yes," responded Miss Jemima, reluctantly; for she still retained her dislike for "those stupid Dudgeons."

"Do you know, Jemima, I have it on my mind to send for Tommy at once, and ask him what he really meant."

"Send for him—to come in here?"

"Yes; why not?"

"Well, you must do as you like, I suppose."

A moment's reflection had convinced the good lady that she had really no sound reason to advance against the proposal her brother had made; and she knew that, in any case, he would do as he thought fit.

Accordingly a messenger was despatched for Tommy Dudgeon with all speed; and the little huckster turned over to his brother, without compunction, an important customer whom he happened to be serving at the time, and hurried away to the bedside of his honoured friend.

The servant who, in obedience to orders received, showed Tommy up at once to "Cobbler" Horn's room, handed in at the same time a telegram which had just arrived from Mr. Burton, saying that he and Mrs. Burton might be expected about three o'clock in the afternoon. "Cobbler" Horn placed the pink paper on the little table by his bedside, and turned to Tommy, who stood just within the doorway, nervously twisting his hat between his hands.

"Come in, Tommy, come in!" said "the Golden Shoemaker," encouragingly, "you see I am almost well."

Tommy advanced into the room; but being arrested by the sight of Miss Jemima, who stood at the bed-foot, he stopped short half-way between the bed and the door, and honoured that formidable lady with a trembling bow. Miss Jemima's mood this morning was complacency itself, and she acknowledged the obeisance of the little huckster with a not ungracious nod. Greatly encouraged, Tommy moved a pace or two nearer to the bed.

"I'm deeply thankful, Mr. Horn," he said, "to see you looking so well."

"Thank you, Tommy," responded "Cobbler" Horn, with a smile, as he reached out his hand. "The Lord is very good. No doubt He has more work for me to do yet."

As Tommy almost reverently took the hand of his beloved and honoured friend he thought to himself, "I wonder whether he has considered what I said?"

"The last time we met, Tommy," began "Cobbler" Horn, as though in answer to the unspoken question of the little man—"But, sit down, friend, sit down."

Tommy protested that he would rather stand; but, being overborne, he effected a compromise, by placing himself quite forward on the edge of the chair, and depositing his hat on the floor, between his feet.

"You remember the time?" resumed "Cobbler" Horn.

"Oh yes; quite well!"

"It was the afternoon of the day I was taken ill."

"Yes; and Mrs. Bunn said you *would* go out in that dreadful rain."

Tommy did not add that he himself, watching through his shop window, in the hope that his friend would come across to ask the meaning of his mysterious words, had, with a sinking heart, seen him walk off in the opposite direction through the drenching shower.

"Well," said "Cobbler" Horn, with a smile, "I've had to pay for that, and shall be all the wiser, no doubt. But there was something you said that afternoon that I want to ask you about. At the time I thought I knew what you meant. But I am inclined now to think I was mistaken, and that your words referred to something quite different from what I then supposed. Do you remember what you said?"

It was impossible for Tommy Dudgeon to conceal the agitation of his mind. He rejoiced at the opportunity to make known his great discovery to his friend; and yet he trembled lest he should prove unequal to the task. He thought, for a moment, that he would gain time by seeming not to understand the reference his friend had made.

"What words do you speak of, chiefly, Mr. Horn?" he asked tremulously, "I said so many—"

But Tommy Dudgeon could not dissemble. He stammered, stopped, wiped his forehead, and stretched out his hands as though in appeal to the mercy of his hearers.

"Of course I know what words you mean!" he cried. "I wanted to tell you of something I had seen for weeks, but that you didn't seem to see. And I can see it still; and there's no mistake about it. I'm as certain sure of it, as that I am sitting on this chair. It was about the sec'tary, and some one else; and yet not anybody else, because they're both the same. May I tell you, Mr. Horn? Can you bear it, do you think?"

"The Golden Shoemaker" regarded the eager face of his little friend with glistening eyes; and Miss Jemima, leaning towards him over the framework of the iron bedstead, listened with an intent countenance, from which all trace of disfavour had vanished away.

"Yes," said "Cobbler" Horn, in grave, calm tones; "tell us all. We are not unprepared."

"Thank you," said the little man, fervently. "But, oh, I wish you knew! I wish God had been pleased to make it known to you," he added with a reminiscence of his Old Testament studies, "in a dream and vision of the night. Oh, my dear friend, don't you see that what you've been longing and praying for all these years has come to pass—as we always knew it would; and—and that she's come back! she's come back? There, that's what I meant!"

"Then it really was so," said "Cobbler" Horn. "I'm surprised I did not perceive your meaning at the time."

Tommy thought him wonderfully calm.

"But I must tell you, Tommy, that we have now very much reason to think that your surmise is correct."

"*Surmise* is not the word, Mr. Horn; I know she's come back!"

"Of course you do," interposed Miss Jemima, in emphatic tones.

Tommy looked gratefully towards the hitherto dreadful lady; and she regarded him with eyes which seemed to say, "you have won my favour once for all."

"Can you tell us, Tommy," asked "Cobbler" Horn, "what has made you so very sure?"

"Yes," replied Tommy, with energy, "I'll tell you. Everything has made me sure—the way she walks along the street, with her head up, and putting her foot down as if a regiment of soldiers wouldn't stop her; and her manner of coming into the shop and saying, 'How are you to-day, Mr. Dudgeon?' and her sitting in the old arm-chair, and putting her head on one side like a knowing little bird, and asking questions about everything, and letting her eyes shine on you like stars. Begging your pardon, Mr. Horn, she's just the little lassie all over. Why I should know her with my eyes shut, if she were only to speak up, and say, 'Well, Tommy, how are you, to-day?'"

"But," asked "Cobbler" Horn, whose heart, secretly, was almost bursting with delight, "may you not be mistaken, after all?"

"I am not mistaken," replied Tommy firmly.

"But it's such a long while ago," suggested "Cobbler" Horn; "and—and she will be very much altered by this time. You *can't* be sure that a young woman is the same person as a little girl you haven't seen for more than a dozen years."

Herein, perhaps, "Cobbler" Horn's own chief difficulty lay. "How," he asked, "can I think of Marian as being other than a little girl?" Tommy Dudgeon did not seem to be troubled in that way at all.

"Yes," he said, "I can be quite sure when I have known the little girl as I knew that one; and when I have watched, and listened to, the young woman, as I have been watching and listening to the sec'tary for these months past."

"Cobbler" Horn and Miss Jemima exchanged glances.

"This is truly wonderful!" said he.

"Not at all!" retorted she. "The wonder is, Thomas, that you and I have been so blind all this time."

"The Golden Shoemaker" smiled gently, as he lay back upon his pillows. The image of a small, dark-eyed child held possession of his mind; and he had not been able readily to bring himself to see his little Marian in any other form. As for any real doubt, there was only a shred of it left in his

J. W. Keyworth

mind now. Yet he still said to himself that he must make assurance doubly sure.

"Well, Tommy," he said, "we are very much obliged to you. And now, will you do us another kindness? We are expecting some friends this afternoon who may be able to give us a good deal of light on this subject. Will you come, when we send for you, and hear what they have to say?"

"That I will!" was the hearty response, "I'll come, Mr. Horn, whenever you send."

"You have met these friends before, Tommy," said "Cobbler" Horn. "They are Mr. and Mrs. Burton—at the 'Home,' you know."

Tommy nodded.

"They found Miss Owen when she was a very little girl; and brought her up as their own child; and we hope that what they may tell us about her will help us to decide whether what we think is true."

Tommy nodded again with beaming eyes, and shortly afterwards took his leave.

"Now, brother," said Miss Jemima, "you must take some rest, or we shall have you ill again."

"Not much danger of that!" replied "Cobbler" Horn, smiling. "I think, please God, I've found a better medicine now, than all the doctors in the world could give me."

"Yes; but you are excited, and the reaction will come, if you do not take care."

"Well, perhaps you are right, Jemima. But first, don't you think she had better be out of the way when Mr. and Mrs. Burton come?"

"Yes, I've thought of that; she can take that poor girl along the road for a drive."

"A capital idea. Have it arranged, Jemima."

"Very well. I'll go and see about it at once; and you get to sleep."

# CHAPTER XLI

## NO ROOM FOR DOUBT!

At the appointed time, Mr. and Mrs. Burton arrived. Being, as yet, ignorant of the purpose for which their presence was desired, they were full of conjectures. Miss Jemima received them in the dining-room, downstairs. The first question they asked related to "Cobbler" Horn's health. "Was he worse?"

"No," said Miss Jemima; "he is much better. But he wishes to consult you about a matter of great importance."

Then, upon their protesting that they were in no immediate need of refreshment, Miss Jemima conducted her visitors upstairs to her brother's room.

Though "Cobbler" Horn had not been to sleep since the morning, he was greatly refreshed by the quiet hours he had passed. He turned to greet Mr. and Mrs. Burton, as they came in.

"This is very good of you," he said, putting out his hand.

Miss Jemima placed chairs for the visitors, and they took their seats near the bed.

"I think I must sit up," said "Cobbler" Horn.

Miss Jemima helped him to raise himself upon his pillows, and then sat down on a chair at the opposite side of the bed.

"There now," said "the Golden Shoemaker," "we shall do finely. But, Jemima, how about our friend, Tommy?"

"He'll be here directly" was the concise reply.

Mr. and Mrs. Burton waited patiently for "Cobbler" Horn to speak. Mrs. Burton was a shrewd-looking, motherly body; and her husband had the appearance of a capable and kindly man. They were both conscious of some curiosity, and even anxiety, with regard to what "Cobbler" Horn might be about to say. The peculiarity of the situation was that he should have sent for them both. Perhaps each had some vague prevision of the communication he was about to make.

"Now, dear friends," he said, at last, "no doubt you will be wondering why I have sent for you in such a hurry."

Both Mr. Burton and his wife protested that they were always at the service of Mr. Horn, and expressed the assurance that he would not have sent for them without good cause.

"Thank you," he said. "I think you will admit that, in this instance, the cause is as good as can be."

Looking upon the kindly faces of these good Christian people, "Cobbler" Horn wondered how they would receive the news he would probably have to impart. He must proceed cautiously. At the same time, he was thankful that his little lost child—if, indeed, it were so—had been committed by the great Father to such kindly hands.

"You will not mind, dear friends," he resumed, "if I ask you one or two questions about the circumstances under which my—Miss Owen came into your charge when a child?"

"By no means, sir!" The startling nature of the question caused no hesitation in the reply. Indeed, though startled, these good people were not so very much surprised. They had not, perhaps, been actually expecting that this would prove to be the subject on which they had been summoned to confer. But, ever since their adopted daughter had entered the household of this man, whose own little daughter had been lost, just about the time that she must have left her home, both Mr. and Mrs. Burton had secretly thought that perhaps, as the result, she would find her own parent, and they would lose their child. Perhaps it was on account of the vagueness of this thought, or because of the painful anticipations to which it gave rise, or for both these reasons, that the good couple had made no mention to each other of its presence in their respective minds. They glanced at one another now; and, by some subtle influence, each became aware that the other's mind had been occupied by this disturbing thought.

"You will believe," said "Cobbler" Horn, "that I have good reasons for the questions I am going to ask?"

"We are sure of that, sir," responded Mr. Burton.

"Yes, indeed," said Mrs. Burton.

"Well, can you tell me in what year, and at what time of the year, you found the child?"

"It was on the 2nd of June, 18—" said Mrs. Burton, promptly.

"Cobbler" Horn and Miss Jemima exchanged glances. It was the very year in which, on that bright May morning, little Marian had vanished, like a flash of departing sunshine, from their lives.

"About what age would you suppose the child to have been at the time?"

"She told us her age," said Mr. Burton.

"Yes," pursued his wife, "she was a very indistinct talker, and her age was almost the only thing we could actually make out. She said she was five; and that was about what she looked."

"Do you think, now," continued "Cobbler" Horn, with another glance at his sister, "that you could give us anything like a description of the child?"

"My wife can do that very well," said Mr. Burton. "She has often told Miss Owen what she looked like when we found her crying in the road."

"Yes," said Mrs. Burton, "I remember exactly what she was like. She had black hair—as she has now, and her eyes were very dark; her skin was even browner than it is now, being so dirty; and she had very rosy cheeks. It was evident that some of her clothes had been stolen. Indeed they were almost all gone, and she had scarcely anything on but an old, and very dirty shawl, which was wrapped round her body so tightly that it must have hurt her very much. She had lost one of her shoes, and her foot was bound up with a filthy piece of rag. She had both her socks on, but they were in dreadful holes. She was wearing a torn sun-bonnet, which was covered with mud; and—let me see—one of its strings was missing. And, yes, her one shoe was cut about over the top, as if it had been done on purpose with a knife. She had evidently been in very bad hands, poor little mite!" and the honest, kindly face was darkened with a frown, as Mrs. Burton clenched her plump fist in her lap.

Miss Jemima had been listening with intense interest, from her position on the other side of the bed; and now interposed with a question, in her own quick way.

"What was the pattern of the sun-bonnet? Was it a small, pink sprig, on a white ground?"

"Why, you must have seen it, ma'am!" was Mrs. Burton's startled reply. "That was the very thing!"

"Perhaps I have," responded Miss Jemima, "and perhaps I haven't."

Mrs. Burton hardly knew what to say.

"Well," she resumed, at last, "Miss Owen has kept the sun-bonnet, and the one shoe, and two or three other little things; and I'm sure she will be glad to let you see them. But, may I ask, Miss Horn, what—"

But "Cobbler" Horn interrupted her.

"I think, Jemima, we had now better tell our kind friends why we are asking these questions."

"Yes," said Miss Jemima; "I should have told them at first."

"Well," resumed "Cobbler" Horn, turning to Mr. and Mrs. Burton, and speaking with an emotion which he could no longer conceal, "we have reason to believe that your adopted daughter—don't let me shock you—is our little lost Marian, of whom you have several times heard me speak; and we are anxious to make sure if this is really the case."

In the nature of things, Mr. and Mrs. Burton were not so much surprised as they would have been if the course of events had not, in some measure, prepared them for the announcement which "Cobbler" Horn had now made. Yet they experienced a slight shock; for even an expected crisis cannot be fully realized till it actually arrives.

For a moment, there was silence in the room. Then Mrs. Burton was the first to speak.

"Excuse us, dear sir," she said calmly, "if we are somewhat startled at what you have said. And yet we are not altogether surprised. You will not think that strange?"

"No, ma'am," said "Cobbler" Horn, in a musing tone, "not altogether strange, perhaps. But, shall I explain a little further? It was only last evening that I was led to entertain the thought that Miss Owen might actually prove to be my lost child. She was telling me, as she had done several times before, all about how you found her, and of your goodness to her; and she spoke last night, for the first time, of the one shoe she was wearing when you found her in the road. Now you may judge how I was startled, on hearing this, when I tell you that, just after Marian was lost, we picked up one of her shoes in a field, over which she must have wandered away. So, this morning, without telling her my reason, I asked her to let me see the little shoe she had worn so long ago. She at once fetched it; and here it is, and with it the one we found in the field."

So saying, he drew, from underneath the bed-clothes, the two little shoes; and placed them side by side upon the counterpane.

Mr. and Mrs. Burton rose and approached the bed.

"Yes," said Mr. Burton, "that is undoubtedly Miss Owen's little shoe."

"And this," said Mrs. Burton, "is unquestionably its fellow," and, taking up the shoes, she held them towards her husband.

"You are certainly right, my dear."

Then there was silence for a brief space, while these two simple-hearted people bent, with deep emotion, over the little baby shoes which seemed to prove so much.

Mrs. Burton was the first to speak.

"Well," she said, calmly, but with a quivering lip, "we are to lose our child; but the will of the Lord be done."

Mr. Burton's only utterance was a deep sigh.

"Nay," said "Cobbler" Horn, "if it really be as I cannot help hoping it is, you will, perhaps, not lose so much as you think. But I am sure you will not begrudge me the joy of finding my child."

"No, indeed, dear sir. On the contrary, we will rejoice with you as well as we can—and with her."

These were the words of Mrs. Burton, and they received confirmation from her husband.

At this point, Tommy Dudgeon quietly entered the room, and took his seat, at a motion from Miss Jemima, behind the chairs on which Mr. and Mrs. Burton were sitting.

"I have been anxious," resumed "Cobbler" Horn, "thoroughly to assure myself that there was no mistake. Here is our friend, Dudgeon, now. You saw him the day we opened the 'Home.'"

Perceiving Tommy for the first time, Mr. and Mrs. Burton gave him a hearty greeting.

"Our friend knows," continued "Cobbler" Horn, "that I've been very sceptical about the good news."

"Very much so!" said Tommy, nodding his head.

"Cobbler" Horn smiled.

"He was the first to find it out. You must know that he took much kind interest in my little girl; and it was a great grief to him that she was lost. And when your adopted daughter came to us, he was not long in forming conjectures as to who she might be. In a very short time, as a matter of fact, he had quite made up his mind. He tried to tell me about it; but I was too stupid to understand him, and so it was left for me to find out the happy truth by accident. Tell our friends, Tommy, how you came to discover who Miss Owen really was."

Thus enjoined, Tommy, nothing loath, recounted once more the story of his great discovery. Mr. and Mrs. Burton listened with deep attention, and, having put several questions to Tommy, admitted that what he had said afforded much confirmation to the supposition that Miss Owen was the long-lost Marian.

"I have a thought about the child's name," said Mrs. Burton after a brief pause. "It comes to me that what she gave us as her name sounded quite as much like *Marian Horn* as *Mary*

*Ann Owen.*"

"Why yes," said Miss Jemima, "now I think of it, she used to pronounce her name very much as though it had been something like *Mary Ann Owen.* As well as I can remember, it was 'Ma—an O—on.'"

"I believe you are right, Jemima," said her brother.

"It must be admitted," interposed Mr. Burton quickly, "that *Mary Ann Owen* was a very reasonable interpretation of that combination of sounds."

"Undoubtedly it was," assented "Cobbler" Horn.

"Yes," said Mrs. Burton, "what you say, Miss Horn, is very much like the way in which the child pronounced her name. And there's another thing which may serve as a further mark. She had on, beneath the old shawl, a little chemise, on which were worked, in red, the letters 'M.H.'"

"I know it!" cried Miss Jemima. "I always marked her clothes like that. You used to laugh at me, Thomas; but what do you say now?"

"Well, well!" said "the Golden Shoemaker" softly.

"And listen to me," resumed Miss Jemima. "I am beginning to recollect, too. Marian's hair was very stubborn; and there were two or three tufts at the back which always would stand up, like black feathers."

"I remember that very well," said Mrs. Burton, with a smile.

"Of course," agreed her husband; "and many a joke we used to have about it. I called her my little blackbird."

"And then," continued Miss Jemima, "there was another thing. A few days before the child's disappearance, she fell down and hurt her knee; and there were two scars, one on the knee, and another just below."

"Ah," said Mrs. Burton, "I remember those scars. Don't you, John?"

"Yes; and I used to tell her she was an old soldier, and had been in the wars."

"So you did; and—dear me, how old memories are beginning to come back!—she talked a great deal, not only of her 'daddy,' but of 'Aunt 'Mima.' I wonder I didn't think of that before. Perhaps, ma'am—"

"That's me!" cried Miss Jemima. "My name's Jemima; and 'Aunt 'Mima' was what she always called me. There, Thomas, do you want any further proof?"

"Cobbler" Horn was lying with his hands over his face, and the bed was shaking with his convulsive efforts to repress his strong emotion. Fear had impelled him to withstand his growing conviction that his long-lost child had been restored to him—fear of the consequences of a mistake, both to himself, and to the bright young girl whom he had already learnt to love as though she were indeed his child. But now, one after another, his doubts had been beaten down. He had listened eagerly to every word that had been spoken around his bed, and conviction had taken absolute possession of his mind. Yet, for the moment, the shock of his great joy seemed almost more than his weakened nerves could bear.

His friends stood around the bed, fearing for him. But, in a few moments, he withdrew his hands from his face, which was wet with the gracious tears of joy.

He clasped his hands, and looked reverently upward.

"'My soul doth magnify the Lord; and my spirit hath rejoiced in God, my Saviour.'"

That was all.

"You would like us to leave you, brother?" asked Miss Jemima.

"For a very short time."

He was quite himself again.

"She is out still, isn't she?"

"Yes," replied Miss Jemima. "She will be in soon, no doubt. You would like to see her. Well, leave that to me."

Then they left him to his blissful thoughts.

For many minutes, he gratefully communed with God. He was thankful his child had come back to him so beautiful, and clever, and good. He could regard her with as much pride as love; though he told himself he would have loved her, and done all in his power to make her happy, whatever she had proved to be. And then, how glad he was that she had found her way into his heart before he knew she was his child.

Great, indeed, was the joy of "the Golden Shoemaker!" That very day he was to clasp his long-lost child to his heart!

The door of his room had been left ajar. Presently he heard the front-door open downstairs; and then there were voices in the hall, one of which he recognised as hers. The next moment he knew that she was coming upstairs. They had not told her the great news yet, of course? No; she was going direct to her own room.

He took up the little shoes, which had been left lying on the bed. How well he remembered making them! He had selected for the purpose the very best bit of leather in his stock. He was proceeding to examine more closely the shoe that had been mutilated, when he heard the sound of a door being opened which he knew to be that of his young secretary's room.

Would she come to him before going downstairs? In truth, he wished not to see her until she had been told the great news. He breathed more freely when he heard her foot on the stairs.

When "Cobbler" Horn had been alone about half an hour, Miss Jemima returned to the room. Mrs. Burton, she said, was in the dining-room, with—Marian. There was just the slightest hesitation in Miss Jemima's pronunciation of the name. Her brother's tea would come up in a few minutes. After he had taken it, he would perhaps be ready for the interview he so much desired.

"Tea!"

"Oh, but," said his matter-of-fact sister, "you must try to take it—as a duty."

"I'll do my best," he said; "but I must be up and dressed before she comes, Jemima."

Miss Jemima demurred, but ultimately agreed.

"I should like Mr. Durnford to be here," he continued, "and Tommy Dudgeon, and Mr. and Mrs. Burton."

"They shall all be present," said Miss Jemima.

"And you, Jemima, you will take care to be in the room at the time."

"Brother," responded the lady, "you may trust me for that."

# CHAPTER XLII

## FATHER AND DAUGHTER

Mrs. Burton, closeted with her adopted daughter, in the dining-room, found, to her surprise, that Miss Owen was not unprepared for the communication she was about to receive. Since her discovery of the little shoe—the fellow of her own—in her employer's safe, and the startling conclusion at which she had thereupon arrived, the young secretary had been in a vaguely expectant state of mind. The great fact she had discovered could not long remain concealed from the person whom, next to herself, it most concerned. Of course, it was impossible for her to speak out. But she had only to wait, and all would come right.

She saw now why "Cobbler" Horn had been so much agitated to hear that, when she was found by Mr. and Mrs. Burton, she was wearing only one shoe; and she was not surprised, the next morning, when he asked to see the shoe itself. As the day passed, she was instinctively aware that something unusual was going on. The visit of Tommy Dudgeon; the circumstance that she was not summoned to "Cobbler" Horn's room as usual, during the day; and her being unexpectedly despatched to take Susie Martin for a drive—were all signs pointing in one direction; and when, on her return from the drive, she was greeted with the announcement that Mrs. Burton was waiting to see her in the dining-room, she felt sure that the great secret was known. And she could not be much surprised, therefore, when, in the end, Mrs. Burton proceeded to make in set terms, the communication with which she was charged.

"My dear," said the good lady, fondly kissing her adopted daughter, "I'm sure you will be surprised to see me."

"I'm delighted, at any rate, dear mother," was the pardonably evasive reply.

"Not more than I am!" exclaimed the good creature. Notwithstanding the loss she expected to sustain through the discovery which had been made, she had schooled herself to rejoice in the happiness which had come to her child. "But," she added, "you, my dear, will be more delighted still, when you hear the news I have to tell."

As she spoke, she led the young secretary to a chair, and, having caused her to be seated, sat down on another chair by her side. Then she took her companion's hand and held it tenderly in her lap.

"My dear, I want to ask you something."

The good lady tried to be calm, but her tones grew tremulous as she spoke. Miss Owen, too, was becoming excited, in spite of herself.

"Yes, mother dear," and the girl seemed to put special and loving emphasis on the word "mother."

"Do you remember," continued Mrs. Burton, "how, when you were all at Daisy Lane, at the opening of the 'Home,' we were talking about Mr. Horn having lost his little girl in some mysterious fashion; and you said, laughing, what fun it would be, if you turned out to be that very little girl?"

"Yes, mother," was the reply, uttered in low and agitated tones, "I remember very well."

"You didn't think that such a wonderful thing would ever come to pass, did you, dear?" asked Mrs. Burton, gently stroking the back of the plump little brown hand, which lay passive in her lap.

"No," replied the girl, "I certainly did not; and it was just a mad joke, of course."

As she spoke her whole frame quivered, and she made as though she would have withdrawn her hand and risen to her feet. Mrs. Burton tightened her grasp upon the fluttering hand in her lap, and gently restrained the agitated girl.

"I haven't finished yet, dear," she said. "You know the saying that 'many a true word is spoken in jest'?"

"Yes, yes—"

"Well—try to be calm, my child—it has been found out—"

"I know what you are going to say, mother," broke in the young girl. "It is that I have found my father—my very own; though I can never forget the only father I have known these years, and I haven't found another mother, and don't want to."

Then the woman and the child—for she was little more— became locked in a close embrace. After some minutes, Mrs. Burton unclasped the young arms from her neck, and, sitting hand in hand with her adopted daughter, she told her all the wondrous tale.

"So you see, my child," she concluded, "your name is not Owen after all; it is not even Mary Ann."

"No," said the girl, with a bewitching touch of scorn. "Mary Ann Owen, forsooth! I always had my doubts. Horn is not much better in itself. But it is my father's name; and Marian is all that could be desired. And so I really am that little Marian of whom I have heard so many charming things! How sweet! But, mother, you must be the very same to me as ever; and I must find room for two fathers now, instead of one."

"Yes, my dear, I feel sure you will not love us any the less for this great change."

"Mother, mother, never speak of that again! If it had not been for you, I might never have come to know anything about myself, to say nothing of all the dreadful things which might have happened. Oh, God is good!"

"He is indeed, dear! But you will be longing to go to your father."

"Yes," said the girl, with a quiver of shy delight; "what does he say?"

"My dear, he is thankful beyond measure."

"But can he bear to see me just yet?"

"He is preparing to receive you now. Come!"

"Cobbler" Horn had finished his tea, and was dressed, and sitting in an easy-chair in his bedroom. Those about him had feared that the coming effort would be too much for his strength. But there was no need for their apprehension. Joy was proving a splendid tonic. He sat calm and collected, awaiting the appearance of his child.

His friends were all around him. Mr. Durnford, Tommy Dudgeon, Mr. Burton—all were there; and there, too, was Miss Jemima, no longer grim, but subdued almost to meekness.

Then it was done in a moment. The door opened, and Mrs. Burton entered, leading the young secretary by the hand. An instant later the girl ran forward, with a little cry, and flung herself into the outstretched arms of her waiting father.

For some seconds they remained thus. Then she gradually slipped down upon her knees, and let her head fall upon his breast, while her arms embraced him still, and his hand held closely to him her nestling face. Speech was impossible on either side. She was weeping the sweet tears of joy, while he vainly struggled to find utterance for his love.

One by one, their friends had stolen out of the room. Even Miss Jemima had been content to go. The memory of that chastened lady was very vivid to-night, and she felt humbled and subdued.

Observing the silence, "Cobbler" Horn looked up, and perceived that they were alone.

"They have all gone, Marian," he said, gently. "Won't you look up, and let father see your face?"

She lifted her face, bedewed yet radiant; and he took it tenderly between his hands.

"It is indeed the face of my little Marian," he said, fondly. "How blind I must have been!"

J. W. Keyworth

He gazed long and lovingly—feasting his eyes upon the brown, glowing face, in every feature of which he could now trace so plainly those of his little Marian of days gone by. The hope which he had never quite relinquished was fulfilled at last! His gracious Lord had justified his confidence, as, indeed, there had never been any reason to doubt that He would.

"You feel quite sure about it, my dear; don't you?" he asked.

"Yes, father dear," she answered, in a thoughtful, contented tone. "There are so many things that help to make me sure."

Then she told him of her strange feeling of familiarity with the old house and street. She spoke of the little shoes, and of her having seen the one in the safe. She told him what she had overheard in the tent at Daisy Lane about her resemblance to himself.

"And besides," she concluded, "after all that—mother has told me, how can I doubt? But now, daddy—I may call you that, mayn't I?"

"The Golden Shoemaker" pressed convulsively the little hand he held.

"That is what Marian—what you always called me when you were a child, my dear. Nothing would please me better."

"Then 'daddy' it shall be. And now, do you know, daddy, I'm beginning to remember things in a vague sort of way. I'm just like some one waking up after a good sleep. Things, you know, that happened before one went to sleep, come back by degrees at such a time; and, in the same way, recollections are growing on me now of my childhood, and especially of the time when I was lost. Let me see, now! I'm like some one looking into a magic crystal to see the future, only I want to recall the past. After thinking very hard, I've been able to call up some remembrance of the day I ran away from home. I seem to remember being very angry with someone, and wanting to get away. Then there was a woman, and a man, but chiefly a woman, and some dark place that I was in. And I think they must have treated me badly in some way."

"Cobbler" Horn thought for a moment.

"Why," he said, "that dark place must have been the wood, on the other side of the field where I found your shoe."

"Yes, no doubt; and wasn't it in that wood that you picked up the string of my sun-bonnet?"

"To be sure it was!"

"Yes; and perhaps it was there that I was stripped of my clothes. When I fell into the hands of Mr. and Mrs. Burton, my chief garment was an old ragged shawl. My one shoe, and my socks, and my sun-bonnet, were almost all I had besides. I've kept all the things except the socks, and you must see them by and bye, daddy."

"Of course I must."

But, having found his child, he did not greatly care just now about anything else.

Presently she spoke again.

"Daddy!"

"Yes, Marian?"

"I'm so thankful it has turned out to be you!"

"Yes, my dear?" responded the happy father, in a tone of enquiry.

"I mean I'm glad it's you who are my father. It might have been somebody quite different, you know."

"Yes," he answered again, with a beaming face.

"I'm glad, you know, daddy, just because you're exactly the kind of father I want—that's all."

"And I also am glad that it is you, little one," he responded. "And how thankful we ought to be that we learnt to love one another before getting to know who we were!"

"Yes," she said, "it would have been queer, and—not at all nice, if we had first been introduced to each other as father and daughter, and told it was our duty to love one another without delay. And then there's another thing. Though, at first, it seemed cruel to you, daddy, that your little girl should have been lost for so many years, when I think how much more—very likely—we shall love one another, than we ever should have done if I had not been lost, and how much happier we shall be together, it seems quite kind of God to have allowed us to be separated for a little while—especially as He found such good friends to take care of me in the meantime."

"Cobbler" Horn gently stroked the dark head, which still nestled against his breast.

"We at least, little one," he said, "can say that 'all things work together for good.' But now, there are other things that we must talk about. You have come back, Marian, to a very different home from the one you left. Your father was a poor man when you went away; he is a rich one now. Are you glad?"

"Oh yes, daddy," she answered, simply, "for your sake, and because I think my daddy is just the best man in the world to have charge of money. And you know," she added, archly, "that, in that respect, your daughter is after your own heart."

"I know that well."

"You must let me help you more than ever, daddy."

She seemed scarcely to have realized the fact that she was heiress to all his wealth.

"You shall, my dear," he said, fondly; "but you mustn't forget that all I have will be yours one day."

She started violently.

"Well now, I declare!" she gasped. "I had scarcely thought of that. I was so glad and thankful to have found my father, that I forgot he had brought me a fortune. Well, daddy, that won't make any difference. We'll still do our best to put all this money to the right use. And, as for my being your heiress— you must understand, sir, that you've got to live for ever; so there's an end of that."

She had withdrawn herself from his embrace, and, kneeling back, was looking at him with dancing eyes.

"Well, darling," he said, with an indulgent smile, "we must leave that. But there is something else that I must tell you. When I was arranging about the disposal of all this money, in case I should be taken away, I thought of my little Marian;

and I had it set down in my will that you were to have everything after me, if you should be found. But, beside that, I directed the lawyers to invest for you the sum of L50,000. But, let me see, I think I must have told you about this at the time."

"Of course you did, daddy, the very day you came back from London, just before you went to America!"

"So I did. Well, now, Marian, that money is all your own from this time."

"Oh, daddy! daddy! How shall I thank you? So I shall be able to do something on my own account now!"

Did no stray thought flit through her mind of all the gaiety and pleasure so much money might buy? Perhaps; but she was her father's own child.

After a little more loving talk, the young secretary suddenly sprang to her feet.

"I am forgetting myself sadly! The evening letters will be in."

"Cobbler" Horn started. He had forgotten that she was his secretary.

"I shall have to look out for another secretary, now," he said, with a comical air of mock dismay.

"And, pray sir, why?" she demanded, standing before him in radiant rebellion. "I would have you to know there is no vacancy."

Then she laughed in her bewitching way.

"But, my dear—"

"Say no more, daddy; it's quite settled. I shall very likely ask for an increase of salary; but there must be no talk of dismissal."

Again she laughed; and, in spite of himself, the happy father joined in her merriment.

"Well now, I must go," she said, with a parting kiss. "I'll send Miss Horn—Why, she's my aunt! I declare I'd quite overlooked that!"

"Yes, my dear; and a very kind aunt you'll find her."

"I'm sure of that. But I'm afraid she'll be thinking me a very undutiful niece."

At this moment, the door opened, and Miss Jemima herself walked in.

"I thought it was time I came," she said, in her usual matter-of-fact way. "You must be thinking of getting back to bed, Thomas."

Her niece interrupted her by throwing her arms around her neck, and giving her a hearty kiss.

"Aunt Jemima, I have to beg your pardon," and she kissed her again; "but you didn't give me time, you were all off like a flock of sheep."

"I think it is my place to beg your pardon, and not yours to beg mine," replied Miss Jemima, in the most natural way in the world. "I fear it was largely through me that you ran away from home."

"Did I actually run away, then?"

"I think there's little doubt of it. But, whether you ran away or not, the fact remains that my treatment of you had been anything but kind. I meant well, but was mistaken; and I'm thankful to have the opportunity of asking you to forgive me."

"Don't say another word about it, auntie!" cried Marian, kissing her once more. "It's literally all forgotten. And I dare say I was a troublesome little thing. But let me see. You haven't seen my treasures yet—except the shoe. I'll fetch them."

In a few moments she had brought her little sun-bonnet, and the other relics of her childhood which she had preserved. It will not be difficult to imagine the tender interest with which Aunt Jemima, and even "Cobbler" Horn himself, gazed on those simple mementos of the past. The severed bonnet-string was lying on the bed. Marian caught it up, and fitted it upon the bonnet.

"I must sew my bonnet-string on," she said, gaily.

Her father laughed indulgently, and even Aunt Jemima smiled.

"Ah," she said, "and I too have a store of treasures to display," and she told of the little box in which she had kept the tiny garments Marian had worn in the days of old.

"How delicious?" cried the girl. "You will let me see them, by and bye, auntie, won't you? But now I really must be off to my letters."

# CHAPTER XLIII

## THE TRAMP'S CONFESSION

Before "the Golden Shoemaker" had returned to his bed the doctor arrived, and despotically demanded how he had dared to leave it without the permission of his medical man. At first the doctor prognosticated serious consequences from what he was pleased to call his patient's "intemperate and unlicensed haste." But, when he came the next day, and found "Cobbler" Horn considerably better, instead of worse, he changed his mind.

"My dear sir," he said, "what have you been doing?"

"I've been taking a new tonic, doctor," replied "Cobbler" Horn, with a smile; and he told him the great news.

"Well, well," murmured the doctor; "so it has actually turned out like that! I have often thought that there were many less likely things; and ever since you told me how closely the young lady's early history resembled that of your own child, I have had a sort of expectation that I should one day hear the announcement you have just made. Well, my dear sir, I congratulate you both—as much on the fitness of the fact, as on the fact itself."

J. W. Keyworth

"Cobbler" Horn's "new tonic" acted liked magic, and he was soon out of the doctor's hands. In a few days' time he was downstairs; and at the end of a fortnight he had resumed his ordinary routine of life.

As far as outward appearances were concerned, the great discovery which had been made produced but little difference in the house. The servants had, indeed, been informed of the change in the position of the young secretary. It was also understood that she was to have things pretty much her own way. It was moreover tacitly admitted that almost unlimited arrears of filial privilege were due to the newly-recovered daughter of the house; and she herself evidently felt that the arrears of filial duty lying to her charge were quite equal in amount. "The Golden Shoemaker" regarded his new-found child with a very tender love; and even Miss Jemima manifested towards her an indulgent, if somewhat prim, affection. The gentle affectionateness of the girl towards both her father and her aunt was beautiful in the extreme. Yet, even towards Miss Jemima, she was delightfully free from constraint; and it would have been difficult to decide whether to admire more the loving familiarity of the niece, or the complaisancy of the aunt.

In the matter of the secretaryship Marian was firmness itself. "Cobbler" Horn wished her to give it up; and Miss Jemima was shocked at the idea that she should propose to retain it for a single day. But she dismissed their remonstrances with a fine scorn. What did they take her for? Was she any less fit for the post of secretary than she had been before? Her duties had been a pleasure from the first; they would afford her greater delight than ever now. And why should they bring in a stranger to pry into their affairs? They might give her more salary, if they liked—and here she laughed merrily; but she wasn't going to give up the work she liked more than anything else in the world.

One perplexing question yet remained unsolved—What had happened to Marian between the day when she had left home and the time when she had been found by Mr. and Mrs. Burton? The girl's own vague memories of that unhappy period, together with the condition in which she had been found, indicated that she had fallen into the hands of bad characters of some kind. Was the mystery ever to be fully solved? To this question the course of events brought very speedily a complete reply.

One evening, about a fortnight after the last-recorded events, an elderly tramp was sitting against a haystack upon some farm premises, at no great distance from the town of Cottonborough. His age might be sixty, or, allowing for the rough life he had led, something less. He looked jaded and unwell. The day had been very warm, and the man was eating, with no great appetite, a sumptuous supper of German sausage and bread. The sausage had been wrapped in a piece of newspaper, which spread out upon his knees, was now doing duty as a tablecloth. Having finished his meal, the man lazily glanced at the paper; but finding its contents, at first, to possess no particular interest, he was about to crumple it up and throw it away, when his eye lighted on a paragraph which induced him to pause. He smoothed out the paper, and raised it nearer to his eyes.

"Well," he muttered, "I ain't much of a scholard; but I means to get to the bottom o' this 'ere."

With intense eagerness, he began to spell out the words of the paragraph which had arrested his attention. It was headed, "'The Golden Shoemaker' recovers his daughter, supposed to have been stolen by tramps in her childhood." From line to line he laboured painfully on. Many times his progress was stayed by some formidable word; and again and again he was interrupted by a violent cough; but at

J. W. Keyworth

length he had ascertained the contents of the paragraph. It contained as much as was known of the history of Marian Horn. It told how, at the age of five, she had, as was supposed, run away from home, and, as recently-discovered circumstances seemed to indicate, fallen into the hands of evil persons; and how all trace of her had then been lost until a few weeks afterwards, when, as had now become known, she was found, a wretched little waif, upon the highway, and adopted by Mr. and Mrs. Burton. The circumstances of her after life were then set forth; and the narrative concluded with a glowing account of her re-union with her friends. The tramp deeply pondered this romantic story.

"Ah," he said to himself, "that must ha' been the little wench as me and the old woman took to. It was somewhere here away. I remember about the shoe as she'd lost. They must ha' found it. The old woman cut the other shoe, same as it says here. It were a bad thing of us to take the kid, that it were."

At this point the man was seized with a violent fit of coughing. When it had subsided, he resumed his half-muttered meditations. "Well, I'm glad as the little 'un got took care on, arter all, and has got back to her own natural born father at last; for she were a game little wench, and no mistake. She were a poor people's child when we got hold on her. But I've heerd tell o' 'the Golden Shoemaker,' as they calls him. It must ha' been arter she was lost that he got his money. Well, I feels sorry, like, as we didn't try to find her friends. But the old gal were that onscrupulous, she didn't stick at nothink, she didn't. As sure as my name's Jake Dafty, this 'ere's a queer go."

Thus mused Jake, the tramp, sitting against the haystack; and his musings were, ever and anon, disturbed by his racking cough. He felt indisposed to move. As he brooded over the past, his mind became uneasy, he was conscious of a vague desire to make confession of the evil he had done. Did he feel that the sands of his life were almost sped? And was conscience waking at last?

At length, between his fits of coughing, he was overtaken by sleep. The night was chilly after the warm day. The sun went down, and the stars peeped out serenely upon the frowzy and wretched tramp asleep against the haystack; and the dew settled thickly on his ragged beard and tattered clothes. Every now and then he was shaken by his cough; but he was weary, and remained asleep. And, in his sleep, the past came back more vividly than it had ever re-visited him in his waking hours. He seemed to be present at the despoiling and ill-using of a dark-eyed child, whom he might have delivered, and did not; and, from time to time, he moved uneasily in his sleep, and groaned aloud.

Thus passed the night; and, in the morning, Jake, being found by the farm people, in his place against the haystack, delirious, and evidently ill, was conveyed to the workhouse.

The next day "the Golden Shoemaker" received word that a man who was dying in the workhouse begged to see him at once. "Cobbler" Horn ordered his closed carriage, and drove to the workhouse without delay. The man, who was Jake, the tramp, had not long to live. His delirium was over now, and he was quite himself. His eyes were fixed eagerly upon the face of "Cobbler" Horn, as the latter entered the room.

"Are you 'the Golden Shoemaker'?" he asked.

"So I am sometimes called," replied "Cobbler" Horn, with a smile.

"Well—I ain't got much time—I'm the bloke wot stole your little 'un; me and the old woman."

"Cobbler" Horn uttered an exclamation of surprise.

"Yes. The old woman's gone. She died in quod. I don't know what they had done to her. Perhaps nothink: maybe her time was come. I warn't that sorry; she'd got to be a stroke too many for me. But I want to tell you about the little 'un. I'm a going to die, and it 'ull be as well to get it off my mind. There ain't no mistake; cos I see'd it in the paper, and it tallies. I've got it here."

As he spoke, he drew from beneath his pillow the crumpled piece of newspaper on which he had read of the restoration of Marian to her father.

"There," he said, "yer can read it for yerself."

"Cobbler" Horn took the paper, and glanced at its contents. He had seen in various newspapers, if not this, several similar accounts of the adventures of his child.

"Ah," he said, handing back to the man the greasy and crumpled paper, "tell me about it."

"Well, you knows that field where you found one of her shoes?"

"Yes."

"Well, we wos a sitting under the hedge, near that field, one morning, a-dining, when the kid came along. She stopped when she see'd us; and we invited her to go along with us, and somehow she seemed as if she didn't like to refuse. Arter that, we took her into the wood; and the old woman stripped off her clothes, and did her up like as she was when she was found. She'd lost one of her shoes, and I went back for it; but I couldn't find it nowheres. You may be sure as we got out o' these parts as fast as we could. We thought as the kid 'ud be a rare help in the cadging line. But she was that stubborn and noisy, we soon got sorry as we'd ever taken on with her; and, if she hadn't took herself right away, one arternoon when we was having of our arter-dinner nap in a dry ditch, I do believe as the old woman 'ud ha' found some means o' putting her on one side."

Having finished his story, the dying tramp lay still for awhile, with his eyes closed.

"Cobbler" Horn looked down with pity upon the seamed and wrinkled face, from which almost all expression, except that of utter weariness, seemed to have been worn away.

Presently the dying man opened his eyes.

"That's all as I has to tell, master," he said faintly. "Do yer think, now, as yer could find it in yer heart to forgive a cove, like? It 'ud be none the worse for me, if yer could; nor, mayhap, for yourself neither. I'se sorry I done it."

"Cobbler" Horn was deeply moved. But, as he now knew as much of what had happened to Marian as was likely ever to come to light, he could afford to let the matter rest; and already he found himself thinking more of the miserable case of the dying waif before him, than of the confession the poor creature had made. So he gave himself fully to the congenial task of trying to bring this miserable being, into a fitting frame of mind in which to meet the solemn change which he must so soon undergo.

"I forgive you freely," he said. "But won't you ask pardon of God? My forgiveness will be of little use without His."

The dying tramp looked up with a listless stare.

"It's wery good o' yer," he said, "to say as yer forgives me. But, as for God, I've never had much to do with Him, yer see; and it ain't likely as He'll mind me now. And I don't seem to care about it a deal."

"Cobbler" Horn was troubled, but not surprised. Breathing a prayer for Divine guidance and help, he set himself to make clear to this dark soul the way of life. In the simplest words at his command, he strove to make the wretched man understand and feel his need of a Saviour; and, when, at length, he quitted the chamber of death, he had good reason to hope that his efforts had not been altogether in vain.

Marian was profoundly interested to hear of the dying tramp and the story he had told, which latter agreed so well with her own vague remembrances, that she joined her father and aunt in regarding it as indicating what had been the actual course of events.

Little, now, remains to be told. Father and daughter united to render the vast wealth which God had intrusted to their charge a source of greater and yet greater blessing to increasing multitudes of needy and suffering people; and Aunt Jemima insisted on participating in all their generous schemes.

Marian is still secretary; but, as she receives many offers of marriage, it is possible the post may become vacant even yet.

\* \* \* \* \*

# Choose from Thousands of 1stWorldLibrary Classics By

A. M. Barnard
Ada Leverson
Adolphus William Ward
Aesop
Agatha Christie
Alexander Aaronsohn
Alexander Kielland
Alexandre Dumas
Alfred Gatty
Alfred Ollivant
Alice Duer Miller
Alice Turner Curtis
Alice Dunbar
Allen Chapman
Alleyne Ireland
Ambrose Bierce
Amelia E. Barr
Amory H. Bradford
Andrew Lang
Andrew McFarland Davis
Andy Adams
Angela Brazil
Anna Alice Chapin
Anna Sewell
Annie Besant
Annie Hamilton Donnell
Annie Payson Call
Annie Roe Carr
Annonaymous
Anton Chekhov
Archibald Lee Fletcher
Arnold Bennett
Arthur C. Benson
Arthur Conan Doyle
Arthur M. Winfield
Arthur Ransome
Arthur Schnitzler
Arthur Train
Atticus
B.H. Baden-Powell
B. M. Bower
B. C. Chatterjee
Baroness Emmuska Orczy
Baroness Orczy
Basil King
Bayard Taylor
Ben Macomber
Bertha Muzzy Bower
Bjornstjerne Bjornson

Booth Tarkington
Boyd Cable
Bram Stoker
C. Collodi
C. E. Orr
C. M. Ingleby
Carolyn Wells
Catherine Parr Traill
Charles A. Eastman
Charles Amory Beach
Charles Dickens
Charles Dudley Warner
Charles Farrar Browne
Charles Ives
Charles Kingsley
Charles Klein
Charles Hanson Towne
Charles Lathrop Pack
Charles Romyn Dake
Charles Whibley
Charles Willing Beale
Charlotte M. Braeme
Charlotte M. Yonge
Charlotte Perkins Stetson
Clair W. Hayes
Clarence Day Jr.
Clarence E. Mulford
Clemence Housman
Confucius
Coningsby Dawson
Cornelis DeWitt Wilcox
Cyril Burleigh
D. H. Lawrence
Daniel Defoe
David Garnett
Dinah Craik
Don Carlos Janes
Donald Keyhoe
Dorothy Kilner
Dougan Clark
Douglas Fairbanks
E. Nesbit
E. P. Roe
E. Phillips Oppenheim
E. S. Brooks
Earl Barnes
Edgar Rice Burroughs
Edith Van Dyne
Edith Wharton

Edward Everett Hale
Edward J. O'Biren
Edward S. Ellis
Edwin L. Arnold
Eleanor Atkins
Eleanor Hallowell Abbott
Eliot Gregory
Elizabeth Gaskell
Elizabeth McCracken
Elizabeth Von Arnim
Ellem Key
Emerson Hough
Emilie F. Carlen
Emily Bronte
Emily Dickinson
Enid Bagnold
Enilor Macartney Lane
Erasmus W. Jones
Ernie Howard Pie
Ethel May Dell
Ethel Turner
Ethel Watts Mumford
Eugene Sue
Eugenie Foa
Eugene Wood
Eustace Hale Ball
Evelyn Everett-green
Everard Cotes
F. H. Cheley
F. J. Cross
F. Marion Crawford
Fannie E. Newberry
Federick Austin Ogg
Ferdinand Ossendowski
Fergus Hume
Florence A. Kilpatrick
Fremont B. Deering
Francis Bacon
Francis Darwin
Frances Hodgson Burnett
Frances Parkinson Keyes
Frank Gee Patchin
Frank Harris
Frank Jewett Mather
Frank L. Packard
Frank V. Webster
Frederic Stewart Isham
Frederick Trevor Hill
Frederick Winslow Taylor

Friedrich Kerst
Friedrich Nietzsche
Fyodor Dostoyevsky
G.A. Henty
G.K. Chesterton
Gabrielle E. Jackson
Garrett P. Serviss
Gaston Leroux
George A. Warren
George Ade
Geroge Bernard Shaw
George Cary Eggleston
George Durston
George Ebers
George Eliot
George Gissing
George MacDonald
George Meredith
George Orwell
George Sylvester Viereck
George Tucker
George W. Cable
George Wharton James
Gertrude Atherton
Gordon Casserly
Grace E. King
Grace Gallatin
Grace Greenwood
Grant Allen
Guillermo A. Sherwell
Gulielma Zollinger
Gustav Flaubert
H. A. Cody
H. B. Irving
H. C. Bailey
H. G. Wells
H. H. Munro
H. Irving Hancock
H. R. Naylor
H. Rider Haggard
H. W. C. Davis
Haldeman Julius
Hall Caine
Hamilton Wright Mabie
Hans Christian Andersen
Harold Avery
Harold McGrath
Harriet Beecher Stowe
Harry Castlemon
Harry Coghill
Harry Houidini

Hayden Carruth
Helent Hunt Jackson
Helen Nicolay
Hendrik Conscience
Hendy David Thoreau
Henri Barbusse
Henrik Ibsen
Henry Adams
Henry Ford
Henry Frost
Henry James
Henry Jones Ford
Henry Seton Merriman
Henry W Longfellow
Herbert A. Giles
Herbert Carter
Herbert N. Casson
Herman Hesse
Hildegard G. Frey
Homer
Honore De Balzac
Horace B. Day
Horace Walpole
Horatio Alger Jr.
Howard Pyle
Howard R. Garis
Hugh Lofting
Hugh Walpole
Humphry Ward
Ian Maclaren
Inez Haynes Gillmore
Irving Bacheller
Isabel Cecilia Williams
Isabel Hornibrook
Israel Abrahams
Ivan Turgenev
J. G.Austin
J. Henri Fabre
J. M. Barrie
J. M. Walsh
J. Macdonald Oxley
J. R. Miller
J. S. Fletcher
J. S. Knowles
J. Storer Clouston
J. W. Duffield
Jack London
Jacob Abbott
James Allen
James Andrews
James Baldwin

James Branch Cabell
James DeMille
James Joyce
James Lane Allen
James Lane Allen
James Oliver Curwood
James Oppenheim
James Otis
James R. Driscoll
Jane Abbott
Jane Austen
Jane L. Stewart
Janet Aldridge
Jens Peter Jacobsen
Jerome K. Jerome
Jessie Graham Flower
John Buchan
John Burroughs
John Cournos
John F. Kennedy
John Gay
John Glasworthy
John Habberton
John Joy Bell
John Kendrick Bangs
John Milton
John Philip Sousa
John Taintor Foote
Jonas Lauritz Idemil Lie
Jonathan Swift
Joseph A. Altsheler
Joseph Carey
Joseph Conrad
Joseph E. Badger Jr
Joseph Hergesheimer
Joseph Jacobs
Jules Vernes
Julian Hawthrone
Julie A Lippmann
Justin Huntly McCarthy
Kakuzo Okakura
Karle Wilson Baker
Kate Chopin
Kenneth Grahame
Kenneth McGaffey
Kate Langley Bosher
Kate Langley Bosher
Katherine Cecil Thurston
Katherine Stokes
L. A. Abbot
L. T. Meade

L. Frank Baum
Latta Griswold
Laura Dent Crane
Laura Lee Hope
Laurence Housman
Lawrence Beasley
Leo Tolstoy
Leonid Andreyev
Lewis Carroll
Lewis Sperry Chafer
Lilian Bell
Lloyd Osbourne
Louis Hughes
Louis Joseph Vance
Louis Tracy
Louisa May Alcott
Lucy Fitch Perkins
Lucy Maud Montgomery
Luther Benson
Lydia Miller Middleton
Lyndon Orr
M. Corvus
M. H. Adams
Margaret E. Sangster
Margret Howth
Margaret Vandercook
Margaret W. Hungerford
Margret Penrose
Maria Edgeworth
Maria Thompson Daviess
Mariano Azuela
Marion Polk Angellotti
Mark Overton
Mark Twain
Mary Austin
Mary Catherine Crowley
Mary Cole
Mary Hastings Bradley
Mary Roberts Rinehart
Mary Rowlandson
M. Wollstonecraft Shelley
Maud Lindsay
Max Beerbohm
Myra Kelly
Nathaniel Hawthrone
Nicolo Machiavelli
O. F. Walton
Oscar Wilde

Owen Johnson
P.G. Wodehouse
Paul and Mabel Thorne
Paul G. Tomlinson
Paul Severing
Percy Brebner
Percy Keese Fitzhugh
Peter B. Kyne
Plato
Quincy Allen
R. Derby Holmes
R. L. Stevenson
R. S. Ball
Rabindranath Tagore
Rahul Alvares
Ralph Bonehill
Ralph Henry Barbour
Ralph Victor
Ralph Waldo Emmerson
Rene Descartes
Ray Cummings
Rex Beach
Rex E. Beach
Richard Harding Davis
Richard Jefferies
Richard Le Gallienne
Robert Barr
Robert Frost
Robert Gordon Anderson
Robert L. Drake
Robert Lansing
Robert Lynd
Robert Michael Ballantyne
Robert W. Chambers
Rosa Nouchette Carey
Rudyard Kipling
Saint Augustine
Samuel B. Allison
Samuel Hopkins Adams
Sarah Bernhardt
Sarah C. Hallowell
Selma Lagerlof
Sherwood Anderson
Sigmund Freud
Standish O'Grady
Stanley Weyman
Stella Benson
Stella M. Francis

Stephen Crane
Stewart Edward White
Stijn Streuvels
Swami Abhedananda
Swami Parmananda
T. S. Ackland
T. S. Arthur
The Princess Der Ling
Thomas A. Janvier
Thomas A Kempis
Thomas Anderton
Thomas Bailey Aldrich
Thomas Bulfinch
Thomas De Quincey
Thomas Dixon
Thomas H. Huxley
Thomas Hardy
Thomas More
Thornton W. Burgess
U. S. Grant
Upton Sinclair
Valentine Williams
Various Authors
Vaughan Kester
Victor Appleton
Victor G. Durham
Victoria Cross
Virginia Woolf
Wadsworth Camp
Walter Camp
Walter Scott
Washington Irving
Wilbur Lawton
Wilkie Collins
Willa Cather
Willard F. Baker
William Dean Howells
William le Queux
W. Makepeace Thackeray
William W. Walter
William Shakespeare
Winston Churchill
Yei Theodora Ozaki
Yogi Ramacharaka
Young E. Allison
Zane Grey